PETERSON'S

3rd edition

The guide that turns learning into earning

LIBERAL ARTS JOBS

PETERSON'S
Princeton, New Jersey

Burt Nadler

About Peterson's

Peterson's is the country's largest educational information/communications company, providing the academic, consumer, and professional communities with books, software, and online services in support of lifelong education access and career choice. Well-known references include Peterson's annual guides to private schools, summer programs, colleges and universities, graduate and professional programs, financial aid, international study, adult learning, and career guidance. Peterson's Web site at petersons.com is the only comprehensive—and most heavily traveled—education resource on the Internet. The site carries all of Peterson's fully searchable major databases and includes financial aid sources, test-prep help, job postings, direct inquiry and application features, and specially created Virtual Campuses for every accredited academic institution and summer program in the U.S. and Canada that offers in-depth narratives, announcements, and multimedia features.

Visit Peterson's Education Center on the Internet (World Wide Web) at
http://www.petersons.com

Copyright © 1998 by Peterson's

Previous editions © 1986 and 1989; 1985 as *Liberal Arts Power*

Library of Congress Cataloging-in-Publication Data

Nadler, Burton Jay, 1953-
    Liberal arts jobs / Burt Nadler. — 3rd ed.
        p.   cm.
    Includes bibliographical references and index.
    ISBN 0-7689-0148-0 (pbk.)
    1. Vocational guidance—United States.   2. College graduates—Employment—United States.   3. Bachelor of arts degree.
    I. Title.
    HF5382.5.U5N25   1998
    331.7′0235′0973—dc21   98-37661
                                                                            CIP

Printed in the United States of America
10 9 8 7 6 5 4 3 2

DEDICATION

To those who taught me that a liberal arts job search could be simple and effective, though not necessarily easy, and that words, specifically the "five phrases forever," can be transformed into true accomplishments.

To those true friends and colleagues who showed me through academics, professional achievements, and personal expressions that liberal arts power can also be a state of mind, a set of memories and motivations, and forgiveness in addition to being a job search strategy. Thanks Jud, Shellie, Bruce, Skip, Mary, Norma, and Terry.

To Dan Malley, a good friend and role model for many, as well as family members who have passed on since the last edition of this work. You will be remembered.

While WOW (Weeks of Work) is an acronym for an innovative and effective strategy for accomplishing your job search goals, the word upside down means a great deal.

And, finally, to Teri, Jordan, Justin, and Rickety.

CONTENTS

INTRODUCTION

THE LIBERAL ARTS PERSPECTIVE

One of the characteristics that differentiates some liberal arts majors from their counterparts who have majored in business or technical fields is their inability (or their unwillingness) to articulate career goals in terms that potential employers understand. Let's explore why this is so.

In the effort to define a "liberal arts major," some cite *inclusive* fields or departments: English and literature as well as the social, physical, and natural sciences. Others look at *exclusive* areas—business, computer science, and engineering—and identify liberal arts as all remaining curricula. You will never find universal agreement. Taking a different perspective, I define a liberal arts major as someone who can, *if desired* (although most likely only after a great deal of graduate study), add the suffix *ian* or *ist* or the word *teacher* after the field he or she studied to determine the most obvious career options.

If you are a liberal arts major who seeks alternatives to these suffixes, as well as to teaching, you must identify career alternatives and assume full responsibility for setting goals, developing strategies, and taking action. If your goal is to become an *ian, ist,* or *teacher,* great! These professions are worthy undertakings. Most people, however, wish to explore other options. This book is not meant to dissuade or persuade but simply to educate, to motivate, and to help those who want to explore alternatives.

Liberal Arts Jobs is designed to introduce you to the concepts that are associated with the job search *process.* It will set in motion the research required for successful goal setting and job search efforts, offer information on job and career options, and help you set realistic job search goals. It is critical that you understand your responsibility to become more *goal articulate* than your peers and that you believe in your *response-ability*—simply, your ability to respond—to accomplish the undertakings associated with setting career goals and finding employment.

FROM PLIGHT TO POWER: DISPELLING MYTHS AND ARTICULATING GOALS

Too many students express unnecessary anxieties over the belief that liberal arts fields are the best of majors and the worst of majors. Students, parents, and, increasingly, faculty members and admission professionals continue to bemoan what some call "the plight of the liberal arts graduate." Well-meaning parents discourage students from exploring traditional "arts and sciences" or "humanities" majors, fearing that sons or daughters won't get "good jobs" or "good-**paying** jobs" after graduation. Faculty members within these subject areas are increasingly pressed to justify their offerings and, at some institutions, are forced to promote enrollment in their majors or perish. With regularity at graduation time, newspapers, magazines, and radio and television stations print and broadcast pieces that

1

underscore difficulties that liberal arts graduates have in securing employment. While myths continue to spread throughout our "show me the money" cultural consciousness, in truth, all liberal arts graduates have qualifications that employers seek, and they have the capacity to market themselves effectively.

Many experienced colleagues reveal that while some liberal arts job seekers may have difficulty getting started, once they are armed with the right job search tools, an understanding of how to implement an effective and comprehensive job search campaign, and the positive attitudes required for success, they have little trouble finding, keeping, and growing within exciting and rewarding career fields.

Unfortunately, however, many talented individuals begin the job search with self-doubt and anxiety. Having heard horror stories of the "unemployability of liberal arts grads," they come to believe that they have few marketable skills and that their credentials, therefore, are not strong enough to conduct easy job searches. The simple truth is that far too many liberal arts grads are victims of self-fulfilling prophecies. Fearing the future and not really expecting to be successful, they make timid, unfocused, and, as a result, ineffective efforts. These liberal arts job seekers prolong the job search process, end up unemployed for extended periods or, perhaps worse, become underemployed, settling for jobs beneath their capabilities.

RESPONSIBILITIES AND RESPONSE-ABILITIES

Liberal arts graduates have repeatedly proven that they can find challenging and rewarding career-focused employment. "What can I do with a liberal arts degree?" is a question that reflects two important issues that concern the job search for liberal arts graduates. First, liberal arts graduates bear the burden of presenting their career goals and job qualifications to potential employers. Second, liberal arts majors (and prospective majors) who ask the question reveal a real difference between themselves and peers who have majored in technical or business fields.

Liberal arts majors are more responsible for communicating goals than those who graduate with more vocationally oriented majors. Names of majors—whether English, history, political science, psychology, or sociology, to cite a few—do not project to employers the breadth of skills that the liberal arts graduate has to offer, nor do they clearly project career goals. It is the responsibility of liberal arts students to identify the fields they wish to explore or enter as well as the qualifications they possess to perform specific job functions.

By utilizing broad-based skills, especially those related to research, analysis, communication, and project management, liberal arts graduates are very able to respond to and meet all the challenges associated with the job search and, ultimately, with lifelong career development. I characterized this **"response-ability"** as "liberal arts power" in an earlier book. Liberal arts power is the ability to use the talents and perspectives that, by virtue of broad academic experiences, are ingrained within liberal arts graduates and thus make up integral components of their portfolios. It is the power to accomplish job search–related tasks, including goal setting, resume writing, employer identification, correspondence development, networking, and interviewing. It is the power they possess to convince employers that their skills can be translated into job performance.

While many myths about the employability of liberal arts graduates prevail, it is definitely true that most liberal arts majors do not develop as large a "career vocabulary" as those who have majored in other fields. They have not taken courses with career-related titles (e.g., Principles of Marketing, Writing for Public Relations, and Information Systems Business Applications) in which basic theories, applications, job titles, and job functions are examined as part of subject-area overviews. The tables of contents for business and engineering texts regularly illustrate the career-oriented nature of the concepts they cover. Students who take these courses, therefore, develop a career vocabulary and, by circumstances of curricula, possess and use terminology that eventually allows them to communicate effectively—and in many cases passively—with potential employers. With initial contacts, these job seekers can "let their majors do the talking." Too many liberal arts students depend upon serendipity for developing a career vocabulary. They are exposed to certain careers by chance. Either through personal contact with someone—usually a family member, friend, or that notorious "friend of a friend"—or through random employment experiences, they learn to speak the languages of some fields. But chance is not enough! The *Glossary of Liberal Arts Options* in Chapter 4 is intended to motivate readers to use their liberal arts power—the abilities and attitudes instilled in them by their education—to very quickly develop the vocabulary that is required for a successful job search campaign.

WYSIWYG: HOW TO USE THIS BOOK

WYSIWYG is a phrase that was coined not too long ago by one of the original Silicon Valley whiz kids who then wore horn-rimmed glasses and pocket protectors yet now owns enough Initial Public Offering shares to have Ralph Lauren Polo logos embroidered on every article of clothing. This software developer differentiated user-friendly word processing software (usually Macintosh programs that were designed for the technologically challenged) from applications that only rocket scientists could (and did) use. He said, "What You See Is What You Get." When you formatted words as *italicized* or **boldface,** what appeared on screen was what was printed on paper. While this may not seem miraculous to charter members of the Internet Generation, this was quite an advancement at the time.

Nice Silicon Valley trivia, but what does this have to do with liberal arts careers and jobs? From a job search perspective, this intriguing acronym offers two very powerful lessons. First, one of the simplest concepts associated with career exploration can be characterized by the phrase "What you see is what you get." When you review field and job descriptions in books and make career observations through shadowing, externship, and, most critically, internship experiences, you enhance your career focus and ultimately, the success of your job search. Too often, individuals look deeply and inwardly, attempting to find a goal through intense self-assessment and introspection. While this is an important part of what career counselors often call "the career focus process," the steps of research must be taken boldly. Examining your options through reading and observing is what yields realistic and attainable goals. In so many wonderful ways, what you see "on the job" can truly help you hone in on your vocational aspirations.

Second, WYSIWYG can be translated to mean, "What you **say** is what you get." **You must be able to describe the nature of the job(s) you seek, whether the jobs are internships or postgraduation employment.** Goal statements must reflect knowledge of self and, most critically, knowledge of job functions. Knowing and communicating job titles and functions is the most significant key to success! If you actively solicit information about jobs through information conversations and reading materials, you will naturally identify fields and functions you wish to pursue. Afterward, a thorough assessment of skills and character traits that qualify you for these positions is appropriate. While some career counselors prefer that students conduct a thorough self-assessment prior to exploration (and this is ideal), I believe that too many career explorers and job seekers spend too much time on this assessment phase of the process. Don't dwell on your Myers-Briggs or Holland codes. Examine your options and prepare yourself as soon as possible to state your next steps for the short and long terms.

Yes, it is easy for career counselors to say, "Set goals, identify the fields and jobs you want, and learn to speak in terms that potential employers will understand," but this is difficult if you don't know where to begin. This book is intended to:

- Introduce you to concepts that are associated with a successful job search
- Set in motion the research required to set goals and initiate internship or postgraduation job searches
- Offer information on more than 300 realistic job and career options
- Highlight the top twelve fields for liberal arts graduates
- Assist you with setting realistic and attainable goals
- Provide step-by-step guidelines for resume writing, interviewing, and completing all the steps involved in comprehensive and successful job search campaigns
- Identify and refer you to print and online resources that are of value to you throughout your job search efforts

This book will help you make informed decisions about the next steps of your career path. You may be thinking, "There's a lot of material here. How do I get started?" To get the maximum from this publication:

Read the book to become familiar with its contents, its rationale, and the steps you will be taking to set goals and, eventually, find an externship, internship, or job that is right for you. For now, skim the worksheets and exercises in Appendix 1. In particular, spend time reading the job descriptions, writing in the margin, underlining passages, circling words or phrases, and noting questions. You should return to these sections often.

Complete the worksheets and exercises. Photocopy these items before you start so that you will always have clean copies for revisions and whenever you might wish to start anew.

Refer to the other publications that are cited in Job Search Resources to complete the research efforts that are required to identify and achieve job search goals. These resources could form the basis for a simple yet very effective collection of materials.

Follow the Ten Steps, discussed in Chapter 1, and other structured efforts to initiate and complete the actions that are required to transform your goals into realities. You will develop and implement job search strategies, create job search tools, build and utilize communication skills, and gain the comprehensive perspective that is required for immediate and lifelong job search success.

Enhance and project your liberal arts power to yield meaningful employment!

During the undergraduate years, liberal arts students rarely seek career planning advice and, consequently, with graduation upon them, they are thrust into an unknown world. The purpose of this book is to motivate readers to establish goals and prepare the necessary documentation to showcase their experience. This is intended to be a workbook, to be read from beginning to end and over again as necessary.

Best of luck!

I

Launching a Successful Job Search Campaign

In Part I, you'll discover how to start a successful job search campaign. Chapters 1 and 2 offer general advice on how to get organized, create a step-by-step plan, and perform the critical research that must accompany a successful job search.

1

I'm a Liberal Arts Grad: Now What?

▶ My experience has shown me that liberal arts job seekers may have difficulty getting started but that once they are armed with the right job search tools, an understanding of how to implement an effective job search campaign, and the positive attitudes required for success in any endeavor, they have no trouble finding and keeping excellent jobs. Liberal arts graduates have the qualifications employers seek, and, whether they know it or not, they all have the capacity to market these qualifications successfully.

Liberal arts graduates have proven that they can find jobs that are just as challenging and rewarding as the work secured by their peers who majored in other disciplines. It is true that if one looks at broad statistics, such as the number of recruiting organizations that request interviews with liberal arts graduates or the average salary offers for liberal arts graduates, it is easy to be pessimistic. But if one focuses on each liberal arts job seeker as a person who is capable of finding satisfying employment, a truer picture begins to emerge.

In order to succeed in the job search, however, liberal arts students must learn to be self-directed and to implement aggressive job-hunting techniques. They have to adopt a new mind-set. They should not, for example, expect to be recruited directly off the college campus for their first job, as many engineering students may be. Although many students do find employment through the on-campus recruiting system, relying on it will put them at a disadvantage. The truth is that many liberal arts students have to work harder at the job search process in two ways: forming and articulating career goals and learning how to effectively utilize job-hunting techniques.

TEN STEPS TO SUCCESS

1. Set and Articulate Goals

Successful job seekers know and say what they want to do and where they want to work. They set functional and geographic goals. Goal setting involves self-assessment (clarification of values, interests, personality traits, and skills) and, most important, research of career fields and job functions prior to the job search. Introspection is not enough! The ability to clearly and concisely present job search goals (by stating fields of interest and job titles) is critical! Stating, "I want to work anywhere, doing anything," diminishes the potential for success. Remember What You **Say** Is What You Get! Often, candidates' majors "speak" for them, particularly when their majors parallel a career field, yet marketing majors proudly, and too often inarticulately, restate over and over their interest in marketing without clearly citing fields or functions of interest. Restating one's major title over and over like a mantra does not enhance one's job search potential. Whether a liberal arts or a technical grad, conducting research is critical to defining one's goals. Because of the importance of this phase of the career focus and job search, a great deal of additional attention will be paid to strategies and approaches in Chapter 2. Remember, research must take place prior to an effective job search.

2. Develop Job Search Tools

Successful job seekers project goals and qualifications via well-written job search documents, such as resumes, cover letters, and follow-up correspondence. Resumes can be multipurpose (without an objective) or targeted (with an objective that cites goals). Cover letters communicate goals and qualifications for specific positions (letters of application) or potential opportunities (letters of inquiry and letters of introduction) as well as writing talents. Follow-up correspondence maintains communication while projecting strong writing skills, positive motivation, enthusiasm, and focus. The very best tools are finely sharpened, pointed toward particular goals. Targeted resumes and cover letters are the most effective. Each should be able to stand alone when reviewed by prospective employers, but together, they form a unified presentation of qualifications and motivation and an illustration of one's writing abilities. Chapters 6 and 7 expand upon the development of the very best job search tools for liberal arts students and graduates.

3. Identify a Hit List of Potential Employers

Directories and other printed and online resources help to develop a list of employers to contact. (Please refer to Appendixes 2 and 3.) Phone communication can help initially identify the nature of some jobs within organizations, the availability of opportunities, the people to contact, and the procedures to follow. *Phone skills are often the most significant characteristics that distinguish successful job seekers from not-so-successful ones!* The more a job seeker uses the phone, the more likely and quickly he or she will succeed. Identification of and initial communication with prospective employers is what allows liberal arts job seekers to conduct proactive as well as reactive efforts.

4. Establish and Use a Network

Successful job seekers ask friends, family members, faculty members, and alumni to assist in their research and job search efforts, including scheduling information conversations and writing referrals to potential employers. These job search support persons should be constantly updated on the job seeker's efforts and status. For liberal arts students and grads, "NETworking or NOT working" means utilizing existing contacts and expanding one's support group, and now more than ever, it also means using the Internet for job search activities. Job seekers identify and use Web sites that are designed to identify appropriate postings and offer advice whenever possible. Networkers send e-mail "cover notes" (shorter than formal cover letters) and resumes that are copied and pasted into e-communiqués in addition to faxes and mailed job search correspondence. Liberal arts candidates who conduct effective e-search campaigns locate home pages of potential employers and conduct research activities, identify postings, and electronically transmit resumes and cover notes. They complete search engine–driven exploration to identify postings, general field information, and employer-specific data to help with hit list and interview preparation efforts. Also, many gain and then market HTML and Java programming skills to potential employers.

5. Respond to Posted Opportunities

Liberal arts job seekers locate and use job postings such as printed and electronic want ads, employment agencies, job fairs, and on- and off-campus recruiting programs. They use professional association newsletters to identify opportunities. "Reactive" job search strategies encompass the identification of and effective response to clearly identifiable opportunities that are advertised in newspapers and newsletters and through college career services offices or third-party employment organizations. Liberal arts job seekers must not depend on paper or electronically published postings, but they cannot ignore them! They should become effective at reactive as well as proactive (goal-directed) methods. They make sure that initial communiqués are dynamic and focus on the skills they possess for specific jobs, but they don't simply make initial contact and hope for an employer response.

6. Call First, Then Fax or E-mail, and, Finally, Mail Resumes and Cover Letters to People on the Hit List and in the Job Search Network

Successful job seekers inform as many people as possible, as often as possible, about their job search goals. They keep the flow of communication persistent yet appropriate. They don't assume that contacts will remember them; they always add a resume to their correspondence or follow-up e-mail or fax notes. The more they feel comfortable using the phone (and increasingly e-mail), the better. They call for additional information and for a more thorough job description in response to a posting and prior to screening or subsequent "call back" interviews. They aren't shy about calling to confirm interviews and asking, "What can I expect? Are there questions I should think about? Could you provide me with some helpful information prior to my interview?"

7. Follow Up, Follow Up, and Follow Up Again

Job seekers continue to communicate with potential employers until an interview (by phone or in person) is given. Communication is done by phone, letter, and fax and e-mail communiqués. Successful liberal arts job seekers are persistent but not pests, communicative yet not obnoxious. Scenarios outlined in Chapter 8 reveal how easy it is to conduct effective follow-up efforts. Over the years, I have identified this as one of the less-than-obvious factors that differentiates successful individuals from those who are not so successful. Most liberal arts grads have well-established verbal communication skills yet, for some reason, are ambivalent about using these skills within the context of a job search. While "What can I do with a major in . . .?" is clearly the most frequently asked question, "Don't you think it would seem too pushy to call now?," "Why haven't I heard from them?," and "When do you think I should follow up?" are queries that clearly are in the top-ten-most-often-heard-list. Assertiveness must be applied to research, networking, and job search efforts.

8. Ace the Interview

Successful job seekers project focus and communicate their motivations and their qualifications to perform the specific job(s) during initial and follow-up interviews. Liberal arts candidates who succeed prepare and practice prior to their interview "conversations with a purpose" in order to identify key points and examples of when skills were used to achieve results. Successful job seekers cite examples of their accomplishments. They "work off" of their resumes during interviews, utilizing three Qualifications Connections (QCs); three anecdotes with Actions, Results, Tasks, Skills (ARTS) examples; and three Employer Questions (EQs), which are discussed in detail later. Chapter 8 will reveal how easy it is to prepare for this often anxiety-provoking conversation without too much perspiration.

9. Volunteer, Serve as an Intern or Extern, or Take Courses to Support Your Job Search Goals

Successful job seekers continue skill-building by taking one or two classes in goal-related areas and by finding part-time paid or volunteer experiences. A few classes in accounting, advertising, desktop publishing, spreadsheet programs, or counseling can be critical to one's success. By working, even in an area unrelated to their majors, successful liberal arts job seekers project positive work ethics. Grads and soon-to-be grads often springboard from internships into ideal paid positions after three to six months. **This is the most critical yet often most ignored step to success. Experiential learning outside of the classroom in the world of work will springboard job seekers, regardless of their majors, into the jobs of their dreams.**

10. Conduct Post-Offer Analysis, Negotiate, *Then* Accept an Offer

Yes, more than one offer of employment can be obtained if a job seeker is effective. Post-offer analysis (taking into account such factors as career goals, salary, personalities of co-workers and supervisors, and job setting) is done after a liberal arts graduate receives a job offer.

DEVELOPING A TIMETABLE: WEEKS OF WORK

While your major may not be the most important factor in securing a job, your motivation and actions are critical. The Ten Steps offer a proven structure to help you with your job search. Having said that, some tasks are easier than others to complete. Devising a timetable will help and, therefore, I offer one that has proven successful—the Weeks of Work (WOW) strategy. This five-week process will mobilize you and maximize your results through exploration, resume writing, communication skills enhancement, and networking. The outline is intended to provide a clear, realistic, and optimistic timeframe. Should you wish to spend a bit more time completing the tasks associated with each week, do so, but don't lose momentum or let fear of focus and other negative factors fixate you on a particular set of tasks.

Week One: Information Conversations

These exchanges are the simplest yet most effective method for exploring options and initiating job search efforts. Whether you are a Career Explorer (one who cannot yet clearly state three fields or jobs of interest) or a Job Seeker (a WYSIWYGer who can articulate job search targets), first identify five individuals, ideally alumni of your alma mater. Then, call or e-mail these five individuals. Through easy-to-follow guidelines, you should identify basic questions and arrange for information conversations. By asking questions like those below, you gain a sense of whether or not you wish to identify a profession as an educational, career, or job search target worthy of the next steps. Also, by communicating with someone in a field of interest, you develop a relationship that will serve you better as you begin to network. An Information Conversation Partner can become a role model, a mentor, and perhaps someday, your boss! Imagine asking:

What do you really do?

How did you get this job?

How did you get your first job in the field?

What would a typical first job in this field be today?

Does it require any specialized education or graduate training?

What advice would you give to someone who is looking for this type of job?

Can you suggest someone else with whom I can have an information conversation?

Would it be possible to shadow you at work for a day or two so that I can get a sense of your day-to-day activities?

The more people you talk to, the more focused you become and the more likely you will someday soon find a great job. Alumni are most often very willing to share information about their backgrounds, and they are usually happy to receive such requests.

Week Two: Shadowing

Shadowing offers you the opportunity to literally "walk in someone's footsteps." By doing so, you will gain a keen understanding of what his or her job entails—what does the average day consist of, what functions does that person perform, what expectations are placed upon him or her in a given day? All of this information is critical for formulating an opinion about whether or not you are suited for such a position. If you can arrange for such an opportunity, it is advisable to shadow as many as four individuals; at least two should represent the roles and responsibilities associated with entry-level positions (years 1–3), while the others should give you a taste of what more advanced positions might be like.

Shadowing is perhaps the most underutilized yet most valuable of all exploration and job search preparation activities. It is intended to make it easier for you to prioritize options, identify the top three job search targets, and initiate the efforts that are required to obtain an externship. Once priority fields and job functions are established, it is easier to develop targeted resumes with appropriate objective statements and a summary of your qualifications. Now is the time to develop these fine-tuned job search tools.

Weeks Three and Four: Externships and More

Simply, an externship takes place after you request **an opportunity to complete a one- to two-week project that offers exposure to the day-to-day activities of your potential job.** After accomplishing the WOW tasks of the first two weeks, you should have strong feelings about who would be your best contact for an externship. Those you shadowed or who served as Information Conversation Partners might be ideal, but you may now feel confident enough to communicate with others and establish new relationships. While internships, with preestablished learning objectives, writing assignments, and projects, are clearly ideal, project-by-project opportunities are often just as valuable. Externships are less formal and shorter internship-like forays into the world of work. They can be the most powerful approach to securing a job but, to date, have not become a commonly implemented step to success. To obtain an externship, you must utilize effective job search strategies and appropriate tools and techniques (resumes, cover letters, and phone interviews). To do so, the first four of the Ten Steps to job search success should be used. To briefly restate:

1. **Set and articulate goals.** Clearly state three externship targets, including fields, job functions, and cities where you would like to work. By stating what you would like to do next, not "for the rest of your life," you will be best prepared to develop and implement goal-specific job search strategies.
2. **Develop job search tools.** Draft, edit, and then finalize multipurpose and targeted resumes as well as effective cover letters and follow-up communiqués. Project goals and qualifications via well-written job search documents.
3. **Identify a hit list of potential employers.** Use internship directories and other printed and online resources to develop a list of potential externship sites to contact. Identify options, prioritize, then act!
4. **Establish and use a network.** Identify and ask friends, family members, faculty members, and alumni to assist you in your job search efforts.

Externships can be critical to your success. They can be a bridge to a job or to a lengthier internship experience. During your externship, you should expand upon your list of relevant employers. When externships are completed, you will clearly and actively document your projects on updated targeted resumes. Network with the people you interacted with during this experience; ask for referrals and expand your hit list of potential full-time employers. Don't be shy! If the externship doesn't provide you with the information or inspiration you require to gain focus, ask to stay longer, seek another project, or complete another externship in a different field or setting.

Week Five: To Thrive, Your Search Begins, Then Ends and Begins Again

After you complete the research and skills-building efforts of the first four weeks, you should be more clearly focused, better able to state goals, and more "qualified." Your resumes, which project the skills you enhanced through your externship, are revised and ready to distribute. Now you are prepared to complete the remainder of the ten steps. To review:

5. **Respond to posted opportunities.** Locate and use job postings, such as printed and electronic want ads, employment agencies, job fairs, and on- and off-campus recruiting programs. Identify and use professional association newsletters. Use third-party employment agencies. Don't depend on postings, but don't ignore them!
6. **Call, fax, or e-mail and then mail cover letters and resumes to those on your hit list, to network members, and in response to postings.** Keep the flow of communication persistent yet appropriate. Always add your resume to correspondence and follow-up e-mail or faxed notes.
7. **Follow up, follow up, follow up.** Continue to communicate with potential employers by phone, letter, and fax communiqués until an interview is given.

8. **Interview by phone or in person** Communicate your motivations and your qualifications to perform a job during your initial and follow-up interviews. Prepare and practice prior to your interview in order to identify key points and examples of when skills were used to achieve results. Work from your resume and cite examples of your accomplishments.

9. **Volunteer, serve as an intern or extern, or take courses to support your job search goals.** Continue to build your skills by taking one or two classes in goal-related areas and by finding part-time paid or volunteer experiences.

10. **Conduct post-offer analysis, negotiate, then accept an offer.** Analyze such factors as career goals, salary, personalities of co-workers and supervisors, and job setting.

The above activities are meant to inspire effective attitudes and actions. Don't let the five-week time frame frustrate you. While some people can complete all the activities within the thirty-five-day period, others do take longer. You are encouraged to find security within the structure of this step-by-step calendar and confidence in the fact that many have proven it successful.

Be Proactive, Not Reactive
Too many liberal arts students and graduates fail to implement the comprehensive approach that is required to optimize their outcomes. Reactive job search efforts (step five of the Ten Steps) involve responding to electronic and printed postings, attending job fairs, participating in on- and off-campus recruiting, and using third-party agencies. It is a passive rather than powerful job search strategy.

Proactive job search strategies involve primarily steps one, three, six, and seven. With clearly focused goals, liberal arts job seekers can identify lists of potential employers, initiate communication, and follow up in order to obtain interviews and, ultimately, offers. If, as an example, the liberal arts job or internship seeker identifies advertising as the field of interest and account management and media planning as functional areas of interest, a very effective proactive campaign can be mounted. Without this type of focus, one is limited to reactive methodologies.

The Heart of the Job Seeker and the Head of the Job Seeker
Certain motivations underlie job search strategies, and these dynamics can be characterized as "the heart of the job seeker and the head of the job seeker." The *heart* of the liberal arts job seeker is revealed by statements, queries, and unrealistic hopes that include:

- I want to keep my options open and not limit myself to anything too specific
- I'm hopeful I can do a great many things, so I'll send out a lot of resumes, respond to a number of postings, and let employers see the potential I possess
- I don't have experience in this field, but the posting looks so interesting, and I know I can do the job
- I really would like to work overseas. Is there a listing of jobs outside the U.S. or employers with international options?
- I hear that there are some fields that like to hire candidates with my major; what are they?

The *head* of the liberal arts job seeker is illustrated by strategic thinking and actions revealed in statements that include:

- I'll focus my proactive efforts on three fields and functional areas, yet I will respond creatively to a variety of postings and be open-minded to other reactive options
- I'll identify the specific skills and field-related knowledge I possess, project these in targeted resumes, clearly present a goal-directed image to appropriate employers, and take responsibility for personifying my desires to enter chosen fields
- I'll be realistic about securing entry-level and internship options while remaining optimistic about other opportunities, but I'll maintain awareness of how potential employers review resumes and grant consideration to selected candidates
- Regardless of my geographic goals, whether domestic or international, I will identify employers, communicate by phone, and clearly realize and meet the challenges associated with long-distance job searches
- I will conduct the assessment and research required to develop realistic goals, identify the skills that are required to enter my fields of interest, promote or expand upon my existing qualifications, and present myself as a focused candidate to employers who offer opportunities in my fields of interest.

Liberal arts power allows you to merge the attitudes, aspirations, and actions that are associated with the heart of the job seeker with those that are associated with the head of the job seeker. It is the power to accomplish tasks related to your job search, including goal setting, resume writing, employer identification, correspondence development, networking, and interviewing. It is the power you possess to convince employers that your personal portfolio of skills are applicable to your on-the-job performance. The following information will inspire your heart and educate your head about reality-based liberal arts job search strategies.

Do Your Research!

▶ As a liberal arts student, you probably have the skills to research and write excellent term papers. If you think of the research involved in setting goals and finding a job as similar to that involved in writing a paper, you may become more motivated to complete these tasks and more optimistic about the results. Too often, the job of setting goals is seen as Herculean, requiring more time and energy than you have. It is a process that you would rather not undertake, in part because you fear limiting yourself. However, if you skip the critical step of research, your job search will lack direction just as a term paper would lack structure and content.

TAKING YOUR FIRST STEPS: FIVE SIMPLE PHRASES

As you consider the process of job search research, you may not know where to begin. Consider the following five phrases as a guide for gathering critical information.

If You Can Describe a Job, You Can Get That Job!
You need to gather information about a job by following the suggestions in Chapter 1 and then articulate what you've found. WYSIWYG—What You Say Is What You Get—applies here. The more you know about a particular career you are pursuing and the better you can describe what you're looking for, the better your odds are of securing such a position.

If You Have Met Someone with a Job You Would Like, You Can Get a Similar Job!
This phrase illustrates the power behind conducting information conversations and identifying role models and mentors. Often, liberal arts graduates begin a job search by using academically oriented goals, and, too often, they are reluctant to speak in realistic terms. As an example, a psychology major expresses interest in organizational behavior or organizational consulting without any evidence that entry-level opportunities exist.

If you meet individuals who hold positions in which you are interested, it allows you to envision yourself in that position and plan your job search accordingly.

The More You Talk to People Who Work in Your Field of Interest, the More Likely You Will Someday Enter That Field!

Now we are focusing on the quantity as well as the quality of information conversations and on the need for the continuation of your efforts. By committing to an ongoing investigation of your chosen field and seeking to meet people within these fields, you enhance the potential of someday networking into jobs, internships, or externships.

Look *at* Jobs Before You Look for Jobs!

A reactive search is a knee-jerk approach because it is easy to look at and respond to job postings and to fool yourself into thinking that the job search is underway. It is very important that you use, but not limit yourself to, reactive approaches. To be powerful and successful, you must utilize the traditional liberal arts talents associated with research, analysis, and communication to conduct research efforts.

If Imitation Is the Sincerest Form of Flattery, It Is Also the Most Effective Career Development and Job Search Strategy!

You can only replicate your role model's success if you truly understand the circumstances that led to it. This can help you learn from someone's past and turn it into your future. Also, you should locate and utilize a job search coach. Often, your coach will be a career services professional at your school, but it can also be a reference librarian, a faculty member, an alumnus, a friend who graduated from another institution, or someone with whom you had an information conversation and who evolved from role model to mentor. This person can share with you a variety of success stories and outline numerous paths for you to follow.

For some, these five phrases will make a great deal of sense immediately. For others, the insights contained within these words may take a bit of time to perceive. Students, graduates, and career services colleagues who read this book should review all five phrases after finishing the entire text and then reexamine their understanding of these phrases. Liberal arts power is the power to comprehend and personify these phrases.

GAINING FOCUS FROM RESEARCH: THE TRUE LIBERAL ARTS POWER

To take the first steps on the path to success, the more motivation you have to connect goal-setting to job search activities, the better. It is critical that you understand your responsibility to become more "goal articulate" than your peers and that you believe in your "response-ability" to do so. You have the ability to respond to circumstances and challenges associated with setting goals to find meaningful and fulfilling employment.

The same type of approach that you would take with writing a term paper will work here. Generally, a step-by-step approach in which you choose a subject, narrow it, and gain a specific focus through additional research is recommended. The following steps are no doubt familiar to you. Use your existing knowledge in your job search campaign and it will be no more difficult than an academic project you've completed in the past.

Choose Your Subject

After reviewing the listing of liberal arts jobs in Chapter 4, you should narrow your options to five to ten fields or job functions that you would like to examine further. The descriptions that appear in Chapter 4 are not comprehensive enough to use as the basis for your job search or internship goals, but they offer enough information to initiate your research and to motivate you to complete your efforts. The Research and Job Search Goals Worksheet in Appendix 1 asks you to identify the fields and job functions of most interest to you. This and other worksheets and exercises in this book have been developed to help you track the data you collect and, as you progress, to provide you with a means to facilitate the analysis required to prioritize your ultimate job search or internship goals.

Narrow Your Subject

As with research papers, *too much* information prohibits you from accomplishing your final goals. It is critical that you quickly identify and narrow the premise or thesis that is associated with your paper and then continue until completion. With your job search, it is crucial that you use initial data collection to focus on the areas of most significant interest and then transform your research options into job search and internship search goals. The Skills Inventory and Majors and Careers Matrix (also in Appendix 1) assist you with the required analysis, and the Research and Job Search Goals Worksheet asks you to ultimately cite three goals. Before you can complete these exercises, you must be inspired to clarify your options and enhance your focus on a manageable number of goals.

Provide a Focus for Gathering Material

To begin the process that will lead to your job search goals, first explore the fields and job functions that you outlined in your Research and Job Search Goals Worksheet, based on the following seven criteria:

Job Description

What duties and responsibilities are associated with the job(s) within a field? How does a person in that field spend a typical day? You must have a clear understanding of what a job involves in order to determine whether or not it is a realistic goal and to effectively set and implement strategies to attain that goal. Remember the first of our five phrases, "If you can describe a job, you can get that job." In addition to general resources, you should contact organizations that hire people to perform these jobs, request job descriptions, and review written and online literature. Initially, focus on obtaining information only, not on obtaining employment.

Qualifications

What skills, attributes, or personality characteristics would be valuable for performing the tasks associated with a job? From job descriptions, you can interpret the qualifications required. At this stage, you are simply identifying the general qualities associated with the job. You are not yet judging whether you are qualified for a post. Later you will analyze your strengths and weaknesses and then assess your chances for job search or internship search success.

Education/Training/Experience

How much and what type of education are required? Is additional training necessary? If so, where can it be obtained—through a certificate program, a seminar, or via one course at a time? Is career-related experience necessary? How may experience be obtained—through internships or externships? Again, do not judge yourself as unqualified if you do not have the stated education, usually cited as a major, nor the required experience. You are simply identifying requirements. Later, if you decide a job is a realistic goal, you can develop a strategy to deal with the issues associated with education and experience.

Organizational Structure

Where does the job fit into the typical organization that hires for these positions? What division or department houses these jobs, and to whom would someone holding this post report? Identify pregraduation internship options, postgraduation opportunities, and future options that comprise a career path. Don't be too concerned with the long-term because your first job will not be your last. Realistically, you are seeking to identify the next, not the last, opportunity.

Entry-Level Options

How does one enter the field or obtain the internship or job in question? Do you begin through a formal training program or in a lower-level position, eventually to be promoted to the desired post? What are the entry-level options?

Work Environment and Conditions

Where does one work? In an office, in a store, over the Internet, or on the road? In what city? What is the physical environment like? Does a geographic move accompany promotions? Consider these factors when you are narrowing your options, but remember that they are most important when you take job search actions, not when you are identifying research or job search goals. Also, don't let perceived negatives inhibit you from taking initial actions. Post-offer analysis is when you can negotiate alternatives or, if desired, reject offers.

Earnings and Outlook

What is the range of starting salaries for your job functions and fields of interest? What are potential long-term earnings? Where are opportunities now, and where will they be in the future? Is the field one with predicted growth, or are there variables that could negatively affect the field? Are there potential bonuses and performance-linked incentives associated with the job? Do not let these answers be the strongest variables in determining your job search goals. If you are motivated, you will find a job within a field, even if it is overcrowded by some arbitrary standards, and you will receive the appropriate financial rewards in time.

Find References and Compile a Bibliography

References can be "paper and pencil," "people to people," and, "on line." They can be written materials, people who are knowledgeable about jobs and fields, or Web pages, and they can be located at various sites. University and large public libraries contain many publications that can be used during the research process. Locate and use varied career-related publications that contain information on your ten research options, such as large multicareer volumes and small career-specific pamphlets. Increasingly, they are field- and, often, major-focused publications. Reference librarians can be excellent career counselors and job search support persons. They are professional problem solvers who can help locate information on almost any topic of interest. Don't be afraid to ask for help, and don't stop when an obstacle is placed before you. It may take several requests and a few referrals to locate what you are looking for.

Professional associations usually publish "Careers in . . ." materials. Make efforts to identify and contact these groups. Always utilize the phone, regardless of the potential costs, to request membership information, written materials, the names of local members, and access to a membership directory. Information conversations with members of associations in fields related to your interests can be very productive. Remember, sometimes the best information is the hardest to find. Appendix 3: Job Search Resources identifies and describes some of the best resources you can use. This listing is designed to be condensed yet comprehensive.

Gather Notes

Researching career options, like writing a term paper, involves note-taking. Use a notebook, index cards, or folders to organize the information you obtain. By keeping written documentation, you will be able to review the information when you are ready to prioritize your options. Once you have identified your job search goals, you will use this information to write your resume and job search correspondence and in the interviewing phase of your job search.

Categorize Your Notes

Once you've researched the fields or jobs you have selected, rank your notes (entries on the Research and Job Search Goals Worksheet) in order. You must then identify which fields or functions are of most interest to you and which are of least interest to you. This begins the analysis that is required to focus on specific options. Don't be afraid to state and then later change rankings. Eventually, you will identify the top three possibilities and list them in the Research and Job Search Goals Worksheet.

Decide Upon an Approach and a Point of View

The seven criteria—job description, qualifications, education/training/experience, organizational structure, entry-level options, work environment and conditions, and earnings and outlook—and the ideas you gathered from completing the research and Job Search Goals Worksheet should be all you need to gain some focus. Don't be intimidated by this particular stage of the process. You can certainly omit and add options as you continue to gain insight and as you face the realities of your job search. **You should feel comfortable identifying some tentative job search goals.** Even tentative goals will offer much-needed focus, and focus provides control!

Draw Up a Detailed Outline

Knowledge is the best way for you to overcome a lack of training or experience. The more you know about a job, the more likely you are to get that job. With definite goals in mind, you can become increasingly confident of your potential to succeed. You can identify potential employers, develop strategies for communicating with employers, and when required, identify additional education that you might need to break into a field. Also, remain confident that focus—best illustrated by targeted resumes—is an asset, not a liability.

You may be asking yourself, "When do I know that my research is thorough enough to set job search goals or take reactive and proactive next steps?" Offering a summation to our term paper metaphor, your research is complete when you can imagine yourself presenting the findings of your "paper" to a hypothetical group of twelfth graders in ways that motivate them to explore the same options. Your presentation should give these students enough information to pass a career quiz. You should be able to explain a career field and its associated job functions in easy-to-understand terminology that is sophisticated enough for someone who is about 17, without using jargon or buzz phrases that might indicate a lack of knowledge. If you can achieve these hypothetical objectives, then you know enough to make a judgment about job search goals, and you are prepared to progress from research to job search.

II

Considering Your Many Career Options

Now that you have a better idea of what the job search entails, Part II will provide you with comprehensive information on more than 300 career options. Chapter 3 outlines the functional areas that virtually every organization possesses, while Chapter 4 includes hundreds of detailed job descriptions for you to consider. Chapter 5 reviews the twelve suggested opportunities for liberal arts graduates. After completing both Parts I and II, you should have narrowed your choices considerably and be ready to respond to specific job opportunities.

3

Exploring the World of Work

FIELDS AND FUNCTIONS OF INTEREST

▶ Once you begin to focus on specific fields and functions, you should be able to state job titles that are of interest to you. Remember the first of the five phrases from Chapter 2, "If you can describe a job, you can get that job."

To uncover entry-level options, it is helpful to know that organizations and industries are generally composed of seven functional areas. These include administration, communications, finance, human resources, marketing, operations, and sales. These basic functions seem to characterize most organizations, from multinational corporations to nonprofit institutions. While the formal names given to jobs within these areas may vary, you might identify additional options by investigating opportunities from a functional perspective.

Identifying the functional areas that best match your skills, capabilities, motivations, and previous experience is the first step of this approach. Next, determine the work environments in which you wish to carry out these functions and focus on the titles of positions that represent specific functions. For instance, you may soon state, "I want to work in marketing (field), most likely developing product-support materials and publications (function) for a manufacturer of consumer products (firm). I could work, either directly or indirectly, within these capacities for a manufacturer, public-relations firm, marketing consultant, or an advertising agency (firms) as an account executive, copywriter, corporate communications professional, or marketing assistant (titles).

When you can speak the "language of the three Fs" (fields, functions, and firms), you are truly prepared to plan and implement dynamic proactive and reactive strategies.

Administration

This function entails general office management and concerns the oversight and maintenance of the facilities and systems that are required to conduct the day-to-day activities of an organization. It consists of three subfunctions:

Office Services
Overseeing and delivering support services, such as word processing, duplication, mail, recordkeeping, and telecommunications.

Facilities Management
Managing and maintaining a physical plant and its surroundings, including decisions about renovations, expansion, and new site selection. It may also entail responsibility for food services and conference facilities.

Security
Overseeing activities related to safeguarding the physical plant, materials and equipment, documents, and personnel.

Administration requires organizational and analytical capabilities and the ability to make sound decisions about people, procedures, and equipment. Those working in this functional area must be prepared to deal with internal and external personnel, an administrative staff, and outside vendors. Opportunities in this field may appear hidden to liberal arts graduates, but they are often well worth the effort to uncover because administration offers growth potential. Titles include office manager, property manager, mall manager, director of administration, facilities manager, facilities planner, security manager, and security director.

Communications
Communications is a functional area that many liberal arts job seekers find appealing. Realistically, it is an area where liberal arts graduates can use many of their natural talents. It also consists of three subfunctions:

Writing
Developing written materials that are used externally to market a product or service or to support the users of products or services and used internally for training purposes and to disseminate important information to employers, shareholders, and related groups. Brochures, posters, packages, reports, articles, proposals, presentations, courses, training and user-support materials, newsletters, speeches, and correspondence are some of the many forms that written output can take.

Graphics
Illustrating, drafting, and designing for marketing, promotions, production, education, and other purposes. Output includes the written documents listed above as well as plans, charts, slides, computer graphics, and, increasingly, Web-presented designs. Writing and graphics professionals often work together for advertising agencies, public relations firms, graphic design firms, book publishers, magazines, and newspapers, or they serve as independent consultants or freelancers.

Public Relations, Publicity, and Promotions
Developing and transmitting information through various media and special events to customers, investors, employees, the public, and local, state, and federal government

agencies. These activities promote sales or services, secure support for particular points of view, announce and enhance attendance at major events, raise funds, promote a particular candidacy, dispel rumors, and otherwise convey accurate information to specific audiences.

Communications is a functional area that overlaps many fields and exists in many employment sectors, including journalism, publishing, advertising, public relations, politics, education, and hospitality. Liberal arts majors who want to find work within these fields must be prepared to show their talents via portfolios and, whenever possible, related experiences (internships, externships, or volunteer projects). Titles include but are not limited to technical writer, documentation writer, proposal writer, technical editor, course developer, training coordinator, promotional writer, marketing communications specialist, employee benefits writer, copywriter, editor, technical illustrator, designer, art editor, graphics specialist, public affairs director, special event planner, development officer, investor relations director, community affairs manager, press relations specialist, and corporate communications specialist.

Finance

Finance is a business-oriented function, but it is not limited to those who majored in business. It is composed of four subfunctions:

Accounting

Collecting, documenting, summarizing, and analyzing financial data to provide the information that is required to control and plan activities and programs and to provide information to taxation and regulatory entities, investors, and creditors. Accounting includes general accounting, with accounts payable and receivable, payroll, assets, and general ledger responsibilities; cost accounting, with responsibility for determining and monitoring the cost of products and services; and planning and analysis (or managerial accounting), with responsibility for monitoring and forecasting budgets as well as conducting the analysis required to make decisions with financial implications.

Treasury

Managing and, when necessary, obtaining the funds that are required to manufacture products or offer services. Treasury includes planning for optimum use of assets and surplus funds within credit and collections, cash management, strategic planning and acquisitions, and tax minimization areas.

Auditing

Collecting data and monitoring the internal financial control systems to ensure reliability and accuracy and to determine more efficient procedures. Internal auditors, working within an organization, work closely with external auditors who work for accounting firms. Many audit general procedures and policy compliance in addition to financial data and financial compliance.

Information Systems

Providing computer support for all of the above areas, allowing quick and accurate import and retrieval as well as the manipulation of data and development of reports.

Finance roles and responsibilities exist within all types of organizations and, of course, within the accounting firms and financial institutions that provide these functions as services to clients. Liberal arts majors who have taken a few accounting and finance courses (before or after graduation) or who simply have quantitative and analytical skills can get jobs in this broad functional area. Opportunities exist within almost any setting, from retail companies to public interest groups, including the most obvious environments of banks, financial services institutions, tax preparation firms, and investment banks. Titles include staff accountant, internal audit trainee, accounts payable administrator, cost accountant, financial analyst, managerial accountant, treasurer's assistant, acquisitions analyst, real estate analyst, strategic planner, and cash management analyst.

Human Resources
An area with many roles and responsibilities that makes good use of liberal arts talents, human resources involves much more than simply working with people. It has four subfunctions:

Recruiting and Staffing
Identifying, screening, interviewing, and hiring both entry-level and experienced professional and administrative employees. This function involves recruiting from external sources, including colleges and universities, as well as from internal ones (when working within an organization) and provides prescreening and other "value-added" services when working for a search firm or temporary agency.

Compensation and Benefits
Developing and monitoring fair, competitive, and legally sound financial and other reward systems as well as overseeing costs related to these systems.

Training and Development
Training and providing access to training for both entry-level and management personnel so that they can gain the skills and experiences that are needed to enhance their performance and take on additional responsibilities. This function includes monitoring and providing feedback on performance and analyzing the effectiveness of groups as well as individuals.

Employee Relations
Developing and overseeing programs, events, and services that promote company loyalty and enhance the work environment. This function includes orientation as well as social, recreational, health, and educational options.

Traditionally, people who have served within "line" roles (day-to-day business of a given organization, whether sales, manufacturing, retail, or service) can and do evolve to staff positions in human resources. Knowledge of the particular business can help a job seeker overcome a lack of experience, as can an internship. Courses, seminars, and experience at a search firm or temporary employment agency are valuable assets when seeking entry-level options. Titles include college recruiter, director of professional staffing, manager of nonexempt hiring, compensation analyst, benefits administrator, corporate health and safety coordinator, employee relations specialist, employee assistance coordinator, personnel manager, and human resources assistant.

Marketing

The marketing function spans a variety of titles and roles across diverse industries and organizational settings. Although titles within different organizations will vary greatly, roles and responsibilities are common. Marketing has six subfunctions:

New Product Development

Analyzing markets and competitors, determining production and distribution capabilities, judging potential costs and profits as well as liabilities and benefits of future expansion, and conducting the research that is required to create and market a product or service. This function can be an independent area or department or can operate in conjunction with product management or marketing research.

Product Management

Planning, introducing, and managing a product or group of related products and overseeing other functions and responsibilities that are associated with controlling the marketing mix—the product, price, promotional activities, and point of distribution (sales).

Marketing Research

Collecting and analyzing data, identifying trends, and contributing to decision making about issues that are related to the marketing mix. This function involves surveying users (customers), monitoring internal operations (production and distribution), and analyzing financial information (cost versus profit) to identify trends and cite recommendations.

Product and Sales Support

Providing specialized and technical information (via publications, manuals, videotapes, audiotapes, and reports) and assistance (via training, customer presentations, and customer service efforts) to product management and sales personnel, often serving as a link between two function areas. This function could involve monitoring inventory, overseeing ordering procedures, and managing contract development.

Advertising, Promotions, and Public Relations

Developing and overseeing materials and activities that are meant to persuade potential customers to use or purchase an organization's products or services and to keep the organization's image highly visible and well regarded. Advertising involves purchasing broadcast time as well as print and graphic space (on billboards, the Internet, and various other sites) to direct a product or service at primary consumers to increase sales. Promotions involves planning and implementing special events and utilizing related materials and giveaways that directly support sales efforts and new product launches. Public relations is directed at broad audiences, with efforts designed to enhance name recognition, connect an image to positive attributes, and generally inspire appropriate attitudes in the public or targeted audiences. Publicity is often sought for special events through public relations efforts. Public relations also involves shareholder services, crisis management, and press relations efforts.

Customer Service

Providing specialized information and assistance to product or service users through materials or interactions (in person or via the phone). Customer service is often cited as a value-added benefit and is marketed as part of the product or service. Customer service personnel act as liaisons between the organization and the customer. These individuals can address concerns as well as provide support that is designed to enhance user knowledge and positive attitudes about the organization's products and services.

Marketing opportunities abound in organizations that produce or create products or services and in specialized environments, such as advertising agencies, public relations firms, and consulting firms. Because marketing is a broad and diverse functional area, research of the various work settings is as critical as research of the function itself. Liberal arts job seekers should know **where they want to work** as well as **what they want to do!** Marketing titles include product manager, product development specialist, assistant brand manager, marketing research analyst, research assistant, technical liaison, technical support specialist, customer training specialist, customer support coordinator, trade show representative, advertising liaison, public relations specialist, and corporate communications assistant.

Operations

Operations is challenging to describe because it differs in various firms that manufacture goods or provide services. In general, this area consists of three subunits:

Production

Overseeing or directly participating in the efforts to make products or offer services. Production includes management of staff as well as equipment and often involves quality control responsibilities.

Materials and Traffic Coordination

In a manufacturing environment, this area includes purchasing, receiving, and storing raw materials; distributing materials to production sites at appropriate times; monitoring production plans to maintain optimum efficiency; and distributing products to storage sites, sales and distribution facilities, and end users. In a service environment, this area includes coordination of assignments, matching client needs to available human resources, managing the use of subcontractors, and monitoring project status.

Management Information Systems

Operating and servicing computerized equipment; training and supporting users; entering, manipulating, and retrieving data in appropriate forms; creating and implementing software programs and procedural systems; and developing and distributing standardized data. This function could involve working in other departments or as part of a centralized management information systems (MIS) function as a consultant or on-call liaison.

All organizations have operations opportunities that are often hidden but usually challenging and rewarding. In health-care or diagnostic services organizations, for instance, production is the area that provides the services of doctors, nurses, lab technicians, and assistants. Be aware that this functional area might not always be called "operations," particularly in service organizations, where the term could mean something else. Job seekers should keep the functional perspective in mind so that they can better identify their options. Operations titles include production scheduler, traffic coordinator, production assistant, inventory control specialist, quality control analyst, distribution manager, assignment coordinator, programmer, Web master, Web page developer, systems analyst, and MIS coordinator.

Sales

Sales are what generate revenue and profits! This functional area ensures a company's continued existence, so it is of utmost importance in the scheme of things. Because of the potential to move from sales to other functional areas (including human resources and marketing), sales should be prominent in most research and job search strategies. Subunits are determined by the way in which products or services are sold to end users. They include:

Direct Sales

Identifying, contacting, communicating with, presenting to, and following up with potential purchasers or resellers of products or users of services. Inside sales involve telemarketing and, occasionally, showroom sites and trade shows to conduct business with customers. Increasingly, Web-driven sales efforts electronically and directly link the consumer with the service or product provider. Outside sales involve making initial and subsequent contacts by phone but ultimately conducting face-to-face business at the customer's site. Some organizations employ both inside and outside approaches, with inside sales personnel supporting field efforts. This regularly involves managing and motivating others involved in sales, often within product or geographical boundaries. Compensation can involve base salary, commissions, and bonuses or some combination of the three.

Representative Sales

Subcontractors of one or more providers of products or services conduct all sales-related efforts and receive compensation, including commissions, fees, and possibly bonuses.

Distribution and Arbitrage

Also can be a subcontractor who purchases products or services and then resells them to retailers or end users. This function involves buying and selling to make a profit from the resale.

Retail Sales

Direct sales to consumers within a specialized store environment. This function emphasizes customer service and regularly involves a predictable career path to management responsibilities.

Sales are the lifeblood of almost any organization. Sales should be one of the first areas in the minds of many job seekers. Sales is a great way of breaking into an organization and later moving into other functional areas, including marketing or human resources, that do not typically hire entry-level candidates. Titles include sales representative, sales associate, district manager, telemarketing representative, account executive, artist representative, broker, and agent.

Which areas and subfunctions seem most interesting to you? Why are they attractive to you? Can you immediately identify one or two broad fields and specific functional areas you would like to research? Using the functional overview, an organization can be described by the function that drives it. Some organizations are market driven (consumer product manufacturers, advertising agencies, and retailers). Some are finance driven, like banks and financial services firms. Others are production driven, such as manufacturers. You should investigate beyond initial perceptions, however, because advertising agencies have many individuals who serve in operations functions, such as computer support personnel; banks have marketing and public relations areas; and manufacturers hire sales representatives.

Whatever the case, you must determine what drives you, what skills you would like to use on the job, and your motivations and ambitions. Remember, focus arises after paper-and-pencil and people-to-people research, not simply after introspection. The functional approach is not meant to replace the general approach taken in this book, but it will provide you with some additional insights and encourage you to do more research about the job functions as well as the titles that look promising.

4

Narrowing in on Your Perfect Job

A GLOSSARY OF LIBERAL ARTS OPTIONS

▶ The following glossary profiles more than 300 jobs in more than sixty career fields. These fields and jobs were selected from information gathered from my personal experience in counseling and coaching liberal arts (LA) students and from several published, computer generated, and online resources. Most options offer opportunities that require little, if any, additional education. A few citations do require additional education but are included because of the outstanding opportunities they offer and because these fields have traditionally been ignored by liberal arts job seekers. Reading the glossary should motivate readers to discover exciting possibilities and inspire research.

Read through the glossary once. Circle fields and jobs of interest and note your reactions or questions in the margin. Then, review the glossary again. After the second time, complete the exercises and worksheets that appear in the appendix. Of course, this listing cannot cover all opportunities. As a liberal arts graduate, you are truly free to enter any field, with any job title. Additional education allows philosophy majors to become computer engineers and religion majors to become physicists. Your ability to state your goals and effectively act upon them can transform the words that follow into job search realities and, thus, the glossary into a strategic step on your path to success.

Academic Adviser
See **College Administration and Support Services, Education**

Account Executive
See **Advertising, Finance, Market Research**

Accounting
Those with strong quantitative and problem-solving skills who would like a role in business might explore corporate and public accounting. Graduates without previous accounting course work or experience should consider a Master of Accounting program. In just over a year, these programs provide most of the curriculum that takes an undergraduate business major four years to complete. Some programs require sponsorship by a large accounting firm, and others do not. All include an internship period or combine work and study during some portion of the program. Entry positions in public accounting (upon receipt of a graduate degree or completion of a

specified number of credits) are usually in auditing, but opportunities may exist in tax, consulting, or other departments of public accounting firms. Graduates with more limited accounting course work or experience can seek entry-level opportunities in corporate accounting. As few as four accounting courses taken at a local college during the summer and fall sessions after graduation could ease entry into this field. Accounting is a field in which liberal arts graduates can become exposed to the financial (and other) operations of employers and their clients and function as financial analysts, consultants, and managers. Accounting firms have grown more and more diverse, with departments ranging from bankruptcy to entertainment to litigation support, yet auditing remains one of the most common ways of entering the field. As one's awareness of the available options increases from firsthand experience, a career can develop in many different directions. Count this as one of many hidden LA options.

See also **Finance**

Acting/Drama

Opportunities in acting are difficult to find. Knowledge of job functions and effective job search techniques—as well as talent and luck—are needed. LA graduates exploring this field should be prepared to continue their education (perhaps best called an apprenticeship, since acting is a craft) through graduate programs in performing arts, acting schools, or performers' workshops. The more experience one has, the more likely it is to live by means of a salary earned as an **actor** or **actress.** Aspiring actors and actresses should learn about the ins and outs of auditioning and acquiring an agent by talking with as many other actors and actresses (perhaps alumni or friends of the family) as possible. Related entry-level opportunities include those associated with theater administration, modeling, and commercials. Large and small theaters need people to sell tickets; maintain the facilities; work on sets, costumes, and lighting; and promote performances. Modeling, whether "photo" or "show," can be one means of support in a related field while continuing the search for acting jobs. Although difficult to enter, commercial acting—radio or television, voice-over, or performing—may be one of the best means of practicing the craft while getting paid. Those who are trying to break into the business may be prepared to do anything to support themselves while pursuing an acting career, but they do not have to wait tables or starve. They can obtain related experience through many of the options cited in this book (from teaching drama and producing plays in a private secondary school to working in a retail store, library, or advertising agency) while continuing along the long and difficult road to becoming a performer.

See also **Arts/Arts Administration, Modeling**

Actuary
See **Insurance**

Adjuster
See **Insurance**

Admissions Officer
See **College Administration and Support Services**

Advertising (Top Twelve)

Called "the liberal arts of business" by some, advertising offers a great many opportunities to LA graduates. In addition to agencies, retail and consumer product organizations offer entry-level advertising positions. In fact, retailers may offer the most entry-level copywriting opportunities.

The **account executive** (AE) acts as the liaison between an ad agency and its clients and coordinates the activities of the various departments that are working on the agency's ad campaigns. Account executives manage an account by orchestrating the talents and performances of others to create and implement an effective campaign. They guide the development and presentation of ads, based upon analyses of clients' products, images, needs, and finances. They are problem solvers who motivate others to accomplish a common goal. They fit together pieces of a puzzle to create an organized effort. Although the account executive deals with creative people and utilizes creative problem solving to make day-to-day decisions, a good sense of management, strong quantitative and analytical capabilities, and superior communication skills are of great importance. The AE is above all other things a manager, motivator, and persuader, not necessarily a creator.

Advertising copywriters work in advertising agencies, retail organizations, magazines, newspapers, and increasingly, Internet service providers, search engines, Web site developers, and multimedia consultant agencies. Advertising copywriters, as the name states, write copy for ads that appear in newspapers and magazines, on billboards and other displays, on packages, and in some cases, on TV, radio, and on line. Ad agency copywriters work in creative departments. They receive strategic information (target demographics, image studies, etc.) from account executives and are called on to create the total written content of an ad campaign. In many cases, they work as members of a creative team, with artists and others, to create one ad or an entire campaign. Although it is difficult to break into copywriting for a large ad agency, it is not impossible. The obstacle for most LA grads to overcome is the portfolio, which is easier to develop for LA graduates with some experience (in extracurricular activities or employment). Any LA graduate who seeks an ad agency copywriting post should request guidance when creating a portfolio. The portfolio should contain samples of one's ability to communicate in the forms required of advertising copy. It is not a scrapbook but a professional presentation of the type of work one is capable of doing. An experienced copywriter can provide an LA job seeker with exercises and assignments that will lead to an effective portfolio. (An example: Cut out newspaper and magazine ads that could be improved by better copy. Write critical analyses of these ads and rewrite the copy, citing your goals and explaining why your version would be more effective.) Most large retail organizations hire copywriters to write newspaper ads, mail-order publications, and promotional brochures. Because of the large volume of work involved in retail advertising, this is a good place to seek entry-level copywriting opportunities. Some magazines and newspapers have staff copywriters to create or edit ad copy. These copywriters serve as consultants to advertisers who do not use ad agencies or have their own creative staffs. They take the advertisers' ideas and turn them into copy. Some of these opportunities are less sophisticated than others, having titles such as "ad taker" rather than "account supervisor." These opportunities are difficult to find but can be excellent ways of breaking into the field. LA graduates who believe they are good writers may wish to explore this job. Remember, however, that being a good writer does not ensure that one will be a good copywriter.

A **traffic coordinator** doesn't work in a police department or in the traffic control tower of an airport; he or she works in an advertising agency. This job is a typical entry-level opportunity for LA graduates. Traffic is the department that is responsible for seeing that all components of an ad are pieced together properly and forwarded to the appropriate media at the right time. Traffic coordinators are well organized, capable of managing large quantities of information with accuracy. They track the various stages of creating an ad and facilitate the process in order to meet specific deadlines. Traffic coordinators know where a particular ad is, in both the figurative and literal senses, at all times. They coordinate several projects simultaneously, each in different stages of development. As an example, within a 5-minute period, one traffic coordinator might be responsible for shipping a piece of video or film to a television station by a specific date and time and for checking to see that a particular piece of printed copy has been returned from the printer in time for a meeting. To say the least, it is a hectic, demanding, and challenging job. In many ways, it is like the job of air traffic controller, only here, careers and financial livelihoods rest on the skills of one person. Traffic can be a career area in which LA graduates stay for long periods of time, or it can be a first step into other areas of advertising, specifically account management.

An **advertising salesperson,** who works for a newspaper, magazine, a radio or television station, a Web site, or an Internet provider, sells advertising space or time directly to advertisers or to media planners who work for ad agencies. LA graduates who possess sales skills and can assess the demographics of publications or stations and target the markets of potential advertisers are attractive candidates for these posts. LA job seekers can begin with small employers and then move up a career path by progressing to larger ones. Ad salespeople can be paid a salary, a salary plus bonus or commission, or a straight commission. Many LA graduates have sold ad space for school newspapers or yearbooks. This or any sales experience that demonstrates persuasive abilities and the potential to sell to the needs of particular customers is a strength for those seeking these jobs.

A **media planner** determines the most cost-effective means of reaching a target market through print and broadcast media. Media planners must be aware of the demographics of radio and television stations, magazines, newspapers, and other means of advertising. They present their recommendations in written proposals that include analyses and budgets. Many formal account management training programs begin with rotations in media planning. This is a good position to seek in firms that do not have formal programs. The area of media planning can also lead to career opportunities other than account management. Plan well for an advertising job search by researching this option. A **media buyer** (typically one step above the planner position) works for advertising agencies, retailers, or other users of advertising services and buys the appropriate space or time from newspapers, magazines, radio and television stations, and other advertising sources. Buyers negotiate the best deals possible, prepare contracts, and monitor ads to determine whether or not they actually appear. Buyers interact with advertising salespeople as well as media planners, account executives, marketing managers, and sales managers and must have quantitative skills as well as persuasive abilities. Many large ad agencies have separate tracks for those interested in careers in media. Occasionally, one can move from an entry-level media position into account management, but this may require going from one agency to another. Research of potential employers will show whether or not an agency has a media training program.

While the preceding titles offer the most obvious entry-level opportunities for LA graduates, production- and creative-related positions also exist for those with the requisite talents and skills. Creative jobs involve the translation of concepts into storyboard (layout, scene-by-scene sketches, and computer-generated graphics that illustrate potential print, online, or broadcast ads) or other forms (including photographic, video, and musical) that clearly identify for account executives and clients how ideas could be transformed into real campaigns. Production jobs involve transforming these ideas into advertising realities—the creation of print or media ads—and can include various responsibilities. Most entry-level production posts hold the title of "assistant" or "assistant to" and involve some very "basic" (a euphemism for "things more experienced people don't want to do") responsibilities. LA grads should uncover as much as they can about this field and consider other options, including direct mail. The trend toward international mega-agencies with one-stop shopping for advertising, public relations, and other marketing-related services has made the entry-level job search a bit more difficult. Firms in transition tend to be more concerned with current employees and with finding their new identities than with hiring recent graduates. Be persistent. Learn by reading publications like *Ad Age* and *Advertising Weekly,* by meeting with and talking to people in the field, and, if possible, by taking courses or attending seminars.

See also **Graphic Arts, Marketing, Public Relations, Sales/Sales Management**

Adviser

See **Education**

Agent

See **Insurance**

Airlines

Those who wish to work for air carriers can locate positions in diverse areas, including cargo, customer service, data processing, flight operations, food services, in-flight service, marketing, personnel, and purchasing. The **cargo staff** handles the administrative responsibilities that are associated with transporting airfreight. People who work in this area complete the paperwork involved in transporting objects by air, route freight via the most cost-effective connections, handle damage claims, answer inquiries concerning rates and services, and market these services to potential users. The airfreight industry has been growing at phenomenal rates in recent years. Both specialized freight carriers and passenger carriers with freight operations are seeking qualified personnel to handle the increasing volume of work. **Customer service personnel,** including reservations agents, ticketing agents, and passenger agents, handle telephone and direct ticket sales, serve passengers' ticketing and boarding needs, and take care of the special concerns of passengers. Customer service can also involve public relations and station agent positions. Customer service positions are excellent entry-level opportunities for LA graduates who seek airlines jobs. Data processing jobs involve programming and maintaining the computer systems that are used in the airline industry. Descriptions of computer-related jobs appear later in this book. LA graduates with some computer science course work or experience should consider these opportunities. **Flight attendants,** perhaps the most visible of all airline personnel, provide in-flight service to passengers and implement emergency procedures, as necessary. Many LA job seekers obtain entry-level positions as flight attendants. Hiring needs vary from year to year and airline to airline, and job requirements also vary from airline to airline. LA graduates should examine the application procedures and requirements of each carrier. Training is structured, and most entry-level hires are admitted into training programs, with employment contingent upon completion of training.

Flight operations positions, regulated by the Federal Aviation Administration (FAA), include **flight dispatcher** and **air traffic controller.** These involve directing flights to their destinations by means of radio contact with flight crews and reporting information received via radar and other monitoring equipment. LA graduates who are interested in these positions must learn of application procedures and requirements by contacting a local FAA office or an airline's Office of Personnel Management. Food service positions, like those of restaurant management, are involved in the management of airline food service operations and in the preparation of food served during the flights. Marketing positions include **sales agent, revenue control analyst, and sales representative.** Sales agents (reservationists and ticket agents) deal directly with customers who wish to purchase passage or cargo space. They are involved in making reservations, issuing tickets, operating computerized reservation systems, and keeping records of transactions. Revenue control analysts handle the computer entry of group sales and analyze passenger and cargo records to determine cost-effective means of scheduling flights and allocating resources (personnel and planes). This requires some computer competence as well as analytical skills. Sales representatives call on travel agencies and other users of group services to sell the airline's products. **Personnel and purchasing opportunities** also exist in the airlines field.

See also **Computers/Data Processing, Human Resources/Personnel, Marketing, Merchandising (purchasing agent)**

Air Traffic Control

Air traffic control offers opportunities to anyone through a competitive examination system. Applicants must pass physical, psychological, and aptitude tests in order to qualify for positions as controller trainees. **Air traffic controllers** direct airport traffic (takeoffs and landings) as well as monitor and regulate flights in progress. Day-to-day requirements include verbal communications skills (to give instructions to aircraft via radio), analytical and retention capacities (to receive, interpret, remember, and organize the data received minute by minute), and the ability to react immediately and calmly to circumstances at hand. Trainees receive on-the-job and classroom training through a progression of positions that lead to certification as an air traffic controller. This field combines mental and physical qualities and could be a hidden gem for many LA job seekers. It is important to research the field thoroughly to know when test deadlines are and to understand the application and training process.

Alumni Affairs Staff
See **College Administration and Support Services**

Analyst
See **Banking, Census/Survey Work, Consulting, Finance, Investment Banking, Real Estate, Telecommunications**

Animal Care

Obviously, jobs that involve animal care exist anywhere animals are cared for—farms, stables, veterinary clinics, boarding facilities, and zoos. LA graduates with a knowledge of animals and a desire to work in the environments associated with their care can locate jobs. These opportunities are not for all. They are for those who enjoy physical labor and the intangible rewards of doing a job a bit out of the mainstream.

Veterinarian's assistants help veterinarians in the day-to-day activities that are involved in treating animal injuries and diseases. At least four years of graduate study are required to become a veterinarian. Because of this commitment of time and money, those interested in the field may wish to first obtain employment as an assistant in order to judge whether or not the realities of the field match their perceptions and then determine whether or not to go on to graduate or specialized study. Community colleges offer course work related to veterinarian's assistant responsibilities, and on-the-job training is common.

Zookeepers must learn techniques for breeding, capturing, caring for, and exhibiting animals in a zoo setting. They must be comfortable with the animals under their care. LA graduates with an interest in working in this unique environment can obtain entry-level positions, which involve on-the-job training. Some course work in zoology, biology, or a related area and experience working with animals are preferred but not required. Some community colleges offer courses in animal care and offer experiences similar to internships, and some graduate programs in zoology and related areas offer internships for those interested in zoo curator/director jobs.

Animator

See **Graphic Arts**

Architecture

This field offers opportunities for LA graduates who are willing to undertake additional studies. Because licensure requires at least a Bachelor of Architecture degree and some practical experience, postgraduation opportunities for LA job seekers are limited to drafting positions. Graduates who wish to become architects must explore additional education.

Architectural drafters/technicians, who work in architectural firms and occasionally for contractors, prepare plans and detailed drawings for building projects. A drafter must have specialized artistic talents as well as the ability to take drawings and create reproduction-ready copies and to identify errors and make corrections in original plans. Mathematical capabilities—for working in scale dimensions and calculating stress variables—and the ability to pay attention to detail are also required. Drafters/technicians usually work under the supervision of an architect and start as tracers, checkers, detailers, or junior drafters, correcting and preparing drawings for reproduction; they move up while on the job. Specialized course work is available through technical institutes, community and junior colleges, extension programs, and undergraduate departments that offer architecture-related courses, but an LA graduate with sufficient artistic and intellectual abilities can find entry-level employment without the specialized courses. A few courses taken during the summer after graduation, however, can serve as a test of one's interest and capabilities and make the job hunting easier. Specialized studies can continue (in the evening or through special programs) while holding one of these jobs. Those with an interest in design who wish to explore the possibility of an architectural career will find these jobs very appealing. Remember, interest is not enough. One must have the special skills and talents that are required to perform the tasks that are associated with this job.

Art Director

See **Graphic Arts**

Arts/Arts Administration

A variety of settings and jobs are available in this field. Think of the arts as being associated with disciplines and settings, including art, history, crafts, dance, literature, the media (film, video, and audio), museums, music, photography, theater, and visual arts. Arts administration, on the other hand, involves the management of facilities or organizations that promote the arts or display works of art. Entry-level jobs can be those of **artists,** involving the creation or performance of artistic pieces, or can be arts related, involving administration, management, production, or teaching. Positions in museums, a setting where both arts and arts administration jobs exist, include the following titles: **assistant director, artist, registrar, business manager, public relations worker, editor, curator, fund-raiser/development worker, research assistant,** and **educational director.** Types of museums include art, children's, history, natural history, and science and technology. Because these fields are so broad and include so many jobs, it is the responsibility of the LA job seeker to research each possibility thoroughly in order to set goals. Employment as an artist is difficult to find and depends on one's talent as well as job search skills. Artists sell their work directly to buyers or to galleries, or they work for employers, including advertising agencies, publishing firms, newspapers and magazines, retail firms, schools, and museums, who use their talents in specialized applications.

Arts-related opportunities, which are also difficult to find, are somewhat more dependent upon one's job search skills. In the past, the best advice for LA graduates was to seek any job in museums, galleries, auction houses, or other arts-related organizations; serve an apprenticeship; and move up to more professional responsibilities. Although this is still possible, it is becoming more and more difficult as the demand for formal training (graduate course work or special training programs) increases. Entry-level opportunities can still be found, but the responsibility for identifying appropriate job functions and settings is definitely that of the job seeker. Too many LA graduates state their preferences for these fields without being able to articulate their specific job search goals. Research is the key for those who seek to enter these fields.

See also **Crafts, Graphic Arts**

Audiology/Speech Pathology

Although audiology/speech pathology requires graduate study as the standard means of entry, this field also offers support positions for LA graduates who wish to explore options before committing to continued schooling. Working as aides or assistants, support staff members assist licensed professionals in the delivery of services. **Audiologists** assess and treat hearing problems, perform diagnostic tests, and assign appropriate treatments (medicinal or mechanical devices). **Speech pathologists** work with those who have speech, language, or voice disorders (from injury, hearing loss, physical defect, or learning disability), and diagnose and treat these disorders by various techniques. In many ways, the speech pathologist is both a teacher and a medical professional. One person can serve the dual functions of speech pathologist and audiologist, or two people can provide both functions as a team. LA graduates with interests in medical opportunities may want to explore these jobs.

Banking (Top Twelve)

There are opportunities for LA graduates in commercial banks, savings and loan associations, mortgage banks, investment banks, and reserve banks. Most banks, especially commercial banks, have various departments that are responsible for specific functions. These include trust—managing trusts and estates for individuals, institutions, and corporations; consumer credit—making and servicing loans to individuals and purchasing contracts that arise from loans or timed payments; operations—involving day-to-day workings of a bank, including supervision of staff and systems, processing daily transactions, check handling, bookkeeping, data processing, and handling customer accounts; real estate—handling mortgages and other real estate dealings, including managing bank-owned properties; and commercial credit—involving all credit transactions with businesses, institutions, and individuals. LA job seekers can find employment within any of these areas as well as other areas of a bank. Although many banks hire undergraduate or graduate business majors, some (especially large money-center banks) provide LA graduates with thorough in-house training and actively solicit liberal arts candidates for employment.

Operations is a growing area for LA opportunities. Most large banks and many commercial banks have operations management career paths and training programs and seek LA graduates for these positions. The operations area of banking (in contrast to credit/lending) involves a great deal of transaction processing in an environment that is labor intensive (though increasingly automated). An **operations manager** must be prepared to meet the deadlines that are associated with internal control procedures, motivate and coordinate the actions of others, and meet the needs of customers daily. Some operations functions include automated teller transactions, check processing, maintaining internal records, reporting account activity to customers, transferring funds within a bank and to other banks, cash management, payroll, and credit card transactions. LA graduates with an interest in bank operations should be familiar with these basic functions of operations divisions. If the emphasis in lending is increasingly on sales, then a major purpose of operations is sales support. The operations division should influence both corporate and individual customers' choice of a bank. The accuracy with which records are maintained, the efficiency of reporting account information, the courtesy with which customer requests are met, and the overall productivity and profitability of a bank help it maintain existing business and develop new customers. LA graduates who seek to use research and writing skills and their ability to manage time, resources, and people—with ever-increasing responsibility—should consider this field. Within operations, **auditors** go from department to department auditing transactions and procedures, making analyses, and reporting recommendations to department heads. Auditing is one of the best (and best hidden) opportunities for liberal arts grads and offers exposure to almost every aspect of banking. Auditors must possess quantitative and qualitative analytical skills and communication skills. Growing specialty areas of banking, such as corporate trust, personal banking, and shareholder services, are often included in operations, although they sometimes function as independent units.

Credit card areas offer many operations, customer service, and marketing opportunities. Enhanced affinity group outreach and the increasingly competitive nature of consumer credit cards requires employees and managers with telemarketing, problem solving, and analytical skills. Liberal arts grads personify all of these traits and more. The responsibilities associated with collections and problem resolution are challenging, but liberal arts grads seem well suited to communicate and negotiate with others. **Retail banking** offers roles, responsibilities, and rewards similar to those described under general retail management. As banking changes in the next decade, these opportunities will continue to require generalists who can serve within the multifaceted roles that are associated with many of the jobs cited in this section. Also, expansion of e-banking will require candidates who can teach and support the efforts of nontechnical users who wish to conduct business over the Internet.

Within credit areas, **lending officer trainee** positions offer good opportunities. Titles for these entry-level trainees (and for loan officers) vary from bank to bank and include **commercial banker trainee, credit analyst, executive trainee, lending analyst,** and **relationship manager trainee.** As a trainee and eventually as a loan officer, this person analyzes potential loan markets to determine how best to "sell the bank's money." Loan officers evaluate the financial status, creditworthiness, and collateral of potential customers (assessing risk) and recommend approval or denial of loans. More and more, lending officers act as liaisons between banks and customers, selling services in addition to those that involve credit. Loan officers must have quantitative and research skills to assess risks and determine the financial status of applicants and sales abilities to continually develop new business. Decision-making and analytical skills and an outgoing, sales-oriented personality are qualities sought by banks in their lending officer trainees. Many large banks in New York, Boston, and Chicago actively recruit LA graduates for their lending programs. Other banks require some course work in accounting, economics, and finance before they will hire an LA graduate as a lending officer. This field offers wonderful opportunities for LA job seekers who want a job that combines financial analysis and sales and offers unlimited opportunities to move into many other areas of commercial banking. History has shown that most LA graduates begin their commercial banking careers in lending.

Money market and securities traders handle all stock, bond, and other financial paper transactions for commercial banks, investment banks, and special trading firms in order to make a profit from the operating funds of the bank. Traders must have excellent quantitative skills, be able to make split-second decisions that involve large quantities of money, and be detail oriented and assertive. They need a knowledge of economics and financial issues, gained through academic course work (some economics, finance, or accounting) or through a training program. Although some LA job seekers can find entry-level positions in trading, it is difficult to break in at this level. A **trust officer trainee,** working in a large commercial bank or a small savings and loan, learns to administer private, corporate, and probate trusts. A trust officer advises customers (both individuals and organizations) about their investments and must be able to research investment possibilities and analyze risks for customers. Few entry-level opportunities exist in trust departments, but one can move from other departments into this one. In smaller banking institutions, **loan counselors** act as lending officers and collections managers by working with borrowers (sometimes delinquent borrowers) to develop plans to repay loans. This position requires financial and interpersonal skills in order to balance the needs of the bank that wants to be repaid with the circumstances of the people and organizations that are unable to do so. "Working your way up" is a phrase to keep in mind when seeking any position within a smaller bank, especially that of loan counselor. **Personal banker** is a new title that encompasses many of the jobs already noted here. Specifically, these individuals are becoming more involved in marketing bank services, providing financial consulting and trust services, and addressing the lending needs of consumers and individuals as well as small-business owners. A **bank examiner trainee** position can be a good one for LA graduates. Examiners work for federal reserve banks or as internal auditors for commercial banks. They review records and procedures to determine whether or not banks are in compliance with federal and state regulations and internal bank policy and must be able to work well with people. LA graduates with strong analytical capabilities, quantitative skills, and some economics background (as few as two courses taken after graduation) can be strong candidates for these jobs.

A **research analyst** looks into various aspects of potential deals. The position involves use of research, financial, analytical, and writing skills and requires attention to detail and the willingness to work long hours. A knowledge of finance and economics and an interest in understanding the elements of financial transactions are required of a research analyst (also known as **financial analyst, corporate analyst,** or **public finance analyst**). Many large Eastern investment banks offer two-year-plus programs that are designed for LA majors who wish to enter graduate school (often graduate management programs). These options are detailed under Investment Banking.

In addition to those jobs already cited, banks have specialist positions, including accountants, public relations and marketing specialists, and personnel and recruiting staff members, which may be appropriate for LA job seekers.

See also **Finance, Insurance, Investment Banking**

Biotechnology and Pharmaceuticals (Top Twelve)

Biotechnology is a relatively new field that deserves a lot of attention. Because the initial activities of biotechnical firms, most of which were founded within the past decade, focused on research and development, their production and marketing efforts will now need to be addressed. Biotechnology firms identify and utilize biologically linked processes that predominantly involve genetic engineering techniques to manufacture pharmaceuticals. Traditional pharmaceutical firms utilize long-established chemistry-linked approaches to do the same. Obviously, liberal arts graduates with strong science backgrounds, including biology and chemistry courses and labs, are very strong candidates. **Research Assistant, Quality Control Specialist, Clinical Research Associate, and Quality Assurance Assistant** are all titles associated with research and development (R&D) as well as manufacturing functions. **Sales, marketing,** and **operations** positions are also available to liberal arts grads with applicable skills. While mergers and acquisitions that result from the increased use of generic and over-the-counter drugs and government regulatory compliance do present challenges, they also generate opportunities. Cycles associated with R&D, proprietary timeframes, biotechnology research, and home health care will create opportunities.

Biomedical Research Staff
See **Health Care**

Book Designer
See **Graphic Arts**

Bookkeeper
See **Finance**

Brand Manager
See **Marketing**

Broker
See **Finance, Insurance, Marketing**

Building/Construction

This field offers opportunities to liberal arts job seekers who wish to be involved in erecting, maintaining, and repairing houses, commercial buildings, and other structures. It includes planning for what is to be built and how it is to be built, preparing sites, and implementing building plans according to specifications and codes. Building and construction jobs can be found almost anywhere—in large companies (contractors), in small companies (builders and repairers), and in related areas (suppliers and manufacturers).

Executive and office staff members work in operational areas in the office of a builder or contractor. LA grads can apply directly for the following jobs at entry level or start as general laborers and later move into these roles. **Accountants** and **bookkeepers** maintain the financial records that are related to a contractor's operations. They can work on general records for many projects or on records for individual projects. **Estimators,** using building plans and specifications, obtain prices for equipment and supplies and estimate the cost of a project for bidding purposes. They must be familiar with the terminology of the field, be prepared to contact many manufacturers and suppliers to obtain the best price, and be able to calculate all related transactions without errors. Estimators work under the pressure of deadlines and must pay attention to detail. Courses to train LA graduates in the skills required for this job are available through technical schools and community colleges, but entry-level employment can be found either with a small organization or as an assistant with a large contractor. **Expediters** develop and maintain schedules for projects and motivate others to perform in accordance with those schedules. Schedules can be for work amounts to be completed, equipment and supplies delivery, the arrival of special subcontractors, or the number of workers and hours to be used on a job during a specified time period. Expediters must be aware of all occurrences that are related to the nature of a particular project. The functions of an expediter may be incorporated into those of a superintendent or similar title.

Landscapers work for a landscape architect, landscape contractor, or gardening service. They design and, in many cases, install the grounds surrounding a building. People working within this area are knowledgeable about design and layout; familiar with plants, flowers, and trees; and prepared to work with clients to develop designs that realistically meet their needs. Entry-level laborer positions are the easiest to locate. Positions in nurseries, which supply plants, trees, and shrubs to landscapers, are also available to LA graduates. A **supply salesperson** works for a supplier or manufacturer of construction-related materials, selling products (and sometimes services) to contractors. The many different types of materials and equipment sold to contractors for each type of project would be impossible to list here. This diversity offers opportunities to LA graduates with an interest in working in this area of building and construction. Depending on the product, some technical knowledge may be required, at least enough to understand how the product is used and how to sell it to knowledgeable buyers. A sales-oriented personality, willingness to make direct contacts with customers, and travel from site to site and contractor to contractor are required. **Surveyors,** working for a contractor or government agency, use specialized tools to locate official land boundaries, mark off site boundaries, research deeds, and identify information for use in developing plans. Specialized training is required in most cases and is available through technical schools. Occasionally, on-the-job training is available.

See also **Architecture (drafter)**

Buyer

See **Marketing, Merchandising, Retailing**

Campaign Worker

See **Politics**

Career Counselor

See **Education**

Career Planning and Placement Staff

See **College Administration and Support Services**

Cargo Staff

See **Airlines**

Cartoonist

See **Graphic Arts**

Catering

Planning and catering special events and providing food services for schools and large employers are expanding areas of the service sector of the economy. Many opportunities within catering also exist in hotel and restaurant management. LA graduates with an interest in managing people and resources and facing the day-to-day challenges of planning, preparing, serving, and cleaning for events that involve two to 2,000 or more people should explore these options. Entry-level opportunities can easily be found as **servers** (**waiters** or **waitresses**) in hotels, restaurants, or other facilities that offer catering services; managerial positions can follow after a while. Many large organizations that provide food services for sporting events, airlines, cruise ships, schools, and other in-house eating facilities hire LA graduates and provide training in accounting, buying, personnel, and related areas. Those who seek this experience with the hope of someday owning and operating a restaurant or catering service should seriously consider these opportunities. In addition to general management opportunities, hotels, restaurants, caterers, and food-service employers also seek individuals for sales positions to develop new business. Of course, LA graduates with entrepreneurial motivations and skills can start their own catering service immediately upon graduation.

See also **Hotel/Motel/Hospitality Management, Restaurant Management**

Census/Survey Work

This field could be a hidden gem for some LA job seekers. Although the national census is conducted only once every ten years, a number of censuses and surveys are undertaken each year by federal, state, and local governments and by private surveying and market research organizations. These involve questioning individuals about their attitudes and requesting information about particular topics. The questions depend on the nature of a survey and vary from "How many bathrooms are in your home?" to "When did you last attend a religious service?" Entry-level opportunities can require interviewing subjects; designing surveys (in questionnaire or interview form); managing interviewers, data collection, and data analysis; and documenting findings. **Project supervisor, analyst, team manager,** and **research assistant** are some of the titles that are associated with these functions. LA graduates with a social science orientation and quantitative, analytical, statistical, and organizational skills should explore these options by contacting as many census/survey organizations as possible to determine their purposes and the nature of their projects.

See also **Market Research**

Chemistry

Chemists work for manufacturers, usually in research and development, production, and inspection; for educational institutions, teaching or performing research; for hospitals, performing research or diagnostic tests; for federal, state, or local governments, in health- or agriculture-related tasks; and for private organizations, providing consulting services in the above-cited settings or conducting research similar to that done in these settings. Chemists use knowledge of theory and laboratory techniques to create new products or improve old ones; to diagnose and treat disease; to analyze the quality of air, food, or water; and to monitor natural or man-made systems. Entry-level opportunities often bear the titles of assistant, analyst, or research assistant. Chemistry majors or liberal arts grads who have completed chemistry courses can serve as **quality assurance** and **quality control technicians** as well as **laboratory technicians** within private laboratories, health-care facilities, biotechnology and pharmaceutical firms, and food, chemical, and related manufacturing environments. Too often ignored, these opportunities can be great "getting started" jobs for those who seek additional time to conduct research or to explore graduate school options. As a result of an increased demand and to serve the needs of recent grads, specialty temporary employment firms, including *Kelly Scientific, YOH Scientific,* and *Lab Support,* have expanded in recent years.

Working as a **chemistry teacher** is also a good possibility for LA graduates with some course work in chemistry and the physical sciences. The need for elementary and secondary school science teachers is strong; LA job seekers who have taken education courses can qualify for certification to teach in public schools. Requirements for certification vary from state to state and can be waived (usually postponed if one is currently enrolled or will enroll in teacher-preparation courses that lead to certification) in some cases (particularly for those interested in teaching in urban or rural settings and for those who wish to teach subjects, including the sciences, where shortages of teachers exist). LA graduates without education course work or certification can more easily locate positions teaching in private schools.

See also **Education**

Claims Representative
See **Insurance**

Clinical Laboratory Staff
See **Health Care**

Coach
See **Education**

Coder
See **Computers/Data Processing, Market Research**

College Administration and Support Services (Top Twelve)

Every LA graduate has been exposed to this field, and it's one that offers many opportunities. College administrative personnel run the services that provide housing, social, cultural, recreational, and special supportive services for college students. These jobs include the advising, counseling, and staff positions associated with student life and extracurricular activities.

One typical entry-level college student personnel job title is that of **admissions officer.** This job deserves special attention because of the number of opportunities available to LA graduates. Admissions officers (also called counselors, representatives, or assistant directors) who work for colleges, universities, and private secondary schools are involved in the recruiting and selection of applicants. Obviously, LA graduates have attended high school and college;

therefore, they possess the most important qualities of a good admissions officer, which include knowledge of the admissions process, the ability to present information about the school they work for, and an awareness of the type of student who would be happy and who would succeed in the academic and social environment of a particular school. Many schools seek at least a few alumni for their admissions staff but consider anyone who is knowledgeable about and motivated to perform the tasks of admissions work. Recruiting potential students by attending special events; creating promotional materials; promoting the school through presentations on and off campus (often involving a great deal of travel); setting admissions criteria; coordinating the work of faculty and staff members, alumni, and others in the admissions process; reviewing applications; and communicating with and interviewing applicants and potential applicants are some of the many responsibilities of an admissions officer. The field is dynamic, with frequent moves and promotions, thus creating numerous entry-level opportunities, only some of which require a master's degree. Although a master's degree in some field, especially fields related to college student personnel work, is increasingly important, entry-level positions are still very much available. The **alumni affairs staff,** working under the Dean of Alumni Affairs or Director of Alumni Activities, provides a variety of services for alumni, including creating and arranging special educational programs, social events, and alumni tours. These jobs often involve writing alumni publications and coordinating some fund-raising and reunion activities. People in these posts are creative, congenial, and well organized and have excellent communications skills.

Career planning and placement staff members assist students in setting and implementing career and job search goals and provide graduate and professional school information and general academic and career counseling. This involves teaching decision-making and job search skills, such as resume writing, interviewing, and job search strategies. In some cases, it also involves arranging on-campus interviews and organizing some form of job-posting system. Titles within career planning and placement offices include **career counselor, assistant director, administrative assistant,** and **career information librarian.** A few good entry-level opportunities exist for LA graduates who have researched the field and had some volunteer work experience while in school. The easiest means of entering the college student personnel area is through graduate study, but it is not the only way to do so. The **college union staff** maintains the facilities and provides the services that are associated with a college union or student center. Jobs can involve such diverse functions as bookstore management, conference coordination, food services, and recreational services, depending on the total offerings of a particular facility. **Counselors** and **advisers** assist students with their problems and develop programs to meet their personal and academic needs. These professionals deal in psychological, social, and administrative areas. Counselors and advisers must be able to work in one-on-one situations or with groups, providing the emotional support needed in particular situations and appropriate information whenever necessary. Counseling and outreach skills, teaching abilities, and a positive, people-oriented personality are associated with these positions. **Development staff members** create and implement fund-raising programs. These people (sometimes considered a part of college administration) may specialize in corporate development or alumni development. They create and administer campaigns that are designed to bring contributions to a school. Persuasiveness and sales ability as well as knowledge of the goals of the school are required for success in this area. More and more, a knowledge of tax laws and estate planning is a plus for those interested in development. **Financial aid personnel** help students obtain financial aid by providing information and administering the paperwork that is involved in the numerous application processes. These people are aware of available options and counsel students about their best possibilities and how to realize them. Counseling skills and a business-oriented perspective, including quantitative and organizational skills, are qualities of financial aid staff members. This could be an excellent opportunity to gain some appropriate experience for a job in business. **Student activities staff members** administer various college activities. These jobs include **fraternity/sorority adviser, disciplinary adviser, international student adviser, student government adviser, student publications adviser,** and the like. For an LA graduate who was involved in extracurricular activities in college, this area offers numerous opportunities. Often, student activity functions may come under the responsibilities of an **assistant dean** or an **assistant to the dean** title. **Student housing** and **student life staff members** administer housing services and promote positive interaction on campus. This involves working in an office or living in housing facilities and acting as an administrator and adviser. These workers develop procedures for assigning space, maintaining facilities, and planning special programs that are associated with campus life by combining real estate management with college counseling and advising skills. Colleges and universities vary greatly in administrative structure; therefore, LA job seekers must be familiar with the range of possibilities in this general area in order to determine the titles and functions at each particular school.

Many of the same administration and support services career opportunities are also available at private secondary schools.

See also **Public Relations**

College Counselor
See **Education**

College Instructor
See **Education**

Commercial Artist
See **Graphic Arts**

Commodities Analyst/Merchant
See **Finance**

Communications
Communications is a very broad field that offers a great many opportunities to LA graduates who can target their specific areas of interest. This field includes written communications (publications) and multimedia communications (film, television, radio, recordings, and online Web-driven) settings.

Entry-level jobs in print media include **ad taker,** which involves work in the advertising department of a newspaper or magazine and assisting those who place advertisements. Ad takers must communicate effectively by phone as well as help create ads; therefore, they must have a creative flair for words and a capacity to think and act quickly. **Advertising staff members** are responsible for activities that generate revenue for newspapers and magazines. They develop rate structures and ad campaigns in order to maintain a desired advertising copy ratio that ensures a profit. Newspaper ad staff members deal with display and classified ads; magazine ad staff members deal mainly with display ads. Salespeople as well as organizers, they must be able to deal with customers; coordinate the receipt of ads and contracts; stay aware of prices; quickly calculate, estimate, and prepare cost statements; and service existing accounts and create new ones. **Circulation personnel,** working for newspapers or magazines, are responsible for the distribution of publications through various means, including subscriptions. Circulation workers compile and analyze statistics that are associated with a publication's readers and take steps to increase its circulation through promotions and ad campaigns.

A **copy editor,** sometimes called **copy reader,** edits a publication's copy for grammatical and style errors. This is a typical entry-level opportunity for LA graduates who have strong grammar and writing skills. Copy editors must be able to identify errors while working under the pressure of deadlines. Abilities to rewrite and to constructively criticize others are also helpful. A **correspondent** or **stringer** can write about a variety of topics. In contrast to a staff reporter, correspondents may work for more than one newspaper or magazine and do not work out of a publication's headquarters. In addition to writing skills, correspondents usually have special knowledge of the subject or geographic area they cover. **Editors** work on newspapers, magazines, or books and determine and coordinate copy, photography, illustrations, and graphics. Editors' responsibilities vary from publication to publication. Some use grammar skills more than managerial skills; others use story development skills more than writing skills. Whatever the primary editorial function, a knowledge of the processes involved in book, newspaper, or magazine publishing is essential. **Editorial assistant** and **assistant editor** positions are excellent entry-level opportunities for LA job seekers. For those without publishing experience, a few journalism courses or the completion of a publishing institute (three- to six-week programs offered at various colleges and universities) during the summer after graduation can ease entry into these positions. These jobs typically entail proofreading for grammatical errors, researching for accuracy of facts, editing for style and clarity, composing headlines, acting as a liaison between editors and writers or reporters, and assisting in layout. Proofreading, organizational, and time-management skills are essential. A portfolio that illustrates one's writing abilities can help when seeking editorial assistant positions.

Freelance writers write for publications on an assignment basis for a negotiated fee. This is not a typical entry-level position for LA graduates; it requires a great deal of self-discipline, and payment is irregular. It is advised to develop a track record as a freelancer while holding another job and then move into full-time freelancing later. The first step—not an easy one—is to get a piece published; after that, a snowball effect is possible. This work requires sending query letters that present ideas for articles to magazines or newspapers and either writing on speculation (with payment contingent upon acceptance of a piece) or for an agreed fee. Samples of one's work, not an entire portfolio, can be included with the query letter. **Reporters** work for newspapers, news magazines, and news services, writing and reporting news and feature stories. Entry-level positions, called **staff writers** by some publications, typically require work on general assignments before being given special subject areas. Reporters who work in print media must be able to research and write stories for a particular audience. The ability to work under the pressure of deadlines and to rework copy quickly as well as a specialized knowledge of a subject are requirements. LA graduates usually begin by working on small publications or as copy assistants, copy editors, or researchers before finding jobs as reporters.

Researchers work for newspapers, magazines, and book publishers and maintain research files on topics and people as well as check the accuracy of stories. This is a typical entry-level print media position for LA job seekers. It requires research skills, the ability to locate hard-to-find information, and an attention to detail. **Technical writers** research, write, and edit publications that communicate scientific and technical—and sometimes financial or legal—information in terms that can be understood by readers with no technical background. Writing proposals, manuals, reports, articles, instruction sheets, and insurance policies and legal documents, technical writers work in departments of corporations, for professional associations, or for public interest groups. LA graduates who have taken science, engineering, or other technical courses and have good writing skills can be strong candidates for these positions.

Production assistants use their design and artistic skills and management abilities to create the most effective and cost-effective publications. **Layout assistant** is an entry-level title that could be of interest to LA job seekers. **Illustrators** and **artists,** mainly freelancers, work for a publication in either its production or design department. **Marketing personnel** who work for book publishers handle many of the activities that are required to market a book. They can work in sales—taking orders over the phone and communicating with retailers, wholesalers, or purchasing agents; in market research—targeting potential buyers; or in advertising and promotions—developing campaigns to sell books and expose authors to the public. Increasingly, Web publishing positions that are similar to those cited above are available to liberal arts grads with HTML, Java, or related programming skills, and graphics, editing, and writing talents.

Entry-level broadcast jobs also offer opportunities. **Announcers** deliver announcements and station-identification spots, provide play-by-play broadcasts of sports events, and report news, sports, or weather. In some cases, announcers research and write their own copy. Previous experience is important for LA graduates who seek announcer posts. It may not be too late to volunteer to work on your college radio or television station or for a public nonprofit station. **Continuity writers** write and edit scripts and prepare the announcer's book, which contains a script of each program as well as the commercials within the program, and they note the sequence and length of each segment. Continuity writers most often work for television stations and production companies. **Disc jockeys** plan and present radio programming, including music and live commentary. Experience is required of disc jockeys. It can be obtained by working at college stations, although some small local stations may hire inexperienced LA graduates in other capacities and allow them occasional on-air experience. Some technical training is available through special schools and institutes. **Production/program assistants** who work with directors and producers are responsible for arranging and organizing radio, film, or television productions. This work involves arranging for props and sets, distributing and editing scripts, scheduling and supervising rehearsals, casting parts, and almost any other form of assistance. These jobs are hard to find; previous experience is a plus. **Researchers** and **copywriters** work in all areas of broadcast media, researching story and script ideas and writing and rewriting scripts. Entry-level copywriting posts are available in news departments and require similar skills to print media researcher, editor, and reporter positions. Additional print and broadcast titles include **art director, broadcast technician, film editor, graphic artist, layout assistant, makeup artist, property handler, set decorator,** and **sound effects technician.**

See also **Advertising, Graphic Arts, Public Relations**

Communications Analyst/Manager
See **Telecommunications**

Community Affairs Director
See **Public Relations**

Compensation Analyst
See **Human Resources/Personnel**

Computers and Technology (Top Twelve)
Computer and technology positions involve the sale and use of machines that store, retrieve, and process mainframe, CD, server, and Web-driven data. Data processing is the functional description of what computers and the people who use computers do. Positions in this field are found almost everywhere in today's computer-oriented society and fall into three areas: hardware, software, and data related. Hardware jobs involve manufacturing, selling, operating, or maintaining computers. Software jobs deal with programming (writing instructions or developing languages for writing instructions), troubleshooting existing programs, analyzing data and systems, and selling "canned" (prepackaged) programs. Data entry jobs deal with transforming raw data into a computer-ready form and with inputting data into computers. Although most jobs require some technical training or at least some technical aptitude, LA job seekers can obtain computer-related positions with as little as one course in computer science (taken while an undergraduate or during the summer after graduation). Some jobs, especially those that are sales related, may not require any related course work.

Entry-level hardware jobs include **manufacturing jobs,** many of which require specialized training that is typical of engineering and computer science majors. These jobs involve the creation of computers and component parts, including microchips. It is possible for LA graduates who have technical aptitude to obtain jobs in quality control, laboratory assistance, and chip processing and move up later into more sophisticated and challenging posts. **Salespeople** identify potential customers, analyze the needs of these customers, and present the strengths of their particular computer product within the context of the customer's needs. Most salespeople are trained in technical areas or work with technical support personnel to answer special questions. Salespeople are usually detail minded, able to convince others of the merits of their products, and also persistent. **Sales-support personnel** make sales presentations, install equipment, and act as liaisons between manufacturers and customers and sometimes between salespeople and customers. In most cases, these positions require a great deal of knowledge about the hardware being sold but not necessarily a technical degree.

Sales-support personnel train customers in the use of equipment, demonstrate hardware at sales presentations or shows, and in some cases, repair equipment. Communication skills, market knowledge, writing skills, and problem-solving capabilities are valuable in sales-support jobs. As computers increasingly become a retail product that is sold to the general public through department and specialty stores, possibilities for LA graduates in both sales and sales-support positions are growing.

Entry-level software jobs include **information systems trainees/consultants.** People in these positions work for large corporations or consulting organizations and make recommendations about hardware use, maintenance costs, staffing, and cost-effectiveness. They are problem solvers with organizational and management skills and are able to recommend how best to use an organization's computer capabilities. Often, these people start with programming responsibilities and add managerial and consulting roles later. LA graduates with some computer course work can find employment with organizations that provide either structured or informal training. **Programmers** work for organizations that use computer hardware or software and write programs that enable a computer to perform particular tasks or functions. Programmers take a specific problem, study and analyze various ways of solving it, and then devise a step-by-step solution procedure in terms a computer can understand (a program). Programmers are problem solvers who have the ability to think in unique ways and to learn and use new programming languages as needed. Four basic types of programmers are business applications, scientific applications, multimedia applications, and systems programmers. Business applications programmers apply computer problem solving to areas such as finance, accounting, marketing, inventory control, and distribution. LA graduates with some programming skills and knowledge of business can be hired into these entry-level positions. Scientific applications programmers, employed by businesses as well as academic and research institutions, apply their skills to scientific and technical problems that are often associated with research and development functions or with scientific or social science research. LA graduates, especially those with scientific or social science backgrounds and some computer knowledge, can find entry-level work of this kind. Multimedia programmers use existing software or programming languages to create graphics and related programs, pages, or presentations that are used in varied settings. Increasingly, "virtual models" are used in design as well as research and development areas of many manufacturing firms. Consulting firms and advertising agencies also hire graphics professionals. Systems programmers, used by computer manufacturers, system software developers, and organizations that use large and complex computer systems, create new languages and programs to ensure that systems run efficiently. These people are responsible for maintaining basic capacities of an entire system and for developing programs that are required to allocate a system's resources among various tasks. Systems programmers often work with applications programmers to determine how to solve large problems and must, therefore, have a larger perspective than other programmers. LA graduates with course work in computer science, math, or research techniques may have the basic programming skills that are required for some systems programmer positions. **Software salespeople** work for manufacturers, developers, and specialized consulting organizations, selling products and services, such as actual programs, technical training and support of computer users, and project-by-project consulting. Like hardware sales, this requires varying degrees of technical expertise in addition to sales skills. All software salespeople must understand computer applications and the concepts behind programming in order to sell products and services. Software products come in many forms. LA graduates with an interest in selling software may work for employers who manufacture and distribute programs that teach foreign languages, create graphics, or train employees, for example. **Systems analysts** work with programmers to solve particular systems problems. They examine how a problem fits into a larger context and act as a liaison between a programmer and the personnel in the operations areas (e.g., marketing or finance). LA graduates with knowledge of computer programming can find positions that eventually lead to systems analyst responsibilities.

Data entry jobs involve transforming data into forms that are ready for computers to use and include **coder, data typist,** and **data entry operator.** Most of these positions are clerical in nature. LA graduates who are willing to start at the bottom and work their way up can explore these options.

Additional computer and data processing titles include **data analyst, data processing trainee, programming trainee, systems consultant, customer service representative, management information systems consultant, Web designer,** and **Web master.**

Retail sales of computers and data processing programs (as well as instruction in their use) is a growing area. Many computers are being sold and serviced through specialized retail outlets and department stores. Retailers need people to sell, demonstrate, and instruct buyers in the use of these machines. LA job seekers with an interest in computers as well as in retailing can locate a growing number of opportunities, including those associated with buying equipment for resale, not just sales-related jobs. Internet-linked opportunities are multiplying as quickly as the number of Web users. Opportunities are expanding in Internet service providers, Web site development, and search engine settings.

Conference Coordinator
See **Hotel/Motel/Hospitality Management**

Consignment Merchant
See **Marketing**

Consulting (Top Twelve)

Consulting involves selling specialized knowledge and analytical services. **Consultants** are hired to solve problems or to supply specialized analyses. Consulting entails the diagnosis of specific problems or situations, research and data collection, and the analysis of data to identify possible solutions or to document views. Consultants offer clients objective outsiders' views, specialized knowledge, and high-level research and analytical techniques. Consulting firms range from small and very specialized to large and general and can be classified into four basic categories. **General management consulting firms** tend to be large and traditional, offering a wide range of services to a variety of industries and organizations. Clients use these firms for analyses that range from market research to worker productivity to site selection. **Specialized consulting firms** may be large, especially in the growing area of computer-related consulting, but are more often medium or small groups. These firms deal with specific types of problems, industries, or functional areas and may also limit their business to particular geographic regions. Examples of specialized consulting areas include health care, human resources, compensation and benefits, the environment, and market research. **Research-oriented consulting firms** range from one-person operations to firms with offices in many U.S. cities and overseas. Research-oriented consultants use sophisticated data gathering and analysis techniques to make projections or to provide data for clients who wish to make their own projections. They include economic forecasting groups, public opinion surveyors, and demographic researchers. **Management information consultants** provide advice about applications of computer-based information and financial control systems. Some provide services in addition to advice, including inventory control or payroll maintenance.

LA graduates can find employment in any of the areas above, with typical job titles and functions as follows. **Administrative and operations staff members** coordinate travel arrangements (a great deal of travel is involved in consulting), develop charts and graphs to illustrate findings, proofread and edit reports, recruit personnel, operate and maintain audiovisual equipment used for presentations, organize and maintain research libraries, and provide clerical support for consulting personnel. The skills required for any such position vary. **Consultants** are the backbone of all consulting undertakings. Some firms (usually specialized and management information firms) hire recent LA graduates directly into consulting positions, but most do not (favoring M.B.A.'s or others with experience). Consultant titles and associated responsibilities follow a hierarchical system and typically include junior, associate, senior, and partner. A consultant has direct contact with clients, defines a problem or identifies the desires of a client, and then develops and implements a strategy for determining a solution or obtaining the necessary information. A consultant can work alone but most frequently is a member of a team. Consultants must have research, analytical, and communications skills and must be diplomatic when seeking information and making recommendations. Consultants' success depends on positive reputations derived from their track records—how often their recommendations result in the desired client goals. **Researcher** positions offer the best opportunity for LA graduates who seek to enter the field. Consulting research may involve broad industry overviews or specialized product analyses. The information acquired is used to determine possible solutions to a given problem and to put particular issues into perspective for consultants as well as for clients.

Many firms have formalized **research analyst** or **research associate** programs (titles vary from firm to firm) that are designed for LA and other graduates who plan on attending graduate or professional school about two years after starting employment. Within these entry-level research positions, LA graduates usually serve for two or more years and then leave, while a select few are promoted to consulting positions. Many go on to M.B.A. programs, with some returning to the field or to their previous firm (which may have provided financial support) after completing their graduate business degrees. Others go on to complete other academic degrees or obtain new jobs. Most firms use researchers, but not all have formalized training programs. Researchers must be able to organize and implement a study (often more than one at a time), locate and utilize available resources, and obtain the information that is needed to complete the analysis required for a particular consulting project. They spend long hours sifting through written materials, completing phone interviews, and manipulating data into a usable form. Researchers must concisely summarize their findings both verbally and in writing. They have less direct contact with clients, although this varies from firm to firm, but a great deal of contact with consultants on their team.

Because LA graduates possess superior research capabilities, they can locate research positions in the field of consulting, but they must resist the "I don't know what I want to do, so I'll get into a diverse field like consulting" motivation. Consulting firms are perhaps the most selective of all employers who hire LA job seekers. They hire only those who project direction and possess strong research, analytical, and communication skills. LA graduates should develop abstracts or brief summaries of their best research papers to document their skills. Those who have a specific interest in specialties such as health care or environmental consulting can use directories and indexes to locate these firms and then project their interest in and knowledge of these areas. Remember that consultants are in the business of selling knowledge; LA graduates must be prepared to sell knowledge of themselves and of the field in order to find a job in consulting.

Consumer Affairs Coordinator
See **Public Relations**

Copywriter
See **Advertising, Film**

Corporate Giving
See **Public Relations**

Corporate Publications
See **Public Relations**

Corrections
There are opportunities for liberal arts graduates who wish to work in the challenging but often hazardous environments of local, state, and federal penal systems. **Corrections officers** maintain order in a facility, enforce rules and regulations, and supplement counseling that is provided by psychology professionals. In fact, many use these positions as springboards to more counseling-oriented careers such as those in parole and probation. Specific job requirements vary from city to city, county to county, and state to state; those for federal positions are standard. In general, they include physical and psychological qualities that most LA graduates possess. Training also varies but usually involves formalized classes at an academy or training facility. Although advancement into supervisory and administrative positions is possible, LA

graduates should be attracted to this field because of their desire to work within a system that is charged with rehabilitating and safeguarding offenders. This is one of the unusual fields that could offer surprising rewards.

See also **Law Enforcement**

Counselor
See **Education**

Courier and Freight Services

As predicted in the first edition of this book, the original incarnation of this field has been all but displaced by electronic information transmission and freight and package carrier industries. While a few opportunities for LA graduates exist in the "old" field, growing numbers are arising in the "new one." National and international **couriers** carry financial and legal papers (less often now, as these can be transmitted via computer systems), jewelry, and other items of value from one location to another, delivering them to their designated recipients.

Easier to locate and increasing in number are opportunities with electronic information transmission and freight and package carrier employers. These industries need aggressive and talented LA grads who can service accounts, sell products and services, and manage the human and other resources that are involved in transmitting messages and delivering packages. Increasing competition has fueled the demand for marketing-driven individuals to serve in customer service and sales-related capacities and has also focused increasing attention on the need for more sophisticated and capable middle-level managers. While LA graduates may be called upon to learn the ropes while working in a service center or on a delivery truck for a while, they will be hired for their potential to serve in roles of greater responsibility. Opportunities exist with the obvious employers, but don't ignore those offered by large airfreight and trucking firms and moving companies. Jobs within this field (within both incarnations) can carry LA graduates to other opportunities via exposure to the variety of clients and industries served.

Crafts

Increasing interest in crafts has been generated in the past few years, with opportunities becoming more available. As a result, **artists** and **artisans** now have more outlets for their creations. In addition to selling their products, craftspeople can teach their skills to others in either formal or informal settings. LA graduates with an interest in this field must undergo an objective assessment of their talents and realize how difficult it is to earn a living in this field but should not let this stop them from exploring this option.

See also **Arts/Arts Administration**

Customer Relations Director
See **Public Relations**

Customer Service
See **Airlines**

Data Entry Operator
See **Computers/Data Processing**

Data Processing
See **Computers/Data Processing**

Data Typist
See **Computers/Data Processing**

Decorator
See **Design**

Dental Assistant
See **Health Care**

Dental Ceramist
   See **Health Care**

Dental Lab Technician
   See **Health Care**

Design

   More LA graduates should consider design, which includes interior and exterior design and decoration of new and existing facilities. **Interior designers** and **decorators** who make plans for and furnish the interiors of houses, hotels, offices, schools, theater sets, and the like possess artistic abilities and the capacity to turn their ideas into reality. They develop plans based on verbal specifications of clients, locate samples, purchase materials and furnishings, and supervise installation. Basic functions of designers and decorators are to make sketches and plans, develop cost estimates, and buy materials while working with clients (and sometimes architects) to implement their plans. The distinction between interior design and decoration is not very clear. An interior designer can become involved in more than the furnishing of a room or building. A designer is frequently involved in the planning stage of a project, working with architects to determine the best approaches to particular problems and choosing the materials or techniques that are needed to meet a client's goals. A decorator is usually involved in the later stages of a project, adding its finishing touches. Professional affiliations of designers and decorators are also different. These people can have specialized training, or they may have started at the bottom as an assistant or salesperson and worked their way up. They may work for retail furniture and department stores as stockroom assistants, salespersons, or assistant decorators; for designers or decorators as assistants; or for architects or builders as design assistants. Whatever the job, individuals in the field must be prepared to work toward professional memberships and affiliations to formally obtain some titles and certifications. Establishing oneself as a decorator or designer is not easy, and the usual method of payment is based on commission, making it a risky field.
      See also **Architecture**

Desk Clerk
   See **Hotel/Motel/Hospitality Management**

Development Staff
   See **College Administration and Support Services**

Distribution
   See **Film**

Drafter/Technician
   See **Architecture**

Drama
   See **Acting/Drama**

Drug and Alcohol Counselor
   See **Education**

Editor
   See **Communications**

Editorial Assistant
   See **Communications**

Education (Top Twelve)

   This field is very familiar to LA students, most of whom have spent at least sixteen years in educational settings. It involves administering educational facilities, providing educational services, and distributing educational materials. Opportunities exist in schools, churches, social service agencies, specialized training services, and businesses—anywhere people are taught formally—and can be organized into the following categories: teaching, involving direct interaction between instructor and student in a classroom; administration, involving coordination and administration of educational institutions and facilities; research and development, involving creating new or improving old educational programs and materials; and distribution, involving sales and distribution of educational materials.

Teaching positions exist in public and private schools, social service programs, vocational training schools, adult education programs, private tutorial services, and training and development departments of businesses. **Preschool and elementary school teachers** teach basic academic and social skills to young children; these jobs require a great deal of patience, creativity, dedication, and strong emotional commitment. Teaching in most public schools requires certification (an examination and licensing process dictated by each state), but a few positions can be located that do not require certification. Some LA graduates have completed most of the academic requirements for certification. State education agencies or college or university education departments can tell LA graduates how much more course work and student teaching they need for certification. Most private schools—and some preschool programs—do not require certification. Preschool and elementary school teachers either instruct classes singly or team teach. Knowledge of the basics in math, English, social studies, fine arts, and physical education is required of elementary and preschool teachers. **Secondary school teachers** instruct high school and junior high school students in specialized subject areas. Most secondary school teachers teach several courses within one subject area; occasionally they teach more than one area. Most public schools require certification; therefore, LA graduates should explore certification requirements of each state or examine private schools and special education programs. More and more waivers (deferrals for those working toward certification) are available for those who wish to teach in rural or inner-city schools. Teachers must possess a knowledge of particular subject areas, be able to present information in compelling ways, be capable of teaching basic concepts and enhancing intellectual development, and demand the respect of students. Many secondary school teachers also supervise school-related functions, sponsor clubs and activities, or coach teams. **College and university instructors** teach college and junior college students. Most teaching at this level requires a doctorate or at least a master's degree; therefore, it is not a likely entry-level option for LA graduates. Some smaller colleges, community colleges, and junior colleges, however, allow LA graduates who possess very specialized knowledge (e.g., computer science) to act as instructors. LA students who want careers in higher education should explore teaching at the secondary level while completing graduate studies. Some private and public schools reimburse teachers for taking graduate courses. **Teacher's aides** assist teachers at all levels in all settings. These posts usually do not require specialized training or certification but do require strong interest in teaching and working with a particular student population. Most aide jobs are in elementary or secondary settings; **teaching assistant** jobs are available in higher education. Assistant jobs are most often given to graduate students. Those who wish to test their commitment to teaching should explore these options. **Substitute teachers** fill in for elementary or secondary school teachers and, depending upon the school, may not need certification, even for public school settings. LA graduates who wish to try teaching or to supplement their income while taking graduate courses should explore this option. A "permanent substitute" position, more like a full-time position because one fills in for a teacher for a longer period of time, can also be found occasionally. Substitute teachers must be prepared to act upon written instructions and deal with the difficulties of being a transient in the classroom.

Coaches are hired at all levels by all types of schools and may not be required to teach. **Special program teachers** instruct students who are enrolled in federal, state, and local government or social service agency programs. These range from preschool head start to special vocational and rehabilitation programs. Other teaching opportunities exist in art and fashion, business, clerical, computer programming, electronics, and miscellaneous vocational schools or through training departments of businesses. These can involve teaching basic skills (e.g., typing and bookkeeping) or specialized skills (e.g., sales techniques or study skills for standardized tests such as the SAT, GRE, and LSAT). Many opportunities may be found in these nontraditional settings.

Administrative positions that are typically associated with titles such as principal, headmaster, and superintendent and that require a great deal of experience and additional schooling do exist for LA graduates who are interested in nonteaching opportunities. These jobs involve counseling and academic advising, library services, administration of special programs, and community relations. **Counselors** and **advisers** provide special services for elementary and secondary school and college students. Positions such as school psychologist and guidance counselor require graduate degrees and certification, but others—including **academic adviser, career counselor, college counselor,** and **drug and alcohol counselor**—sometimes do not have these requirements. Private schools tend to be more likely to employ LA graduates in these areas without certification. Library work involves the administration of school or corporate library facilities. Specialized course work is usually required to be a librarian but not to be a **library aide.** Library aide jobs exist in two functional areas: user services (dealing directly with the people who use library facilities) and technical services (dealing mainly with acquiring and preparing materials). LA job seekers should explore the option of obtaining a support position while deciding whether or not to attend a graduate program in library science. **Special program administrators** develop and administer programs that are sponsored by schools, churches, government agencies, or corporations. These can include arts-and-crafts programs sponsored by a church for senior citizens, drug education programs sponsored by a social service agency for high school students, and after-school athletics programs sponsored by corporations or youth agencies. Many youth organizations, such as Boy Scouts and Girl Scouts, 4-H, and Junior Achievement, have professional administrative positions that offer LA students opportunities to work with young people and adult volunteers. These are excellent entry-level administrative posts and can lead to increasing responsibilities.

Research and development jobs involve developing and using techniques to assess the effectiveness of educational methods and materials as well as creating new methods and materials. People in these positions work for school districts, private schools, manufacturers of educational equipment, and publishers of educational materials. Knowledge of research methodology and educational theory is required for most positions. National testing organizations also have large research staffs, and some test publishers hire for research and development posts. Large youth agencies have personnel who develop and assess programs. LA graduates can also seek research assistant positions with academicians who work on education-related topics.

Distribution jobs exist in schools and organizations that manufacture or distribute educational materials. Sales jobs involve selling books, audiovisual materials, special equipment, and computer hardware and software. **Salespeople** may have direct contact with teachers, administrators, and coaches or may deal with either a centralized purchasing office or a distributor (a middleman who in turn sells directly to schools). People in this area must understand the education field and the goals of educators and possess sales ability. For some LA job seekers, this is an ideal opportunity to sell something they believe in. Distribution positions in academic settings involve getting products from a central facility to teachers, coaches, and other users. In addition, distribution functions include maintaining inventory, purchasing new materials, developing in-house materials, and training users on equipment. Colleges and universities as well as elementary and secondary schools hire for distribution-related posts. English as a second language (ESL) teaching and support positions exist in public and private school settings in various multicultural regions of the United States. Of particular interest to liberal arts grads are the opportunities to teach English expanding worldwide as well as in the U.S. Opportunities to teach English in other countries exist within government-sponsored programs and private schools. Teacher training, experience, and education courses are assets, but they may not be required of all candidates. Certain certifications may be required in many European countries, which can be obtained through colleges and universities as well as through independent specialty schools.

Elementary School Teacher
See **Education**

Emergency Medical Technician
See **Health Care**

Energy/Environment

These two interrelated fields offer diverse opportunities, especially to those with general science and earth science backgrounds. Because these fields are so broad, only a basic discussion will follow. Interested LA job seekers are urged to undertake thorough research efforts. Energy opportunities exist in four basic settings: production/exploration companies, awareness organizations and lobbying groups, government agencies, and consulting firms. They involve working with five major types of energy: oil and gas, coal, solar, nuclear, and electric. (Alternative, including wind and tide, is a sixth category of energy.) One can work for a production company within research and development, production and purification, distribution, marketing, or operations. Many of the jobs discussed elsewhere in this book can be found with energy producers. For example, oil and gas companies hire LA graduates with accounting course work as entry-level accountants or financial analysts. They hire people with scientific skills for laboratory work, and they hire LA graduates to market products and services (including overseeing the sales of products through retail outlets and gas stations).

A title worth noting in oil and gas production and exploration is **landman.** This job involves researching the ownership of the land a company wants to use for exploration, negotiating a contract and royalties, and taking appropriate actions to register the transaction. Although course work in land management is desired by most companies, LA graduates with some knowledge of the oil and gas field can find opportunities. The title land*man* reflects the gender of those who held most positions in the past. Current and future opportunities are available to *all* qualified people. Geologists, field surveyors, and environmental impact study analysts also work for energy companies. In addition to traditional firms, alternative energy providers, including geothermal and solar, offer various options.

Jobs within awareness organizations entail efforts to inform the public of energy-related issues (typically conservation) and lobbying local, state, and federal government officials. LA job seekers can find many opportunities in this area because research and writing skills are highly desirable. Positions in government agencies can require researching energy issues, testing samples, administrating the paperwork involved in meeting guidelines and regulations, and overseeing various programs. Although the red tape involved in locating a government post can be thick, LA graduates should be patient and explore this option carefully. Consulting firms hire LA graduates as research assistants; students with an interest in energy issues or with a scientific and technical background can be attractive candidates. Environment jobs in government agencies, consulting firms, citizens' groups, research laboratories, scientific associations, and industrial companies encompass many titles and functions, including administration and planning, atmospheric sciences, earth sciences and mining, ecology, energy management, environmental engineering and public works, fish and wildlife management, and marine sciences and water pollution. Because the range of titles and functions is too wide to discuss here, these areas should be researched thoroughly. The titles **lobbyist, activist,** and **analyst** are three that quickly come to mind in special interest organizations, regulatory agencies, government organizations, and committees and consulting firms, but they are not the only titles. It is not enough just to care about energy and environmental issues; knowledge of what is involved in working within these fields and some academic background in related areas are required for job search success.

Equal Employment Opportunity Representative
See **Human Resources/Personnel**

Estimator
See **Building/Construction**

Exercise Instructor
    See **Parks and Recreation**

Expediter
    See **Building/Construction**

Fashion Buyer
    See **Retailing**

Fashion Illustrator
    See **Graphic Arts**

Field Interviewer
    See **Census/Survey Work, Market Research**

Field Representative
    See **Insurance**

Film
    This field, like acting and drama, requires talent, luck, and determination to locate entry-level jobs. LA graduates with course work or experience in film (history, production, performance, or management) have strong qualifications to offer employers. Those without qualifications must be realistic about their chances and supplement their weaknesses with a knowledge of the field's job functions. **Production assistants** work with directors and producers to arrange and coordinate rehearsals and filming. They arrange for props and sets, book the rehearsal space, schedule travel, edit and distribute scripts, schedule and supervise rehearsals, and cast parts, generally assisting in any capacity. **Researchers** and **copywriters** review scripts and check for accuracy of facts (sometimes working with special technical advisers), rewrite copy (in some cases immediately adding changes based upon decisions made during rehearsals or shootings), and often work with the people who are responsible for creating storyboard representations of scenes. Although these are typical entry-level opportunities, they are very difficult to find. Taking film courses while holding a non-film-related job may increase one's chances of obtaining such a job. **Distribution and marketing staff members** are involved in the business aspects of film. Distribution involves contracting with theaters (individually owned and large corporate-owned groups) to show a particular film. Marketing involves promotion of a film through various advertising and public relations efforts. With the proper skills, LA graduates can identify and obtain entry-level jobs in these areas. These may not be glamorous, but they can be the first step to more challenging and professional responsibilities. **Technicians** work with the equipment (lights, sound equipment, and cameras) and the props used in creating a film. Most technicians are union personnel and advance through a formal apprentice program. LA students should explore schools that offer film-related course work and consider the possibility of working for documentary, educational, and industrial film producers to learn about the field and obtain specific skills before they "go Hollywood" and seek involvement with major theatrical productions. Also, more and more video opportunities that involve both production and distribution functions are available.

Finance
    Finance offers a great many options for LA graduates. It involves extending credit, granting loans, purchasing, accounts receivable, and managing finances such as accounts receivable and payable, cash flow, and investments (including stock, bond, and dividend transactions). Finance includes the functions of accounting, financial analysis, financial planning, and credit and debt control. Finance opportunities exist in commercial and investment banks, corporations, brokerage firms, schools, government, and social service agencies—anywhere organized financial operations (such as keeping track of incoming and outgoing payments and profits and losses) take place. Because of the breadth of the field, job titles can be confusing. Financial

analysis, for example, can involve simple accounting responsibilities for one organization and investment, cash-flow, and spending responsibilities for another.

The finance-oriented job functions of **accountants** and **bookkeepers** involve recordkeeping for day-to-day transactions. With as few as three courses in accounting or by completing a Master of Accounting program, LA graduates can obtain very challenging jobs in corporate or public accounting. **Brokers** (called *account executives* and *financial consultants* in some financial services firms) deal with stock, bond, or commodities transactions. They analyze the financial status of clients (individuals, organizations, or companies), set investment goals with clients, choose the investments most likely to meet these goals, propose particular investments, and buy and sell (broker) the investments desired by clients. The broker uses analytical, research, organizational, and sales skills daily. Training may be formal—offered as courses, publications, or seminars by the hiring organization—or informal via the learning-by-doing or mentor system, but all brokers must be sponsored and take a licensing examination. Many brokers write newsletter-type publications and correspond directly with clients to present their recommendations; therefore, writing skills are also important. Although brokerage opportunities are more difficult to obtain than in the past (M.B.A.'s and experienced sales professionals are now sought for most entry-level posts), LA graduates can find them. One must be willing to work on a commission basis (perhaps struggling at first while studying for the licensing examination) and project very assertive sales skills to be successful.

Financial analysts work for corporations or institutions and assess the feasibility of specific actions and/or the profitability of given departments or transactions. This involves maintaining and interpreting records and developing reports (including charts and graphs) that document the status of the transactions related to departments or products. Most companies prefer business majors or LA graduates with some accounting, economics, and finance course work for these posts, but this should not stop LA grads from researching options or taking job search actions. A few courses taken during the summer after graduation can ease the way into one of these jobs. Investment banks and brokerage firms also hire analysts. Working in corporate or public finance areas, analysts do the research that is required for brokers and senior associates to be able to advise clients concerning possible transactions. They analyze investment possibilities, complete background work for merger and acquisition and stock and bond deals (underwritings), and help develop the prospectuses used to generate interest in a particular offering. Analysts maintain awareness of the state of the market (by industry, field, or product), general economic trends, and the status of particular companies and/or governments. LA graduates with strong analytical, quantitative, and communications skills who are willing to work in the pressure-filled Wall Street environment (although some opportunities are in cities other than New York) should explore these options. Often, these are formalized programs of two or more years preceding graduate school. While increasing numbers of analyst positions similar to those described above exist within specialized organizations commonly called venture capital (VC) firms, the total number of undergraduates hired into these positions remains relatively small. VC firms typically invest the funds of partners or shareholders, those who contribute their own money or the money of clients to establish a pool of capital, to seed new ventures. Most frequently, these ventures are entrepreneurial start-up organizations and often involve cutting-edge technologies, making traditional financing inappropriate. In return for this seed money, these new organizations agree to pay back portions of future profits and to give members of the venture capital group some say in management through positions that are directly involved in day-to-day operations or on policy boards. Be aware of the differences as well as the similarities between investment banking organizations (or departments of commercial banks) and venture capital firms and how they might influence the work of an analyst or researcher.

Investment counselors advise clients on investment possibilities, sometimes with a broker. While they usually do not have stock and bond purchasing authority and limit their involvement with clients to advice, they sometimes do sell products such as money market funds and insurance. Investment counselors can receive training and affiliation through such institutions as insurance companies and brokerage firms. Because a counselor must be able to project the image of an expert and work on commission, entry-level opportunities are limited.

Often, LA graduates evolve from more sales-oriented positions (sometimes in finance-related fields, such as banking and insurance) into financial advising and counseling capacities. Support-staff positions in investment counseling firms are available.

Researchers work for corporations or financial institutions and maintain and review literature and records that concern departments, industries, and possible transactions and compile statistical reviews and forecasts. Like financial analysts, researchers pass on their findings to brokers or associates who have more direct client contact. Researchers must be comfortable with the research process (able to find the needle in the haystack) and understand techniques of statistical and financial analysis. Increasingly, computer competence is required. LA graduates with a knowledge of finance (gained through course work or work experience or simply through personal interest in the field) can find research jobs similar to the analyst positions described earlier, including formal two-year programs. Be aware that this job, too, like so many in finance, has become M.B.A. oriented. **Traders** buy and sell commodities, bonds, money, or other "financial paper" in order to profit from the "spread" or "margin." Traders have good quantitative skills, can handle the pressure of having to make split-second decisions that involve large amounts of money, and thrive in a high-risk environment. Some commercial banks hire LA graduates for money market trading opportunities, and some brokerage firms hire them for commodities or futures trading.

LA job seekers who wish to enter the field of finance should be prepared to state the specific type of position they want and the skills they have to perform the specialized functions of that job. LA graduates with course work or experience in accounting or finance-related areas can be strong candidates. Those without should consider taking some courses after graduation. Research and additional course work may prove well worth the investment.

See also **Accounting, Banking, Insurance, Investment Banking**

Financial Aid Personnel
See **College Administration and Support Services**

Flight Attendant
See **Airlines**

Flight Operations
See **Airlines**

Forestry
Forestry aides assist foresters in maintaining and managing forests as well as the resources of national and state parks. In the environment field, this job can involve responsibilities in timber production, forest improvement, fire prevention and firefighting, maintenance of recreation facilities and trails, and enforcement of rules and regulations. Training, through forest technician programs at some colleges and universities, junior and community colleges, and technical institutes, lasts from one to two years. Some LA graduates with related experience can gain positions without formal training, but most should explore these programs. Aides begin as trainees or in positions under direct supervision of experienced foresters. Some aides eventually obtain bachelor's degrees in forestry (a prerequisite to obtaining a forester post). LA job seekers who enjoy the environment and the outdoors can turn their avocational interests into a vocation.

See also **Parks and Recreation**

Government
This large field encompasses agencies, organizations, and officeholders with administrative responsibilities for services provided by federal, state, and local governing bodies. Government jobs can be found within agencies, public interest groups, watchdog organizations, and lobbying groups and on the staffs of elected officials. The range of responsibilities and settings associated with this field is extremely wide and diverse; therefore, settings rather than individual titles will be the focus of this discussion. Each level of government—federal, state, and local—has standardized formal hiring guidelines that job seekers should research. In most cases, job

seekers are required to follow certain application logistics to obtain government employment. Federal government jobs are filled in accordance with specific department procedures. This involves testing in some cases and the completion of forms and applications in all cases. The merit system, which involves a rating and roster for potential employees, is one an LA job seeker must become familiar with in order to obtain some federal posts. A great deal has been written on the ins and outs of getting a government job. If federal posts become job search goals, review these publications thoroughly (remember that federal jobs exist outside Washington, D.C.). State government jobs are also filled in many cases by a merit system that involves testing and the completion of forms and applications. To become familiar with the procedures of a particular state, contact its department of employment or civil service office. Local government jobs are filled by various procedures, depending upon the size of the governmental unit. Large cities and counties follow procedures similar to those for federal and state hiring. Smaller cities, towns, and counties have less formal hiring processes. Upon identifying job titles and functions of interest, contact each city, town, or county to learn the appropriate procedures.

Jobs in government generally involve working for agencies, departments, or elected officials. Most LA graduates can successfully complete the tasks that are required to administer federal, state, and local agencies and departments, especially those that are associated with developing and monitoring programs and with writing reports that document activities. Reviewing the functions of these agencies and departments allows LA grads become aware of specific jobs and to target those that would use their skills and match their values. Many LA graduates have obtained jobs and established careers in the State Department in both foreign service posts (having passed the Foreign Service Examination) and other capacities, in the National Security Agency (after passing the Professional Qualifying Test), in the Central Intelligence Agency (after testing and a thorough security clearance), and as aides to senators, representatives, state officials, and municipal officeholders. Individual opportunities on staffs of elected officials are obtained by direct contact rather than through a centralized hiring system. LA graduates who wish to use the research and writing skills they developed during their academic careers should explore these options, especially as analysts for particular agencies and departments. Many agencies, especially those associated with the intelligence community, offer LA graduates excellent opportunities to continue their studies of geopolitical issues. They offer somewhat academic environments, provide the resources to conduct research, and teach specific analytical and writing techniques. It deserves note here that LA graduates often allow stereotyped views of an agency and of working for the government in general to stop them from exploring very challenging and rewarding possibilities.

LA graduates who seek any type of government job must be patient and persistent because the job search can be frustrating. They must follow formal procedures while also conducting an informal, assertive, direct-contact campaign. This involves communicating directly with the agencies or people they wish to work for and projecting their qualifications. If asked, "Did you follow procedures and complete the appropriate forms?," they can answer yes and continue direct communications. Job seekers shouldn't let formal systems frustrate them to the point where they give up or become hypnotized into believing they can sit back and wait for someone to call with an offer. It is their responsibility to take action. Although some agencies, especially the CIA and NSA, actively recruit LA graduates, they should initiate and maintain contact with government employers. When completing the forms and applications that are used to rate a candidacy, an LA grad should attach a resume and any other relevant information and not limit himself or herself to the space provided.

See also **Lobbying, Politics**

Graphic Arts/Computer Graphics

Jobs in the graphic arts involve illustrating and designing advertisements, brochures, books, textiles, and any item that projects visual style.

Illustrators create pictures to appear in publications, advertisements, or on the World Wide Web. Specialists who create illustrations for particular purposes include **animators, cartoonists, fashion illustrators, medical illustrators, record jacket artists, storyboard artists,** and **technical illustrators.** Both generalists and specialists work either as freelancers who provide services on a project-by-project basis or as employees of ad agencies, retailers, book publishers, magazines, newspapers, Web site developers, Internet providers, or printers.

Designers might not draw, paint, or use computer applications, but they create or supervise others who create advertisements and other graphic products. Titles in this category include **art director, book designer, graphic designer, layout artist, letterer, package designer, paste-up artist,** and **textile designer.** The roles of these people vary as greatly as their titles, from selecting and laying out type that projects a particular image to creating packaging that is attractive and functional.

Jobs that don't fit into illustrator or designer categories but that utilize many of the same skills in some of the same settings include **display worker, photographer,** and **printer.** Some unusual employers of photographers include police departments and scientific research laboratories. LA graduates who know how to use photographic equipment can examine this option. Remember that programs are available through colleges and vocational schools. This may be an option that one grows into, someday turning an avocational interest into a vocation. Research is the first step. LA graduates with the appropriate talents can successfully obtain graphic arts and computer graphics jobs. A portfolio that contains work that demonstrates one's abilities is the most important component of the job search. Job seekers who have not created a portfolio through formal training (course work in art or design) should consult with experienced professionals about how best to do so. LA graduates may want to consider taking courses in order to hone their skills and create a dynamic portfolio. Of course, jobs as formal or informal apprentices can be obtained in any setting where graphic artists work.

See also **Advertising, Arts/Arts Administration, Communications, Printing**

Health Care

This field involves providing medical and therapeutic care and administering the facilities where such care takes place. It includes both primary medical care administered by licensed practitioners, such as doctors, dentists, and nurses, and supportive services offered by occupational therapists, physical therapists, laboratory technicians, and researchers. Jobs are located in hospitals and clinics, private practices, corporations, and social service and educational settings. Wherever health-care activities take place—hospitals, college health centers, health maintenance organizations, medical laboratories, nursing homes, pharmacies, or private offices—opportunities for LA job seekers exist. Trends toward home health-care services have also created additional opportunities. Medical practitioners, including nurses, optometrists, osteopathic physicians, physicians, and podiatrists, diagnose and treat physical disorders. This involves specialized training and education well beyond the undergraduate level. Although these are not entry-level options, they are discussed because they are goals that LA graduates can pursue after a few years in other health-care positions.

Aides and **assistants** act as paraprofessionals in health-care settings and assist with diagnosis and treatment as well as with administrative duties. Some of these jobs require specialized training, which is usually brief and easy to obtain. Therefore, the following jobs are realistic options for LA graduates. A **dental assistant** prepares patients, maintains records, assists dentists while they perform treatments, and is involved in a variety of clinical, laboratory, and office duties. Too few liberal arts graduates consider this possibility because of the special training required. Training, through community colleges, junior colleges, trade schools, or technical institutes, can take as little as one year to complete. Many LA graduates have completed some science courses already, and working while completing training (often in a dentist's office) is possible. This can be a good transition job that offers exposure to the field of dentistry and allows hands-on experience before deciding whether or not to apply to dental school or advance to another job. Although formal training in dental laboratory technology is more and more the norm, it is still possible to obtain a job as a **dental lab technician** through a formal apprenticeship program or as a trainee. Dental lab technicians make and repair dental appliances. Some specialize, with titles that include **dental ceramist** and **orthodontic technician;** others remain generalists, dealing with a wide range of appliances, including inlays, crowns, braces, and dentures. Most technicians work in labs, but some work in dentists' offices. Their jobs combine a craft, working with one's hands, and involvement in a health-care field. It should be attractive to those who like to do precise work with tangible materials. Advancement to supervisory and managerial positions, as well as owning a lab, is possible after working as a technician.

An **emergency medical technician (EMT)** or **paramedic** works for a hospital, an ambulance service, or a municipal service such as the police and fire departments and provides emergency medical treatment and transportation. EMTs and paramedics respond to medical emergencies, determine the nature and seriousness of injuries, initiate appropriate treatments, and transport patients to health-care facilities. Other aides work in emergency rooms of hospitals and are not involved in transporting patients but do administer emergency treatment. LA graduates who are looking for direct involvement in medical treatment and who can make decisions in stressful situations, act quickly, work well as a team member, and accept the rather unusual lifestyle that is associated with long hours and difficult working conditions should explore this option carefully. Many LA graduates who explore long-term careers in medicine consider these jobs excellent transition experiences prior to medical or nursing school. Training (involving three to five months) is through specialized programs that are offered by technical schools, hospitals, or organizations like the Red Cross; certification and licensure are required by some states.

A **medical assistant** works for a private practitioner or in a clinic and performs both clinical and clerical duties. This person maintains records, may act as a receptionist, and is involved in some of the most basic diagnostic activities. Medical assistants must be willing to work as subordinate members of a team, have good communication skills, and possess organizational and clerical capabilities. An **occupational therapy assistant** works in a hospital, a social service agency, a nursing home, or a rehabilitation clinic and assists occupational therapists in teaching patients self-care and occupational skills. Occupational therapy assistants are strongly motivated to help others who, due to injury or illness, require training to accomplish day-to-day and job-related tasks. An **optometric assistant** assists optometrists with such duties as fitting lenses and glasses and answering questions about diagnostic and treatment techniques and with administrative duties (keeping records, making appointments, taking histories, and billing). Formal training is through community colleges, technical schools, and sometimes colleges of optometry, but positions that require only informal training can be found. Obviously, this is an ideal job for an LA graduate who is exploring the idea of becoming an optometrist. A **physician's assistant** works in the office of a private practitioner and occasionally in a clinic, small hospital, or school medical office and assists physicians with a variety of tasks, including interviewing patients, taking histories, and performing minor treatment and diagnostic techniques. Physical therapy aide and assistant positions are available to LA grads who have focused interests, related experiences, or specialized courses. Many seek and obtain these options prior to applying to grad school.

A **nurse's aide** provides support services for nurses and participates in some of the less technical activities involved in treating patients in hospitals, nursing homes, and other health-care facilities. No formal training is required. Nurse's aides must be prepared to follow instructions, gaining their rewards from the work itself rather than the salary. A **physical therapy assistant** works with physical therapists to treat patients who need to regain use of their limbs or to learn new ways of interacting with their environment due to illness or injury. Formal means of obtaining such a position require specialized training programs and eventually licensure and certification. Informal means involve locating employers who are willing to hire LA graduates with strong motivation and skills to serve in these posts. **X-ray technicians** perform diagnostic techniques using X-ray equipment, and **radiation therapists** use radiation-producing equipment to perform therapeutic treatments. These jobs generally require a two-year program (perhaps less for LA graduates with science backgrounds) at a technical school, in an allied health department of a medical school, or at a college.

Biomedical and medical research staff members work in hospitals, clinics, colleges and universities, research institutes, and private industry. LA graduates with good research skills and some laboratory experience (usually gained through science course work) can find jobs as **research assistants** or **research technicians.** Knowledge of laboratory procedures and of particular subject areas, such as biology, chemistry, and physiology, are strong qualities for candidates to possess. These people work by detailed instructions and follow prescribed procedures. They keep records, write reports, and often are called on to do library research in addition to laboratory duties. **Clinical laboratory staff members** work for hospital and private labs and perform both routine tests and complex analyses that are related to diagnostic and treatment techniques. Specialized training and licensure may be required by some facilities, but most require simple laboratory experience and basic knowledge of medical subjects.

Dispensing opticians accept prescriptions (written by ophthalmologists or optometrists), assist customers in selecting appropriate frames or contact lenses, write work orders that instruct ophthalmic laboratory technicians how to produce the appropriate lenses, and fit glasses and contact lenses. They also teach customers how to use and care for contact lenses. Although increasing numbers of opticians have completed formal training, opportunities still exist for LA graduates who wish to obtain positions through formal or informal apprentice programs or on-the-job training. Formal training is offered by community colleges and technical or vocational institutes and, in some cases, by manufacturers and large optical retailers and require anywhere from a few weeks to two years. Many schools offer programs that last six months to one year and incorporate practical work experience in addition to course work. Some states require licensure, which involves meeting educational standards and passing examinations. Dispensing opticians can go into business for themselves, become managers of retail optical stores, or become sales representatives for wholesalers or manufacturers. LA graduates who seek a professional customer service and health-care–oriented position should explore this opportunity.

Technologists and **technicians** work in all health-care settings and operate diagnostic and treatment equipment (such as X-ray, EKG, and EEG machines). They also create prosthetic appliances.

Operating room technicians (also called **surgical technicians**) assist surgeons and other operating room personnel, such as anesthesiologists, throughout surgical procedures. They set up operating rooms with instruments, equipment, and supplies; prepare patients for surgery; transport patients to and from surgery; assist in various ways during operations; and clean and restock operating rooms after surgery. Formal training, which involves nine months to two years of course work (depending on courses already taken), is available through community colleges, technical schools, and hospitals and is required in many settings. Informal on-the-job training is also available through hospitals that hire technicians. Advancement from this job to administrative and supervisory roles is possible.

Titles that should also be explored include **admissions clerk, billing assistant, coordinator of volunteer services, medical records administrator, patient representative,** and **pharmacy assistant.** Liberal arts graduates with an interest in future studies in medical fields or those who simply seek a challenging career in health-care settings should examine this field carefully.

Hospital Administration

There are opportunities for LA graduates who wish to work within a health-care setting in business-oriented or administrative functions. Entry-level jobs exist within all functional areas of hospitals and clinics. Admissions, billing, medical records, and personnel are just a few of the places where employment can be found.

In addition, as a result of the increasing awareness of issues related to the needs of the elderly and handicapped, opportunities for **nursing home administrators** are increasing. LA graduates with an interest in providing the best services possible and in participating in the business decisions that are associated with running hospitals and nursing homes in the most cost-effective manner should examine this field.

Hotel/Motel/Hospitality Management

Too few LA graduates consider hotel/motel/hospitality management, which involves coordinating all operations of a hotel, motel, resort, conference center, or other lodging facility. This includes management of staff, resources, and facilities. Positions can be found in large and small hotels and motels, in large lodging corporations, and with individually owned inns and lodges. Of course, many large hotel chains seek graduates of specialized undergraduate and graduate programs, but they would also consider an LA job seeker who appears to be motivated and qualified. Numerous opportunities (that do not require formal training) exist in smaller organizations. **Hotel managers** and **management trainees** are responsible for the day-to-day operations of a facility. This includes assignment of personnel, reservations, and maintenance and decisions that concern granting credit, setting rates, public relations, and advertising. Most large hotel and motel chains have formalized training programs. LA graduates who seek hotel management positions can begin as **desk clerks** or **reservationists** or in some other administrative post, adding more management responsibilities with time, and then springboard into formal programs. Hotel managers must be able to handle many different roles and responsibilities. They must be business decision makers who can address personnel, plant, and profit issues as well as professional hosts who ensure that their facility's image and service will be positive and promote continued patronage. A hotel manager works in basic business areas—accounting, marketing, and personnel—and those more specific to the hospitality industry—food preparation, conference coordination, and interior design.

Catering coordinator, conference coordinator, and **facilities salesperson** are additional titles in hotel/motel/hospitality management that LA graduates can explore. These sales-oriented positions involve soliciting business for a hotel, motel, or conference center and then coordinating the services that that business requires. Sales qualities and patience are required, as is the ability to pay attention to the numerous details that are associated with coordinating programs, meals, and events. Too often, the idea of starting as an evening desk clerk scares away a person who would be excellent in hotel management. There is room for LA graduates in this exciting and challenging field.

See also **Restaurant Management**

Human Resources/Personnel

This is a broad field that encompasses many areas and jobs. Human resources is a term that is difficult to define. It is often used as a modern and sometimes euphemistic label for personnel. Human resources is used here to describe all the functions that are oriented toward the efficient use of employees within an organization. This includes all areas of personnel—hiring and assigning employees to jobs, providing counseling services, planning wage and salary scales and benefit packages, and developing programs and conducting research related to employee productivity and welfare. It involves issues such as equal opportunity employment; performance ratings; staffing policies, including recruitment, selection, and placement; wage, salary, and benefit administration; labor relations and collective bargaining; recreational and safety programs; labor laws and regulations; employee retention; and layoffs. Human resources and personnel jobs can be found almost anywhere, including social service organizations, schools, and businesses. In some settings, specific employees are responsible for one or more human resources function. In others, these functions are carried out by general managers, supervisors, or owners. LA graduates who seek employment in this field are most likely to find positions in larger organizations with a visible human resources or personnel department. Opportunities also exist with search firms (known alternatively as employment agencies, headhunters, and personnel consultants) for LA graduates who are interested in human resources. With pay usually based on some form of incentive system (commission or bonus), these jobs offer a good chance for learning the basics of recruiting and hiring.

Before a discussion of specific entry-level job titles, a brief overview of the field's basic categories is helpful. Employment involves recruiting, interviewing, and hiring; counseling employees about job-related issues; recommending promotions and coordinating transfers; and handling firings, layoffs, and resignations. This area offers a great many opportunities for LA graduates, for the skills involved can be acquired through various academic, extracurricular, and employment experiences. Specialized course work is also available; a few classes taken during the summer after graduation can make LA graduates strong candidates for jobs in this area. Wage and salary administration involves setting pay scales, analyzing and evaluating jobs, judging the appropriateness of compensation, and maintaining salary levels that are competitive within an industry. LA graduates may have some difficulty locating entry-level jobs in this area because it requires some specialized knowledge and skills, but someone with quantitative and analytical abilities (plus some additional course work) can be successful. Labor relations requires specialized training (in some cases, a law degree) to obtain positions beyond the entry level. It involves handling labor issues, such as contract negotiations and labor disputes. Some entry-level opportunities, working as paralegals, researchers, or grievance investigators, can be located in large organizations, labor-law firms, government agencies, or labor unions. The benefits area involves coordination of insurance, pension, vacation policies, and, sometimes, incentive plans. People in this area handle day-to-day administrative details and disseminate benefits information to employees. This can involve publication of in-house newsletters or benefits manuals. As with wage and salary administration, entry-level opportunities are available for LA job seekers, but some specialized knowledge and skills are required by most employers for the more professional jobs. Of course, it is possible to start in a clerical support position and move up. Training involves developing training objectives and policies as well as implementing programs. It sometimes involves development of handbooks and manuals and coordinating classroom-learning programs that take place outside of the organization. Although entry-level opportunities are few and people with experience in the particular organization or industry are often sought for its training positions, LA graduates do have qualifications for this area. Many start in other areas and transfer to a training position after a few years on the job. Research involves analyzing staffing, developing projections, researching such special issues as productivity and worker satisfaction, and monitoring longitudinal studies and statistical reviews. Obviously, LA graduates have research capabilities, but as with training posts, opportunities are few, and many organizations use consultants for research projects.

Some specific entry-level human resources or personnel job descriptions follow. As with any field, LA majors should also explore positions that carry the title "assistant." A **compensation analyst** examines compensation packages, including wages, salaries, and benefits, and compares them with those of organizations in the same field to determine their competitiveness and fairness. This requires research and analytical skills and abilities that are associated with reviewing files and reports, investigating industry-wide salary reports, and writing comparative analyses. This function may be part of a less-glamorous administrative or clerical title, but it is a good starting place for an LA graduate. A growing number of specialized compensation consulting firms hire LA majors with a specific interest in this area. An **Equal Employment Opportunity (EEO) representative** investigates and resolves grievances and coordinates an organization's efforts to comply with EEO guidelines. A knowledge of EEO regulations and diplomacy and mediation skills are qualities associated with this post. One can learn about EEO through either course work or independent research. LA graduates who seek jobs in this area must do their homework. A **job analyst** reviews job descriptions and writes new ones, following company procedures and government or union guidelines. This involves research, analytical, and writing skills for reviewing job responsibilities through interviews, questionnaires, and observation and determining what the description should be. A **labor relations researcher** assists labor relations managers and labor relations specialists (lawyers, government arbitrators, and union negotiators) with detailed research that is required for contract negotiations. This person prepares reports to advise others on aspects of union-management agreements. Although few opportunities exist, LA graduates with proven research capabilities and some related academic background can be ideal candidates. A **personnel generalist** or **personnel assistant** is involved in all aspects of the field, including handling paperwork, interviewing and selecting candidates to fill openings, coordinating wage and salary issues, and administering training, career development, and employee benefit programs. With patience and persistence, LA graduates who are interested in human resources and personnel can locate entry-level generalist opportunities. Some are available through formalized training programs; others are simply learn-by-doing positions.

A **recruiter** interviews applicants on college campuses, at employment fairs, at trade and professional meetings, or in the office. In addition to specific interviewing responsibilities, recruiters may have broader college relations or professional hiring responsibilities. This involves developing relations with colleges, universities, and other institutions or organizations that supply prospective employees. LA job seekers, obviously familiar with colleges and recruiting, can make good candidates for these posts, either immediately upon graduation or later in their career. Few students ask on-campus recruiters about their job, about what they do and how they feel about it. This is a valuable exercise for someone who is interested in human resources and personnel. Remember, these positions exist in various settings, including increasing opportunities in search firms, specifically within specialized technology and science-related career and temporary search agencies. A **training specialist** trains employees or coordinates programs that are designed to teach general information or specific task-oriented skills. Training varies from organization to organization and industry to industry, with the role of trainer varying accordingly. Someone in a retail setting might teach other employees how to analyze inventory statistics, how to complete buying-contract forms, and how to operate a cash register. Someone in banking might teach credit analysis, accounting, and sales techniques. Knowledge of specialized subject areas and teaching abilities are required for this job. It is rare that someone who does not have experience in a particular field will be hired as a trainer, but this option should be explored by LA graduates with an eye to the future.

Job seekers with an interest in human resources and personnel should know a great deal more about the field than is reflected by the typical "I want to work with people" statement. You must become knowledgeable about the theoretical and practical issues that are related to the field and project an ability to handle the day-to-day responsibilities of jobs within the field. Additional course work can be a very strong plus, but knowledge can also be gained through independent research. Human resources and personnel involve more than working with people. A strategic aspect of any organization, the field requires specific skills and the motivation to work with policies and programs as well as with procedures and forms. This option requires a great deal of research and a very persistent and patient job search. Best bets involve starting with temp agencies or search firms.

See also **Consulting**

Human/Social Services

This field consists of jobs with agencies and organizations that provide services or programs that are designed to promote the welfare of individuals, groups, or communities. These include health and psychological services, recreational programs and facilities, and financial and other support services for the poor, the elderly, the physically handicapped, or any group with special needs. These agencies and organizations are often nonprofit. Because it is impossible to list all of the jobs in this field, LA graduates are urged to examine specific options thoroughly through detailed research. Although many jobs in this field require graduate degrees in counseling, social work, or related areas, LA graduates who are familiar with the goals, purposes, and target population of the agencies, organizations, and programs can be strong candidates. **Social work assistants** support the work of professional social workers who provide counseling and referral services to individuals and families. Often, social workers work for government agencies or hospitals, but some have private practices. Most frequently, social workers help individuals deal productively with social institutions (health services, housing, and education agencies) and assist individuals and families to improve situations that are perceived as social problems (e.g., drug and alcohol abuse, racial discrimination, and inadequate child care). Social work assistants can be involved in obtaining intake information, maintaining files, coordinating schedules, interacting with referral agencies, and documenting cases. LA graduates should investigate ways of entering this field without training and explore what graduate or undergraduate programs are required for social work degrees and licensure.

Some jobs in this field involve working with individuals or families who are applying for or receiving services, judging their needs, recommending appropriate aid (financial or professional), following up on cases to determine if the aid is used appropriately, and acting as a liaison between recipients and the agency or organization. Others consist of administering and leading programs for youth and adult groups, including developing goal-oriented activities, organizing resources (money, people, and materials), and selecting and training volunteers or paid workers. Other job functions may include fund-raising, budget planning, and public relations. Still other jobs, often those that require specialized graduate study, involve counseling or advising individuals or groups on issues such as financial planning, housing, stress, drug and alcohol abuse, child abuse, and other social and psychological matters. Interested LA graduates can locate very challenging and rewarding administrative and counseling-related jobs. Most of the well-known youth agencies, such as the Boy Scouts and Girl Scouts, YMCA and YWCA, and Boys Clubs, have professional administrative staffs that offer LA graduates opportunities. (The United Way of America has an excellent management intern program for those who are interested in administration of human/social services. Contact the United Way in Alexandria, Virginia, for details.)

Wanting to work with people is not enough to be successful at obtaining a job in human/social services. LA graduates must be prepared to state the specific abilities they possess to help others effectively and to work within the guidelines of particular services and programs. Titles vary from situation to situation and from organization to organization. Most commonly, they include **program director, assistant director, program staff member, counselor, field worker, community organizer,** and **project assistant.** Volunteering during the summer after graduation could lead to a paid position in the fall. Don't underestimate the power of a volunteer position, which can be a springboard into a challenging professional opportunity.

Illustrator
See **Graphic Arts**

Industrial Sales
See **Sales/Sales Management**

Information Systems Trainee/Consultant
See **Computers/Data Processing**

Insurance (Top Twelve)
The days when sales-related positions were the best (perhaps the only) way to enter the insurance field are gone (if they ever existed anywhere beyond the perception of job seekers). The sooner LA job seekers realize this, the better. Insurance is often defined as the business of financially protecting one's person, life, or property against injury or loss that arises from specified circumstances, such as death, fire, accident, or natural disaster. This involves the development and sale of policies (contractual agreements) that outline the circumstances under which payment will be made and the amount of such payment. Today, insurance is expanding beyond this simple definition to include a wide variety of personal and corporate financial services, including money market funds, pension plans, and real estate. Opportunities can be found in large insurance companies, in small agencies, or in such organizations as health-care facilities, that deal with administrative elements of insurance transactions.

What follows is a listing of some entry-level options. Keep in mind that because the field is so large and increasingly complex, a complete listing is impossible. Thorough research is the way to identify the field's many alternatives.

A good entry-level job for LA graduates is that of **actuary.** Actuaries assemble and analyze statistics, calculate risk probabilities, and determine premium rates for policies and pension plans within the three basic areas of insurance: life, property and casualty, and health. Explore this possibility by contacting the Society of Actuaries or any large insurance company. Graduates who have passed the first few exams are very much sought after. They must have good quantitative skills and be capable of working independently; increasingly, computer skills are associated with the role of actuaries. LA graduates with math aptitude (not necessarily math majors) can be strong candidates for these positions. Actuaries are also involved in many areas of managerial decision making, from designing insurance and pension programs and training sales personnel in marketing these programs to developing new applications for computer models. Almost all large insurance organizations hire actuarial trainees who, as a part of their training process, study toward passing a series of actuarial examinations in addition to completing their work assignments. The exams can be taken while a candidate is in school. Too few LA graduates take these exams when they are best prepared to do well: upon completion of associated course work. The entire examination process can take more than five years, with two exams offered each year and a total of ten exams required to become an associate or fellow of the Society of Actuaries, although many actuaries have excellent careers without passing all of the examinations.

An **agent** or **broker** makes direct contact with potential buyers of insurance and insurance-related services, assessing the client's needs and selling appropriate policies and plans. An agent is employed by one insurance company. A broker is an independent businessperson who acts as a sales and service representative for several insurance companies. Both jobs involve preparing reports, making sales contacts and presentations, maintaining records, and assisting policyholders with claim settlements. Thus, agents and brokers are sales-oriented people who, in addition to selling insurance, must provide services. Since most agents and brokers depend on commissions for income, they are always seeking new business and working under the pressure of commission sales. For entry-level hires, a salary plus commission or a draw arrangement (in which a salary is drawn from future commissions) is possible. Patience and persistence are traits of a good insurance salesperson as well as a good job seeker. Selling insurance, particularly for larger organizations and involving group policies and plans, has become very sophisticated and requires a great deal of financial knowledge and analytical capabilities.

A **claims representative** or **adjuster** investigates claims, negotiates settlements, and authorizes payments. These people are inquisitive, analytical, and well organized and possess the communication skills that are necessary to conduct an investigation. Investigations can involve working with people who have suffered a loss of property, an injury, or the death of a family member. Therefore, claims reps and adjusters must be tactful, sensitive, and businesslike and follow the procedures of their firms or agencies. Claims representatives and adjusters most often work for large insurance companies. A willingness to travel, analytical abilities, and some facility with calculations are desirable characteristics for the job. **Field representatives** (sometimes called **group sales representatives**) work for large insurance companies, out of regional offices, and help agents in the territory to increase sales and provide better services. Although some field representatives have several years of experience in sales capacities, many large companies offer entry-level opportunities in training programs that lead to these posts. In addition to having sales skills, field reps must be able to teach and motivate others to achieve. They are also responsible for passing on information about new offerings and for supporting salespeople who make presentations to potential clients. Field representatives may be called upon to make a number of group presentations to sales staff members or clients in either large or small groups. LA graduates who like the idea of sales but do not want the pressures of commission sales or the responsibilities of contacting clients directly should explore this option.

Underwriters determine whether an insurance company will accept the risk of a particular transaction by analyzing actuarial studies and other information that relates to the potential client. Underwriters price policies and programs in line with determined risk in an attempt to balance the need for business and the demand for profit (with total premiums exceeding losses), answer inquiries from policyholders, and assist in sales-support functions. Analytical and evaluative skills are key for LA graduates who seek underwriting positions. Most large insurance organizations hire entry-level underwriter trainees who eventually specialize in areas such as fire, hospitalization, workers' compensation, and life. Underwriting jobs also involve supervisory and managerial responsibilities as one progresses with a company. Like actuaries, underwriters prepare to continue their studies and pass certification exams. They work for insurance and reinsurance companies. Reinsurance companies (hidden sources of opportunities for LA graduates) underwrite other insurance companies when a particular risk is too great. Often, this involves some very unusual policies—for race horses, satellites, or rock concerts, for example. Reinsurance requires a creative and analytical mind, strong negotiating skills, communication skills, and the ability to work somewhat like an internal consultant or brand manager.

Like any large organization, insurance companies hire people to perform numerous support functions, including **advertising staff members, computer programmers, economic analysts and researchers, investment analysts, legal researchers, mortgage and real estate analysts,** and **trainers.**

The field of insurance has been negatively stereotyped for a number of years. LA graduates shy away from the image of the pushy insurance salesperson who calls people who are listed in a high school yearbook. The field offers much more than that, with a great many nonsales professional opportunities that can ensure challenging and rewarding careers.

See also **Banking, Finance, Investment Banking**

Interior Decorator/Designer
See **Design**

Interpreter
See **Languages**

Interviewer
See **Market Research**

Investment Banking
Related to but distinct from both banking and finance, investment banking offers opportunities to a few select LA graduates. Investment bankers provide financial advice and services to clients and underwrite and sell financial securities. Clients include private companies, corporations, municipal governments, educational institutions, and foundations. Underwriting involves offering and selling securities (stocks, bonds, and other financial paper) that are issued by a client with the ultimate investor (also a client). Investment banks raise long-term capital for clients and act as intermediaries between clients and investors (such as insurance companies, pension funds, bank trust departments, and individuals), earning fees for services and commissions on sales. The two basic sales activities are institutional—involving sales of large blocks of securities to institutional investors—and retail—involving sales of varying sizes to individuals. Investment bankers also act as consultants and intermediaries, suggesting ways to raise capital and coordinating merger and acquisition transactions. Jobs for liberal arts graduates exist in sales, finance, and trading areas of investment banking. Although fewer entry-level opportunities exist for LA graduates in the sales area (brokers often must have sales experience and/or an M.B.A.), they can still locate training positions. These eventually lead to commission-based jobs and require sponsorship and passing licensing examinations. LA graduates who seek these posts must be sales oriented and have a strong command of economic and investment-related concepts.

An increasing number of **analyst** positions are available to LA job seekers. Many larger firms or large investment banking departments of commercial banks (mostly in New York City) offer programs of two or more years for qualified candidates, including LA majors. Analysts work in corporate or public finance or in specialty areas and complete the basic research that is required for investment bank transactions. As discussed, most transactions are related to the securing of funds and/or providing advice that is required to complete deals. Deals often involve the creation and selling of stocks and bonds (or the packaging of these and other financial paper, as in the case of large mergers and acquisitions). Financial institutions and venture capital firms have similar analyst opportunities. Analysts in investment banks (and other environments) work closely with associates, senior associates, and, in some cases, partners to provide analytical and statistical support both in general matters and on specific financial transactions. They are also asked to provide general support for such activities as proofreading documents and delivering materials. Analysts research broad industries as well as the specific financial status of companies or municipalities and prepare documents and other materials that staff members or clients need to make decisions and promote a deal. Analysts may be assigned to a specialized area, such as mergers and acquisitions, utilities, or oil and gas or to a pool, working on projects in various areas as needs arise. Traditionally, investment banks have recruited analysts from the so-called elite liberal arts institutions, but they consider candidates from any school. Those with very strong quantitative, analytical, and written communication skills; the desire to work in a demanding, fast-paced environment (sometimes requiring 70-hour work weeks); a high GPA; and sophisticated work experience should be strong candidates. A few LA graduates obtain positions in the trading areas of investment banking. **Traders** put the capital of an investment bank or a client at risk by "taking a position"—seeking a profitable margin or spread—on various financial transactions. Trading can be in stocks, bonds, commodities, or a variety of other financial dealings. Because of the risk that is involved and the expertise required, few opportunities are available to candidates without an M.B.A. or work experience. Although few, these options should be examined.

Less visible opportunities are available for **operations staff members** of investment banks. These jobs can be in information systems, treasury, records, or public relations areas and can involve writing programs for use by analysts and brokers, maintaining financial records of the firm, verifying and filing transactions with appropriate agencies, and writing and proofreading materials that are used to promote particular deals and inform clients of recommendations. Most investment banks (traditionally called investment houses) have consumer and other marketing-related areas, where entry-level opportunities exist for LA graduates. These are sometimes considered operations positions but not in all cases. LA grads should explore these opportunities, where one "manages" the products that are offered to brokers and to the public, and determine whether the positions match their skills and capabilities.

See also **Banking, Finance, Insurance**

Investment Counselor/Financial Planner
See **Finance**

Job Analyst
See **Human Resources/Personnel**

Journalism
See **Communications**

Laboratory Assistant/Technician
See **Health Care**

Labor Relations Researcher
See **Human Resources/Personnel**

Landman
See **Energy/Environment**

Landscaper
See **Building/Construction**

Languages
Although it's not really a field, this is a skill area that involves knowledge of a foreign language or languages. Many, especially those who have majored in languages, would welcome the opportunity to use a foreign language on the job. What too few LA job seekers realize is that fluency in another language is only one asset to offer an employer. Job seekers sometimes use the word "international" as a prefix before any field, such as international advertising, international banking, international business, international law, or international affairs, and think that they have articulated realistic and obtainable goals. Job seekers must be aware that international does not describe just a year abroad, an academic program, or a cultural exchange experience. It is a realm in which business, political, educational, and other transactions take place. Travel and overseas assignments are often given to those with several years of experience, as rewards for their accomplishments. Language capabilities may be taken into account when

making decisions about who can best serve in an overseas post. LA graduates should first decide which fields and jobs are of interest before they add language skills to a job search strategy. Once a realistic goal has been set, LA job seekers can identify employers who may prefer someone with fluency in foreign languages. As examples, the following job titles may involve use of a second language: **airline flight attendant, buyer, consultant, customs inspector, exporter, foreign service officer, hotel manager, immigration agent, importer, intelligence officer, interpreter, journalist, lawyer, radio announcer, researcher, salesperson, teacher, travel agent,** and **United Nations staff member.** These and similar positions exist in many different fields.

Two areas that may offer the most readily accessible opportunities are government and education. Numerous federal agencies, including the State Department, the Department of Defense, and intelligence-related organizations, seek candidates with language proficiency. Social service organizations, including the United Nations and its various agencies, also look for people with language skills. Of course, jobs that involve the use of foreign languages do not guarantee international travel.

Positions as **foreign language teachers** may be the easiest jobs for LA graduates to obtain. Teaching a language in a private or public school, while continuing career exploration, is an excellent way to hone one's skills and become a stronger candidate for employment.

Interpreters and **translators** express a message in a language other than that in which it was originally transmitted. In general, interpreters work with spoken language and translators with written or printed materials. Interpreters must be able to listen to speeches or conversations and effectively translate them into another language. Translators must be more detail oriented and have knowledge of writing style and grammar. Both interpreters and translators work for government and human services agencies, corporations, publishers, educational institutions, and independent services. Many translators freelance. Depending on the setting, they are involved in transcribing and translating technical, commercial, and literary material. Interpreters and translators often must, in addition to possessing knowledge of both languages being used, be familiar with the subject of the text or conversation. Therefore, research skills are also required for both positions. Many who hold these posts are fluent in more than two languages. Training beyond the undergraduate level, specific to translating and interpreting techniques, is available and should be explored.

Law

LA graduates may have heard recently of the glut of attorneys, with cries for graduates to consider alternatives to law. Obviously, these messages contradict the thoughts of numerous LA graduates who perceive law as a way to apply the skills they obtained through liberal arts curricula and to receive the rewards that are associated with a prestigious career. Law remains a field of great interest to LA graduates, but increasing numbers of grads are seeking law-related (or nonrelated) employment prior to law school. The following are a few law-related options. Explore these as well as the roles and responsibilities of an attorney to determine immediate and long-term goals.

Judicial clerks and **administrators** work for courts and judges and handle administrative duties that are associated with complex federal, state, and local judicial systems. Varying from job to job, responsibilities can include clerical duties, scheduling calendars, recordkeeping, and research tasks. Although many clerkships are filled by law school students, opportunities for LA job seekers do exist. **Paralegals, legal assistants,** and **legal researchers** work in private, public defenders', and prosecutors' offices and perform preparatory work that is required to research a case and develop documentation that is required to write a brief. These are excellent researchers who are able to work long hours under the pressure of deadlines and capable of grasping legal fundamentals and applying them to the particular projects they are working on. Paralegals are involved in a variety of tasks that are associated with researching and preparing cases. Depending on the firm or organization, a paralegal's responsibilities can range from basic to sophisticated and sometimes involve preparation of briefs and interviewing prospective witnesses. Paralegals can be generalists who are involved in a variety of cases, or they can specialize in areas such as antitrust, bankruptcy, corporation law, litigation, and real estate. Many large New York City and Washington, D.C., law firms have formalized programs for graduates who have clear intentions of attending law school after two years of employment. **Law librarians** (who often possess specialized degrees) organize the resources or reference collection of a firm or organization, update these materials, and assist other support staffers and attorneys in using these materials. **Litigation support consultants** work for specialty consulting firms and, on occasion, for accounting firms. They conduct research and analysis for lawyers. These consultants perform services that are similar to attorneys and legal researchers, but they provide some special point of view, analytical approach, or talent. They can conduct economic and financial analyses to determine how much profit might have been lost in a case where there has been a claim of unfair competition; they can provide evidence of the value of a given firm that has sold off assets as part of bankruptcy proceedings; they can determine profiles of (and questions for) prospective jurors who might be detrimental to a given client; and they can create illustrations of very technical data or information that laypersons (members of the jury) can understand. Frequently, research-related positions, like those described for consulting firms and investment banks, exist for LA graduates in these law-related environments.

Law Enforcement

This field has increasing opportunities for college graduates, including LA majors. **Law enforcement officers** work for federal, state, and local police departments and agencies (FBI, ATF, drug enforcement, border patrol, etc.) within various capacities, including direct enforcement jobs. Most opportunities require formal application and testing procedures that job seekers should become familiar with. The increasing sophistication of law enforcement and investigative activities, including the use of computer analyses, makes this a growing field for LA graduates who do not have to become patrol officers to be contributing members of the law enforcement community, although this is where many begin.

See also **Corrections**

Layout Artist
See **Graphic Arts**

Leasing Agent
See **Real Estate**

Letterer
See **Graphic Arts**

Library Aide
See **Education**

Lobbying

Lobbyists promote particular points of view and attempt to influence federal, state, or local legislative processes. They work for business groups, like chambers of commerce; with the many professional associations related to business fields; in labor, civil rights, education, energy, environmental, farm, international, political, public interest, senior citizen, and women's issues groups; and in the offices of professional lobbying representatives. As the existence of these groups indicates, individuals band together in formal ways to attempt to influence policy and project a particular image. Lobbyists research, develop positions, and through written materials and face-to-face discussions, communicate their positions to officeholders and policymakers. LA graduates can work in public relations, political, or informational functions. Organizing jobs are available in public interest, civil rights, and labor groups. **Researchers** identify information that can be used to support particular stands and enhance the efforts of lobbyists. They perform basic library research, monitor specific publications, attend conferences and committee meetings (noting important activities), and write reports or position papers. **Organizers** distribute materials and disseminate information about a particular issue or organization, recruit volunteers, solicit funds, and organize efforts, such as rallies, letter-writing campaigns, and voter registration drives. The increasing role of political action committees and public interest groups, exemplified by Common Cause and the many spinoffs of Ralph Nader's organizations, has created more opportunities for graduates who seek work in this field. Obviously, persuasive abilities and communication skills are of utmost importance.

See also **Government, Politics**

Manufacturer's Representative
See **Marketing, Merchandising**

Manufacturing

Manufacturing deserves special attention because of the negative perceptions of most job seekers. Of late, many manufacturing companies, especially those in the so-called smokestack industries, have not been doing that well; therefore, some people assume that they are not worthy of job search attention. I strongly disagree. Too often, LA job seekers take into account factors that confuse rather than clarify job search issues. One of these factors is the future of an industry or company. Of course, everyone likes security and would like to find a situation that guarantees employment and promotions over many years, but this rarely occurs, and those who spend too much time seeking that degree of security may be missing many excellent opportunities. Any job—particularly a first job—that offers chances for success, even in a difficult environment, should be explored.

Many LA graduates can find good opportunities with manufacturers in finance, marketing, operations, personnel, or sales capacities. These manufacturing companies produce and distribute automobiles, chemicals, clothing, packaging, pharmaceuticals, and other products. Some of the best opportunities for LA graduates exist in technical and industrial sales with firms that manufacture computers, electronics, and other technical products and with those that produce machines and materials that are used by industrial consumers. **Manufacturing managers** are responsible for the day-to-day supervision of personnel, resources, and manufacturing procedures; this is a growing area. An LA graduate with good supervisory capabilities and an interest in working in the trenches, where the actual manufacturing process takes place, can obtain some very challenging jobs. **Quality control inspectors** oversee a production process to ensure that the quality of a given product meets the minimal standards and falls within a specified range. Manufacturers of high-technology products, including computer microchips, as well as pharmaceutical and biotechnology firms would consider LA graduates with some science course work for quality control positions. Entry-level inspector jobs can lead to management opportunities.

See also **Marketing, Merchandising, Sales/Sales Management**

Marketing

Less a field than a process, marketing involves the transfer of goods and services from seller to buyer. Marketing can be divided into six functional areas: advertising, brand management, market research, retailing, sales, and sales promotion. Marketing includes activities from the conception of a product or service to the sale of that product or service as well as delivery and postsales servicing. Although the functions that are involved in marketing are described separately in this book, they are discussed here primarily in relation to the overall marketing process.

Advertising involves development and implementation of activities that are designed to attract the attention of consumers and influence their buying behavior, thus increasing sales. LA job seekers should remember that many nonagency opportunities exist in retail firms and with consumer products and other types of manufacturers. Sales-oriented jobs (also called line positions) can lead to staff positions in advertising that involve marketing strategy formation and implementation. Agenting and brokering involves acting as a middleman who brings buyer and seller together in order to earn commissions on transactions. **Consignment merchants** take goods on consignment from suppliers and resell them to retailers or wholesalers; **brokers** act as temporary representatives for buyers or sellers to negotiate agreements; and **manufacturer's representatives** are independent businesspeople who act for one or more clients in a buying or sales capacity. Brand management involves overseeing the activities that are related to development and marketing of a product, typically one with a brand name. Most **brand managers** work for consumer-products manufacturers, which make and sell cosmetics, drugs, food, and other soft goods. Their work can comprise aspects of production, sales, research and development, marketing research, law, purchasing, warehousing, transportation, advertising, and sales promotion. Brand management (also known as project management) is typically considered an M.B.A. job, but some organizations do hire LA graduates as **assistant brand managers** or **brand assistants** or in other training positions. LA job seekers who are interested in brand management might consider, in addition to continued studies, starting in another marketing area and then moving into brand management.

Retailing involves selling goods directly to consumers. Retailers range from large national chains (department stores, drugstores, shoe stores, etc.) to small independently owned stores, with jobs that encompass a wide variety of responsibilities. Wholesaling involves purchasing products in large quantities from producers and reselling smaller quantities to retailers, institutions, and industrial or commercial buyers. Wholesale jobs include those of buyer and salesperson.

Some LA graduates tend to associate marketing with their negative stereotypes of sales. Sales *is* a part of marketing, and it's one that offers excellent entry-level opportunities. LA job seekers shouldn't be afraid to get their hands dirty in sales in order to gain more managerial and professional positions later. They should research all options within marketing and determine those that are most realistic and that suit their skills and values.

See also **Advertising, Airlines, Film, Merchandising, Retailing, Sales/Sales Management**

Market Research

Gathering and analyzing statistical data to determine the market conditions in relation to a particular product or service is the primary function of market research. It includes analysis of sales records, surveying attitudes and opinions, and test marketing. Market research includes both working with existing data and accumulating new information through methods such as questionnaires, surveys, and sales studies. Market research provides producers and retailers with information on package design, product type, consumer attitudes, demographics, pricing, advertising and promotional effectiveness, store appeal, store traffic flow, etc. This information is used to decide whether or not to market a product and then determines how, where, and to whom to market it.

Entry-level positions in market research firms, advertising agency market research departments, and manufacturers' and retailers' market research areas include **account executive trainee** positions. Like advertising agencies, some market research firms have formalized training programs to develop **account executives, account managers, analysts,** or **project managers.** In fact, market research is one of the areas in which many advertising account executives begin their careers. Market research AEs, like their advertising counterparts, act as liaisons between clients and the market research firm and coordinate all activities of a project. They work with clients and agency personnel to develop the projects or studies that will best meet the needs of client organizations. Once a project is completed, AEs present its results and conclusions via written reports and oral presentations. **Interviewers** and **field interviewers** gather information about the public's attitudes and opinions. By asking predetermined questions, interviewers acquire statistical data that pertains to potential buying behavior, consumer attitudes, and other market-related issues. They may ask questions face to face, in the field, or on the phone. Although somewhat tedious, this is an excellent entry-level option for LA graduates. This is the heart of market research and a position from which job seekers can progress to greater responsibility.

Project supervisors work under an AE or project manager and directly coordinate the efforts of interviewers, tabulators, and coders. Project supervisors ensure that each phase of a project is completed efficiently and on schedule. **Research assistants** undertake the preliminary research for a project, seek information about competitors' products, and organize existing sales records and other data. They also assist in writing final project reports. This is another basic job from which one can grow into more professional responsibilities. **Statisticians**

provide guidance in a market research study and ensure that the obtained results are valid and therefore worthy of interpretation. LA graduates with academic backgrounds in math, statistics, or social science research possess many of the skills that are associated with this job. **Tabulators** and **coders** assign numerical codes to survey results and tabulate the data in ways that will allow for analysis and interpretation. Quantitative abilities and knowledge of computers are essential characteristics of candidates for these positions.

Although these jobs have been discussed independently, functions and responsibilities do overlap. In some market research firms, the titles and distinctions between functions do not exist, with **market researchers** participating in all facets of a study. LA graduates with strong quantitative skills and research backgrounds should explore this job market.

See also **Advertising, Census/Survey Work, Consulting, Marketing**

Media Planner/Media Buyer
See **Advertising**

Medical Assistant
See **Health Care**

Medical Illustrator
See **Graphic Arts**

Medical Laboratory Technician
See **Health Care**

Merchandising
Merchandising is a very broad functional area that includes all buying and selling positions. With buying, it includes assessing the needs of an organization, locating goods or services to meet those needs, and purchasing the needed goals and/or services at the most cost-effective price. With selling, it includes promotion and sale of goods or services, presenting products to the right market or buyer at the most opportune time, and carrying out organized advertising, promotion, and sales strategies. Because the field is so broad and retail options are detailed elsewhere, the following discussion is focused on opportunities in wholesaling and manufacturing. These involve selling goods to retailers for resale to consumers, purchasing materials to manufacture goods, and purchasing large quantities of goods at low prices for resale to retailers or consumers. **Contract administrators** work for manufacturers and administer contracts that are established with suppliers of raw materials and parts required to manufacture products. Contract administrators may be involved in writing agreements as well as coordinating delivery of materials to proper locations at predetermined times. They may also coordinate agreements with retailers or others who purchase the manufactured goods. This is an extremely challenging opportunity for many LA graduates and because few realize it exists and what it involves, it is one that is hidden from most job seekers. **Manufacturer's buyers** assess the needs of manufacturing firms, locate suppliers of raw materials or parts, and working with contract administrators, reach agreements with suppliers on price and delivery. They possess many of the skills of a retail buyer but have additional understanding of the product that is manufactured and of the production process. High-tech industries hire people to perform as buyers and contract administrators, sometimes combining both roles under one title, and have entry-level opportunities for LA job seekers.

Manufacturer's representatives work for manufacturers and sell products to wholesalers, retailers, and occasionally other manufacturers on a commission basis. These are special salespeople who either are knowledgeable about a variety of product lines or specialize in a series of related products. They travel a great deal of the time (and spend a great deal of time on the phone from a central office) and often cover large geographic territories. Manufacturer's reps are comfortable with direct sales techniques and deal both in soft goods, such as clothing and consumer products, and in hard goods, such as heavy equipment, industrial supplies, and electronic parts. **Manufacturer's salespeople** work for one manufacturer and sell the products of that organization. Working within a geographic, product-specific, or customer-specific territory, these people visit potential customers, analyze their needs, promote the products that meet those needs, and take orders. Most manufacturer's salespeople work on commission, but entry-level hires may work on a base-salary-plus-commission arrangement. Inside sales, in which the salesperson stays in an office and communicates with customers on the phone or by telex, is one aspect of this area that LA job seekers should consider. Often, these positions are easier to obtain than those that involve direct customer contact. Once knowledge of a product line has increased, advancement to outside sales with direct customer contact is possible.

Purchasing agents, sometimes called **industrial buyers,** work for manufacturers, government agencies, public and private institutions, or any large organization. They purchase office supplies, furniture, business machines, equipment, and raw materials—anything needed by their employer. A purchasing agent buys goods in desired quantities at the lowest possible prices, with delivery arranged for specified dates and locations. These goods are for the use of the buying organization, not for resale to a consumer. The roles of purchasing agents vary with the nature of employers. In all cases, purchasing agents must be detail oriented, capable of communicating with suppliers and negotiating prices and delivery arrangements, and maintain communication within their organization. LA majors who are good organizers and communicators should explore this option.

Wholesale buyers buy from manufacturers in large quantities at low prices and resell, for a profit, to retailers or consumers. This interesting middleman or jobber function covers diverse fields; wholesale buyers can deal in consumer products or raw materials, anything from dresses to aluminum. **Wholesale salespeople** work for a wholesale distributor and call on retailers and buyers to display their product lines. Similar to manufacturer's reps and salespeople, these people assess the needs of potential customers, promote products, make agreements with buyers (including arranging lines of credit), and coordinate delivery. What differs is the middleman role. One especially interesting segment within this area involves supplying restaurants, hotels, and food services. The field of merchandising offers some of the more interesting and hidden options for LA job seekers.

See also **Manufacturing, Marketing, Retailing, Sales/Sales Management**

Modeling

Modeling involves posing with a product to help create an ad campaign, to display a product for immediate sale, or to promote a mood that will enhance future sales. Depending on where the modeling takes place and the nature of the activities, models can be categorized as **fashion models, showroom or fitting models, photographic models,** or **artist's models.** (Models in television commercials are usually considered commercial actors.) Because modeling is as much an art as a job, talent as well as the obvious physical attributes are required. Although models can work for department stores, clothing and cosmetic manufacturers, and clothes designers, most work for agencies and are assigned jobs through them. Getting an audition with an agency is not easy. A portfolio that contains sample photographs and a resume that notes physical characteristics and related experience are the tools for someone who seeks employment as a model. To understand this search process, job seekers should get firsthand information from a person who works in the field. Modeling schools do exist, and potential models should research them as a means of acquiring the necessary skills before contacting an agency.

See also **Acting/Drama**

Motel Management
See **Hotel/Motel/Hospitality Management**

Music Teacher
See **Education**

Nurse's Aide
See **Health Care**

Nursing Home Administrator
See **Hospital Administration**

Occupational Therapy Assistant
See **Health Care**

Operating Room Technician
See **Health Care**

Optician
See **Health Care**

Optometric Assistant
See **Health Care**

Organizer
See **Lobbying, Union Operations and Management**

Orthodontic Technician
See **Health Care**

Package Designer
See **Graphic Arts**

Paralegal
See **Law**

Paramedic
See **Health Care**

Parks and Recreation
This field offers both seasonal and long-term opportunities for LA graduates. Parks jobs, represented by numerous titles, including **ranger,** involve maintaining national and state parks as well as providing services to visitors at parks and historic sites. **Reservationists, guides,** and **curators** are some other jobs in these settings. LA majors who are interested in these jobs should contact federal or state parks departments and historical societies for information about job requirements and application procedures. Frequently, these are very structured and lengthy procedures.

Recreation jobs include the management of recreational programs and facilities within community or corporate settings, the sale of recreational equipment or services, and the administration of exercise and fitness (including diet-related) facilities. LA graduates who have knowledge of particular sports, experience in recreational programming, or any recreation or sports-related experience can be strong candidates for jobs in this field. With the increasing interest in health and physical fitness, **exercise instructors** have gained increasing occupational respect. LA graduates with experience can obtain entry-level jobs to teach or manage exercise facilities. Some semiformal training that is sponsored by franchised programs is available for those who wish to climb the ladder from student to teacher. Instructors can become managers and sometimes owners of exercise facilities. Teaching opportunities exist in private settings (studios and health clubs), public settings (Ys, youth centers, schools, hospitals, etc.), and corporate settings (as part of wellness programs). Broader positions that involve program management exist in the environments that were discussed under the Human/Social Services, Education, and Human Resources/Personnel headings. Recreation and fitness positions are available in increasing numbers in programs that are offered to children of working parents (day care as well as after-school and summer programs). These are in private or public schools or other facilities. Also, do not ignore growing specialty areas that combine recreation with specialized training or, in some cases, treatment. Wilderness and other challenging group-related experiences are offered more frequently to executives, to people with special physical needs, and to people who are trying to establish new (often better) life patterns. Specialty programs, camps, and tours are springing up daily. While there are academic programs in physical education and recreation administration, training is not always required for entry into this field.

See also **Travel/Tourism**

Parole Officer
See **Corrections**

Paste-up Artist
See **Graphic Arts**

Personnel
See **Human Resources/Personnel**

Photographer
See **Graphic Arts**

Physical Therapy Assistant
See **Health Care**

Physician's Assistant
See **Health Care**

Planner
See **Urban/Regional Planning**

Politics
LA students tend to strongly consider politics during presidential election years but then seem to forget it during other years. They shouldn't; politics can be a good field for LA graduates at any time. **Campaign workers** are involved in planning, fund-raising, doing research, writing issue statements, canvassing, and assessing voter attitudes. Most are volunteers, but some are paid. Often, a volunteer or low-paying position on a campaign can turn into a full-time, well-paying appointment if the candidate wins. Win or lose, the experiences that are gained while working on a campaign can be applied to numerous fields and jobs. Consider this option. Remember that elections are held every year and that working for local, state, or federal candidates can be rewarding and challenging. In addition, political parties at the state and national levels have full-time staff positions for which LA job seekers can apply either directly or after they have worked on a campaign. Entry-level opportunities can also be found within political action committees (PACs) in fund-raising, organizing, and lobbying capacities.

See also **Government, Lobbying**

Preschool Teacher
See **Education**

Print, Electronic, and Broadcast Media (Top Twelve)
Because creative thought, research, writing, and editing skills are the hallmarks of the LA graduate, the fields of print, electronic, and broadcast media offer amazing opportunities for many. Editing and writing posts exist in all three settings. Increasingly, liberal arts graduates have supplemented a traditional curriculum with computer science and technical courses. Those who have good writing skills, knowledge of specialized areas, and the desire to write and create graphics should explore technical writing, Web page development, and related options.

See also **Communications**

Printing
Sometimes confused with publishing, printing offers some interesting possibilities that are related to the production of printed materials (books, magazines, newspapers, brochures,

posters, photographs, etc.). Jobs that are directly involved in the printing process, including that of **press operator,** are available to LA graduates who are willing to participate in formal apprenticeship programs, to learn on the job, or to complete technical training. Jobs are also available in the day-to-day operations of printing organizations, including sales, customer service, layout and design, scheduling, and purchasing. Few realize that many magazines and specialty publications, especially those with circulations in the thousands rather than the millions, are printed by specialized companies. These pieces are not reproduced by their publishers (a title given to the organizational head of magazine or book publishing groups) but by printing firms. These firms need people who are capable of understanding the production, design, and cost aspects of projects to serve in sales and customer service capacities. These **sales and customer service representatives** work with customers and potential customers to estimate costs; act as liaisons between design, production, and editorial personnel; monitor press run schedules; coordinate editorial, production, and delivery deadlines; deal with issues and emergencies as they arise; and generate new business. This is a hidden area of opportunities for LA grads who are interested in publishing, advertising, and other promotions-related fields. Those who want exposure to and the chance to work with people who are responsible for developing books, magazines, brochures, annual reports, newspaper inserts, coupons, posters, advertising and public relations materials, and anything printed in large quantities should examine this related means of entry. Also, the growing number of retail printing and reproduction operations, once thought of as simply copy centers, can provide entry-level opportunities that are similar to large printing firms.

See also **Graphic Arts**

Probation Officer
See **Corrections**

Production Assistant
See **Film**

Programmer
See **Computers/Data Processing**

Project Supervisor
See **Census/Survey Work, Market Research**

Property Manager
See **Real Estate**

Public Affairs
Similar to public relations, public affairs involves creating, implementing, and coordinating programs and events that are designed to provide a service for a community. Public affairs can involve raising funds for a particular charity or program, overseeing a scholarship fund, maintaining a service-oriented facility or program, or sponsoring a youth group. Public affairs activities are often more altruistic than profit related and are more change oriented than public relations efforts. Job seekers can move from settings in education (development) and social services to public affairs capacities within corporate settings.

See also **Public Relations**

Public Interest
See **Lobbying**

Public Relations (Top Twelve)
Although this field is a stated interest of many LA job seekers, most people do not research it enough. Public relations (PR) involves promoting a favorable image for a person, corporation, institution, or organization by developing and implementing programs and activities that create goodwill and favorable publicity. Although similar, public relations is *not* advertising, and job

seekers should be able to demonstrate that they understand the differences. PR opportunities exist in professional agencies and in-house for manufacturers, retailers, hotels, and service-oriented companies. Nonprofit and social service organizations also need to develop and maintain public support and consequently hire people in public relations posts. In addition, schools, government agencies, and sports and recreation organizations have employees who serve in public relations capacities.

Because this field is difficult to break down into general job titles, its broad functional areas are noted here. Assessing and implementing the public relations needs of an organization involve determining goals and coordinating activities to meet these goals. Functions similar to market research fit into this area. Supervising the use of an organization's name and logo is a second function. An organization's name and symbol are keys to the public image of the organization; supervising their use can involve developing new logos and names for products and determining how they will be used. Another PR responsibility is developing and maintaining a positive relationship with the media. A key difference between public relations and advertising is that the results of PR efforts—publicity—may be free. Although a PR department can spend a great deal of money to develop promotional materials and create a media event, its press coverage is free. Attracting such publicity involves interacting with the press and serving as a liaison between members of the press and principals of an organization or company. Often, it entails preparing press releases and press information packets. Making public appearances and coordinating the appearances of those who represent an organization can involve writing speeches, developing programs and presentations, and organizing social events or other outreach efforts. Writing reports, brochures, news releases, and interorganization communications and editing in-house publications and newsletters are good areas for LA graduates to uncover entry-level opportunities. Writing skills can be marketed to a public relations firm or department through the power of a portfolio. Creating and distributing brochures, pamphlets, small gift items, and other materials that represent an organization and its image are additional aspects of public relations. One public relations job may involve all or just a few of the activities cited. Some typical job titles include **PR director, PR coordinator, PR assistant, public affairs director, publicity director, public information specialist, promotions director, press liaison, special events coordinator, alumni affairs director, sports information director, community affairs director, director of corporate giving, consumer affairs coordinator, customer relations director, alumni magazine editor,** and **corporate publications editor.**

LA graduates must possess a clear understanding of the field and be prepared to stress their writing skills and organizational capabilities when seeking public relations jobs. Wanting to work with people is not a sufficient statement of purpose. Part-time and volunteer (as well as full-time and paid) public relations positions are available in social service organizations, youth groups, and hospitals. These are good ways to break into the field; later, job seekers can move into corporate or agency positions.

See also **Advertising, Communications, Public Affairs**

Publishing
See **Communications**

Purchasing Agent
See **Merchandising**

Quality Control
See **Manufacturing**

Radiation Therapist
See **Health Care**

Radio Salesperson
See **Advertising (salespersons)**

Ranger
 See **Parks and Recreation**

Real Estate

 Real estate is the business of buying, selling, and servicing property. Property can be a piece of land, a house, an office building, or an entire shopping center. The breadth of the field makes a listing of job titles difficult. Therefore, a discussion of functional areas where entry-level jobs can be found follows.

 Development involves buying land, securing financing, and supervising construction and other details of a project, either residential (homes, apartments, and town houses) or commercial (stores, office buildings, and factories). A typical entry-level job entails research, sales, or property management responsibilities. Research requires obtaining information about available parcels of land, keeping abreast of the needs of particular communities, exploring the feasibility of projects in a market-research sense, and knowing about contractors and finance sources. People who work in this area have research and writing skills. They are able to examine the diverse issues that are related to a particular project, write a report or proposal that presents their analysis, and state conclusions in ways that will attract potential financial backers. Most research functions support sales in one way or another. Be aware that large real estate development and finance firms and the real estate divisions of financial institutions regularly hire analysts to serve in capacities that are similar to those discussed for investment banking and consulting. While this research goes beyond simply determining optimum selling and buying prices, it is still sales driven. Broader financial research and analytical skills are required.

 Leasing involves the renting of apartments, offices, and stores. **Leasing agents** work for developers or leasing firms. This area is sales oriented and is handled by people who can present the advantages of a particular property or space to a potential tenant in a positive and persuasive manner. Good leasing agents know their properties and the needs of prospective tenants, making matches whenever possible. Because most leasing jobs involve commissions, or draws on salaries that are tied to commissions, those in this area are risk takers, acting virtually as independent businesspeople in many cases.

 Management involves leasing, collecting rents, controlling operating expenses, and supervising people who are involved in maintenance or repairs of office buildings, shopping centers, or multifamily residential properties. **Property managers,** or **agents,** in addition to performing the responsibilities that are described for leasing agents, manage properties after they have been leased. An ongoing relationship with a tenant is established when a lease is signed, and this relationship depends on continued maintenance of the property. Working in real estate management, LA graduates must be prepared to deal with problems and to delegate responsibilities for repair and upkeep while constantly monitoring properties. Management of residential property can involve living in a particular complex; management of commercial property may require having an on-site office. Management personnel work for developers or real estate management firms. Some property managers are paid on a salary basis; others, especially those who combine leasing and management responsibilities, are paid on commission arrangements.

 Sales involves locating sale properties, making arrangements with owners to act as the sales agent, locating potential buyers, and making the match that results in the sale. **Sales agents** contract their services to licensed brokers and work on a commission basis. **Brokers** are people who execute orders from buyers or sellers for the sale or rental of properties. A broker may not do actual selling but instead act as a clearinghouse and headquarters for salespeople. Agents and brokers are licensed, based upon examination, through state-regulated systems. Course work leading to licensure is available through colleges and through private training organizations. People in sales should understand real estate principles, zoning regulations, financing, and sales techniques and must have sales-oriented personalities. The expertise of the salesperson and the job's requirements will vary with the size and nature of the properties that are involved. As with leasing, some form of commission is the likely means of compensation. Sales is perhaps the best way for an LA major to enter the field of real estate, although opportunities exist in all areas. In addition to real estate development, management, and brokerage firms, LA graduates should explore opportunities in investment and commercial banks, insurance companies, and large academic or public institutions (including local and state governments, regulatory agencies, and special interest groups that are concerned with housing issues).

See also **Sales/Sales Management**

Record Jacket Artist
See **Graphic Arts**

Recreation
See **Parks and Recreation**

Recruiter
See **Human Resources/Personnel**

Recycling and Hazardous Materials Management
For many, this field represents both the best and the worst of progress, as evidenced by the use and misuse of resources in our society. Recycling involves the collection, resale, and in many cases, refining of used raw materials, including paper, aluminum, copper, lead, steel, other metals, and plastic. It can also involve the burning of trash in special incinerator plants as alternative energy sources. While some might place this area under the Energy/Environment category, it merits its own listing. Growing concern over the ecology and the related rise in the number of companies and organizations that are dealing with recycling issues and activities indicate that this area will continue to offer increasing opportunities for LA graduates. Titles and functions vary, depending on whether one works for a manufacturer with internal recycling divisions, a scrap metals firm, a special interest group that organizes communities to recycle trash, or a government agency that regulates and monitors compliance. It is therefore particularly important to do thorough research. Independent contractors, special interest groups, manufacturers, and government agencies offer management opportunities in the collection and disposal of chemical and nuclear wastes. Legislation has dictated that this area grow to meet present and future demands; greater awareness of the issues that are related to waste management further ensures that the number of opportunities will grow. Knowledge of chemistry and ecology would be significant skills, but general administrative and supervisory capabilities and the communications talents of LA graduates are also important.

Regional Planning
See **Urban/Regional Planning**

Research Analyst/Associate
See **Computers/Data Processing, Consulting, Investment Banking**

Research Assistant
See **Census/Survey Work, Consulting, Health Care, Investment Banking, Market Research, Real Estate, Urban/Regional Planning**

Researcher
See **Chemistry, Consulting, Film, Finance, Health Care, Law, Lobbying**

Reservationist
See **Airlines, Hotel/Motel/Hospitality Management, Parks and Recreation**

Restaurant Management
Many LA graduates have had part-time experience in restaurant management, but few consider it as a postgraduation opportunity. Restaurant managers administer the staff, resources, and facilities of restaurants or food services. Working for large or small restaurants, fast-food chains, hotel dining rooms, or institutions with dining or catering facilities, managers maintain

financial records, hire and fire personnel, help chefs develop menus, create and implement promotional campaigns, and buy food and equipment. Large chains have management training programs, which usually require a trainee to rotate for specific time periods through numerous positions and areas. These programs can lead to management responsibilities for a single facility and eventually to management of districts and regions of restaurants. Many of the better-known chains are owned by large corporations (e.g., W. R. Grace, General Mills, and Pillsbury), so strong business-oriented approaches are applied to the management of these chains; advancement to other areas within the corporations is possible. Prospective restaurant managers must be willing to get their hands dirty (both figuratively and literally) in order to learn the business. In fact, most managers rise through the ranks through informal means rather than formal training programs. Restaurant managers are familiar with all aspects of a restaurant. They must be good decision makers and good hosts. A knowledge of business fundamentals and a willingness to become totally involved in the day-to-day operations of a restaurant are qualities sought by employers. No organization wants a college graduate to be a waiter or waitress forever, so if job seekers are willing to wait for the opportunities that are associated with an informal job track or for the structured progressions of a formal training program, restaurant management might provide good opportunities.

See also **Catering, Hotel/Motel/Hospitality Management**

Retailing (Top Twelve)

Retailing is the business of selling goods directly to the ultimate consumer of the goods. Job possibilities exist in any store or sales facility, including large department store chains, small specialty shops, automobile showrooms, and mail-order and direct-sales organizations. Retailing's major functional areas include buying and merchandise management, which entail the purchase of goods for resale to customers and the management of the means by which the products are sold. Merchandise management involves management of procedures, resources, and people.

Buyers work for either large or small retailers. They stay aware of the desires of a particular clientele and the goals of the retail organization; go to manufacturers' showrooms, factories, merchandise marts, and fashion and trade shows to select items for purchase; negotiate prices and contracts for delivery; and coordinate the distribution of goods to stores within a chain and the display of goods within a store or stores. Buyers—especially fashion buyers—must buy as far in advance as six months; therefore, they must decide what to buy from predictions of consumer behavior that are based on the forecasts of manufacturers, trade information, and in-house analysis of past records. Buyers must analyze and make decisions about trends and buying habits. This requires attention to detail and a willingness to take responsibility for risky decisions. Increasingly, buyers are using statistical and computerized data analyses to make decisions. As a result, some mathematical abilities are helpful in addition to the ability to review records in order to make judgments and to calculate appropriate price markups. Buyers must be organized and performance oriented in an environment that is constantly changing and chaotic. They must keep track of quantities to purchase, purchase prices, resale prices, delivery requirements, and many other details during a workday that does not end at 5 P.M. Buyers might work directly with store owners in small stores or with merchandising, store, or department managers in larger chains, so they must be able to work with others to accomplish mutual goals. Most LA graduates enter buying through rotational training programs that include both store management and buying assignments. Titles for trainees vary from store to store and chain to chain and include **executive trainee, buyer trainee,** and **management trainee.** These programs often target a career beyond the buyer level, and many organizations would be disappointed if their trainees did not progress beyond their initial functional area.

Department managers and **group managers** work within retail stores and are responsible for particular areas, which are usually distinguished by the goods sold in that area (e.g., Junior Fashion, Bath Accessories and Linens, and Home Furnishings). Department and group managers are responsible for maintaining appropriate inventory levels; displaying products; supervising personnel who have stock, display, and sales responsibilities; and providing buyers, merchandise managers, and store managers with information about sales activities. Group managers are responsible for more than one department and oversee the activities of department managers and sales personnel. Often, these positions are steps in a progressive management training program. People who serve in these capacities must be organized, able to keep track of inventory and personnel, and capable of motivating employees to perform assigned tasks. Most retail settings are hectic. Department and group managers must be able to adapt to an ever-changing environment, ensure efficient and profitable operations, and facilitate courteous customer service, occasionally through direct contact with customers. A manager must be able to balance paperwork and peoplework with ease. LA graduates can enter directly into management tracks as a salesperson or assistant manager (especially within smaller stores or chains) and stay in this area or move on to buying. Some large retailers have developed separate training programs for merchandise management and buying, but most involve a rotation through these areas. LA job seekers too often forget that management skills are as important to retailers as the skills that are associated with buying and consequently fail to project these management skills to potential employers. Buyers work with managers and salespeople; department and group managers must understand how and why particular items were purchased and priced in order to sell them.

Distribution personnel work in centralized locations (large distribution centers for chains and distribution areas for small stores) that coordinate the allocation of merchandise to stores and departments. People who work in this area must be able to maintain accurate records, follow procedures, and communicate effectively with store personnel, buyers, suppliers, and others who are involved in transporting goods from one location to another. This behind-the-scenes support area offers challenges to LA graduates who want a job in an area other than buying or merchandise management. **Merchandisers** work for large retail chains, including food and drugstore companies, and conduct analyses of previous sales to determine store inventories and plan for anticipated purchases. The responsibilities of a merchandiser can be thought of as those of a buyer or head buyer and may bear various titles. Merchandisers or merchandise managers usually work for large chains, travel from store to store, and have an office at a central headquarters. They can act as a centralized buyer or direct the buying activities of others. Although some entry-level assistant merchandiser jobs do exist, most merchandisers have risen through the ranks of an organization, frequently through a formalized training program. Opportunities in smaller firms exist for those who have progressed through promotions to merchandising roles. Merchandisers, like buyers, work for supermarket and drugstore chains, department stores, clothing stores, toy stores, and appliance stores. Being a merchandiser requires skills that are similar to those of a buyer, plus the ability to see a larger perspective. Merchandisers must keep track of more than one buyer and perhaps more than one line of products at a time.

Salespeople work in all retail settings and assist customers with selections, maintain stock and inventory, and keep records of transactions. A sales position is one of the easiest ways for LA graduates to enter retailing. If a job seeker is unable to enter through a formal program as a trainee, the best alternative is to obtain a sales position and apply again as an in-house candidate. Salespeople must be able to handle direct customer contact and administrative responsibilities with equal effectiveness. They must be willing to work the unusual hours that are associated with some retail settings and survive the hectic environment that exists in most stores. For most LA graduates, this is a starting place for progress into other retail jobs. For others, it can be a good way to earn money and test a career field while continuing the decision-making process.

Operations and administration areas include numerous behind-the-scenes jobs, which vary in title and function. In general, they involve maintaining stores and performing tasks other than sales or buying. These include customer service, bookkeeping, data processing, credit, finance, security, and personnel functions. Some large chains hire people to work in real estate departments to determine new store locations and maintain information on leases of current facilities and research workers to perform specialized financial or marketing analyses. Sales promotion, advertising, and display personnel are involved in activities to promote the merchandise that is available in stores. These functions include titles such as **copywriter, artist, photographer, typographer, window and interior decorator, media buyer,** and **demonstrator.** Those who work in these capacities plan special events and develop promotional campaigns, such as fashion shows, exhibits, and sales, or they can be involved in developing the large quantity of routine advertising that is generated by a retail operation. People in these jobs are creative and possess the ability to take ideas and transform them into realities. They combine organizational skills and creativity. Web-driven marketing as well as catalogs, shopping networks, and infomercials have also created some intriguing new opportunities.

See also **Advertising, Marketing, Market Research, Merchandising, Public Relations, Sales/Sales Management**

Revenue Control Analyst
See **Airlines**

Sales/Sales Management (Top Twelve)

Sales involves accepting a price for or making a profit from the exchange of goods or services with a buyer. Sales management involves coordinating the sales efforts of an organization and overseeing the activities of sales personnel. Sales and sales management positions can be found anywhere that selling to retailers or consumers takes place. Some sales opportunities are discussed under the field of merchandising. Additional sales opportunities can be categorized within three functional areas: consumer sales includes all retail sales positions; direct sales positions involve house-to-house or store-to-store sales; and "teleselling" positions include catalog, mail-order, television and radio, phone and Web-driven sales. Route sales jobs that involve the sale of consumer products, such as food, drugs, and hardware to supermarkets and drugstores, offer excellent entry-level opportunities for LA graduates. Although these are in many ways wholesale sales positions because the sale is made to retailers for a price lower than the price ultimately charged to consumers, they are introduced here because of the nature of the products sold.

Large consumer product manufacturers hire college graduates into sales training programs, which begin with **sales representative** responsibilities and lead to careers in sales management, with titles such as **account supervisor, district sales manager,** and **regional sales manager.** Those who are interested in sales should examine these options closely. All consumer sales positions have the potential to lead to additional management responsibilities. Industrial sales involves selling industrial goods or raw materials to manufacturers or wholesalers. Industrial sales includes inside sales (in which the salesperson remains in one office and takes orders by phone, in person, or by some electronic means) and outside sales (in which the salesperson travels from customer to customer in order to service existing accounts and to develop new ones). Specialty sales involves selling intangible items or services, such as advertising space in print media and advertising time on broadcast media. Other examples of specialty sales include selling banking or accounting services, insurance, stocks and bonds, or financial and general consulting services.

Wholesale involves the sale of goods to retailers for resale or to manufacturers and others for ultimate use. Responsibilities of a wholesale salesperson include identifying new accounts and servicing existing ones (by taking orders), coordinating promotional activities and advertising efforts, and coordinating the delivery of goods to the buyer. Most wholesale salespeople, whether **manufacturer's representatives** or **sales representatives,** limit their efforts to either geographic or functional (by product) territories. Of course, the nature of sales positions varies with the type of sales and the products or services. LA graduates with positive and outgoing personalities, good communication skills, the willingness to take risks and face rejection, and the capacity to learn about a special product or subject area can be very successful in sales. Too many LA job seekers perceive sales activities as those of the traveling salesman who in a pushy way convinces people to buy something they do not want or need. Sales is a much more sophisticated and professional field than that.

Sales management involves hiring and supervising other salespeople, overseeing larger territories, and having more strategic planning responsibilities (setting sales projections and developing promotional and advertising campaigns). Management jobs bring less direct sales contact with clients but more interaction with salespeople and senior staff members of a company to develop strategies and overall projections.

Do not be confused by the use of marketing and sales as interchangeable terms. Although they may have different functional definitions within different organizations, they can mean the same thing.

LA graduates should determine what jobs they are seeking and the tasks that are associated with these jobs. If they can sell themselves effectively and convince employers of their abilities, employers will judge them as qualified to sell products. Sales is a challenging and rewarding field. Job seekers shouldn't let stereotypes stop them from exploring options.

See also **Advertising, Airlines, Communications, Computers/Data Processing, Education, Insurance, Investment Banking, Manufacturing, Marketing, Merchandising, Printing, Real Estate, Retailing, Telecommunications**

Secondary School Teacher
See **Education**

Social Action/Public Interest
See **Lobbying, Politics**

Social Work Assistant
See **Human/Social Services**

Software Development and Sales
See **Computers/Data Processing**

Special Events Coordinator
See **Public Relations**

Special Program Administrator/Teacher
See **Education**

Speech Pathology
See **Audiology/Speech Pathology**

Sports Information Director
See **Public Relations**

Statistician
See **Market Research**

Storyboard Artist
See **Graphic Arts**

Student Life Coordinator
See **College Administration and Support Services**

Substitute Teacher
See **Education**

Surveyor
See **Building/Construction**

Systems Analyst
See **Computers/Data Processing**

Tabulator
See **Market Research**

Teacher of English as a Foreign Language
See **Education**

Teacher of English as a Second Language
See **Education**

Teacher's Aide
See **Education**

Teaching
See **Education**

Team Manager
See **Census/Survey Work**

Technical Illustrator
See **Graphic Arts**

Technical Writer
See **Communications**

Technician
See **Film**

Telecommunications
This field includes jobs that are related to planning, implementing, selling, or managing communications systems. These systems can be telephone (long distance in most cases and sometimes local and internal), data communications (transmitting and receiving computer information via telephone lines, cables, or other means), videoconferencing and videotex (transmitting pictures and text via phone), or telegram, telex, and facsimile (also transmitting pictures and text via phone). Opportunities for LA graduates exist with both vendors and users of these systems. Vendors manufacture, lease, or sell telecommunications equipment or provide telecommunications services (e.g., telephone companies). Users are organizations that require telecommunications capabilities, (e.g., banks, insurance companies, manufacturers, and retailers). The increased use of data processing and the growing dependence on speedy, reliable, and cost-effective telecommunications as well as federal deregulation of the industry have made this a growing field. Telecommunications consulting firms that provide expertise rather than hardware also offer opportunities for those LA graduates who seek to enter this field.

Although many who work in the telecommunications field have technical backgrounds, technical training is not always required, and the growth of the field has created more and more opportunities for LA graduates with analytical skills and the desire to understand and evaluate the nature of telecommunications systems. Positions with users of telecommunications carry various titles—**communications manager, director of telecommunications,** or **communications analyst.** With increasing levels of responsibility as one moves up a career path, these jobs involve day-to-day maintenance of existing systems and implementation of new ones, assessing the need for and selecting new systems as well as upgrading existing ones, monitoring system use and making cost analyses to increase efficiency and determine cost-saving approaches, developing budgets, supervising and training those who use or maintain systems, and acting as a liaison between the user organization, vendors, and consultants.

Many opportunities also exist in sales, sales support, operations, and general management capacities with vendors of telecommunications equipment and services. Manufacturers and distributors of equipment offer sales-related opportunities for LA graduates who possess sales skills and appropriate personality traits. These people are called upon to assess customers' needs, match equipment and services to these needs, make sales presentations, and provide customer support after a sale has been made. Of course, numerous sales-related and general management opportunities (supervising systems and personnel that are involved with billing, directory assistance, operator services, etc.) exist in phone companies. The divestiture of AT&T, deregulation of long-distance service, and the growth of competing long-distance phone service and data communication organizations have resulted in increasing options. Whether seeking positions with vendors or users of telecommunications, LA graduates must research this field, become aware of late-breaking information and advances, and project this knowledge to employers.

Textile Designer
See **Graphic Arts**

Tourism
See **Travel/Tourism**

Trader
See **Investment Banking**

Traffic Coordinator
See **Advertising**

Training Specialist
See **Human Resources/Personnel**

Translator
See **Languages**

Travel/Tourism
Travel is the business of moving people from one place to another; tourism is the business of leisure travel and related services. **Travel agents** plan the travel arrangements for and counsel clients on the best travel activities for their particular needs and desires. Travel agents make hotel, airline, train, car, and other arrangements for those who travel for business or pleasure. Detail-oriented individuals who like customer contact and can tolerate customer complaints should consider this option. Travel agents are trained on the job or by course work at community colleges or technical schools. They work for agencies or as independent businesspeople, sometimes spending long hours on the phone, operating computer reservation systems, consulting with clients, and completing the paperwork that is involved in making travel arrangements. They may also be involved in billing clients and promoting services through sales-related activities. Most travel agents work on commissions from arrangements with airlines and hotels, while some agents receive minimal salaries from owners of an agency. Hotel jobs offer tourism- and travel-related opportunities. Many hotels offer some type of travel service, functioning like an in-house travel agency, and most offer reservation services for hotels in the same chain. Some even offer tours of the cities where they are located. Other positions in this field exist in travel clubs, travel information services, state and local tourist bureaus, theme parks, and resorts. These often involve answering questions from travelers and providing assistance for those who are planning trips. Many gasoline companies, credit card companies, travel associations, and tour groups hire **travel consultants, guides,** and **travel assistance personnel** to perform these tasks. Promotions and sales-related opportunities exist with convention centers; with state, regional, and city tourist bureaus; with resorts; and with sponsors of particular events (including fairs, sporting events, and conventions). LA grads who wish to promote events or facilities or sell related products (equipment or mementos) or services (tours, accommodations, and travel) should have sales-oriented personalities and strong communication skills. They are often required to perform tasks that are similar to those that were discussed under Public Relations and Advertising. Although these jobs are glamorous in most peoples' minds, the realities associated with this work should be examined thoroughly.

Underwriter
See **Insurance**

Union Operations and Management

While most union-related jobs are filled by members who have been active in union activities, some entry-level opportunities do exist. **Organizers** promote membership in given unions and conduct seminars to educate members and potential members about the benefits of such groups. Organizational talents and persuasive communication skills are critical to serving within these positions. Knowledge of a particular employment area or industry and a commitment to the philosophies of a given union organization are also critical. **Grievance handlers** work with the labor relations staff of employing organizations to determine if a union member has a legitimate grievance about the breaking of contract stipulations. They investigate situations, write reports, and pass conclusions on to appropriate union and employer personnel. In many ways, these positions can be compared to those that were discussed under Lobbying and involve the solicitation of members (and funds) and monitoring of related activities as well as working for a cause that one believes in.

University Instructor

See **Education**

Urban/Regional Planning

Planners (sometimes called city or community planners) develop strategies for growth and renovation of rural, suburban, or urban areas. They assist officeholders and zoning boards in assessing economic, environmental, social, and other concerns about development by conducting research studies, presenting results, supervising the efforts of others (consultants, architects, builders, etc.), and acting as a liaison between government agencies and systems and community members. Most planners work for government agencies of some kind (federal, state, or local); a few work for consulting and architectural firms. Most planners have graduate degrees in urban or regional planning, and some have degrees in architecture and public policy, but an occasional **research assistant** position may be available for the LA graduate who has excellent research and writing skills and who wishes to get exposure to this area before deciding whether or not to attend graduate school. Because these opportunities are few, it takes a great deal of planning and patience for the LA job seeker to be successful. Planning begins with research.

Veterinarian's Assistant

See **Animal Care**

Web Designer and Web Master

These positions are relatively new positions that create, launch, and maintain Web sites. Liberal arts grads with programming, graphics, editing, and writing skills are possible candidates for these positions. The advent of Web-design software that is as simple as word processing and graphics programs has expanded employment opportunities to those who have learned how to use these packages. Specialized consulting and marketing firms as well as advertising and public relations agencies are now actively seeking employees for these ever-changing and state-of-the-art roles.

Wholesaling

See **Marketing, Merchandising, Sales/Sales Management**

Writer

See **Communications**

X-Ray Technologist

See **Health Care**

Zookeeper

See **Animal Care**

After you have reviewed the glossary for a second time, complete the Research and Job Search Goals Worksheet in Appendix 1.

5

Twelve Opportunities for Liberal Arts Graduates

SOME POPULAR CHOICES

Now that you have completed the first four chapters of this book, it's time to prioritize your options. The main purpose of the first four chapters was to facilitate your goal setting. Reading these chapters should help you to establish research goals, which are essential for completing step one of the Ten Steps to success, listed in Chapter 1. The traditional academic philosophy says that liberal arts students should explore diverse subject areas in order to "learn how to learn." As a result, you are conditioned to seek a well-rounded education and to revel in eclecticism. The only commitment that is required for most liberal arts students is the selection of a major. In the same way that selecting a major did not limit your educational opportunities, defining your job search goals will not limit your employment options. Instead, goals provide much needed focus. The more "open" your goals, the more you limit yourself.

I offer the following list of the top twelve fields to underscore the need to continue to research and refine your goals. I do not presume to know what would be right for you, but a lifelong interest in liberal arts education has provided me with some helpful information. I have selected my top fields as those worthy of special consideration by liberal arts job seekers because they match one or more of the following criteria:

1. They are too often unjustly ignored. Liberal arts majors perceive these fields to be off-limits and usually dismiss them as unworthy of consideration. By including these alternatives on my list, I hope to stimulate exploration of *all* options and selection of job search goals that are right for each person without prejudice. By not limiting one's choices to traditional options, some very promising and creative opportunities may be uncovered.

2. They are traditionally pursued by liberal arts students but sometimes without much thought. While many liberal arts grads enter these fields and do so quite happily, many do so without much research. They simply go for what is popular or easy to identify, or employers actively recruit them on college campuses. By including these fields, I hope to inspire more rigorous decision making. What's

popular at the moment may not last, and, more directly, it may not be the right first job. Even if an option appears on this list, don't rush into it. Meet people who can share their views. Identify role models. Learn through others why a liberal arts graduate would want to begin a career in a specific field.

3. They offer new and increasingly challenging opportunities for liberal arts majors. Because a field is newly established or offers entry-level options is reason enough to explore opportunities. While supply and demand should not play a critical role in making a decision, trends that give evidence of increasing opportunities should be considered. By including these options, I hope to focus attention on emerging areas, but again, decisions should be based on self-assessment and research, not on magazine articles or on what's "in" this particular recruiting season.

4. They are receptive to and can benefit from the talents, energies, and perspectives of liberal arts majors. The capabilities of liberal arts graduates can help revitalize and nurture certain fields. Without an influx of liberal arts talent, the overall quality of services might diminish, and the future of these fields could be jeopardized.

The top liberal arts fields are listed alphabetically. Once you review the list, decide how you would prioritize these opportunities. Does this group contain fields that you have already begun to examine? What is the next research or job search step you might take?

Advertising

Although many liberal arts students and graduates cite advertising as a field that they would like to pursue, too few successfully enter it. Opportunities exist in account management, media, and creative areas in agencies, marketing-oriented media groups, and related employers. Liberal arts job seekers should undertake thorough research to understand the day-to-day functions within an agency as well as the field's relationship to public relations, promotions, and other marketing functions. Internships abound within the field. Those who have completed at least one internship do have an advantage. Leo Burnett stands as one of the most significant employers of liberal arts graduates who enter this field. Annually, this Chicago-based firm hires graduates for media planning and client services training programs. While New York and Los Angeles still remain the "advertising capitals," opportunities within large and small agencies exist in several large and small cities.

While large brand-name firms historically hire liberal arts graduates and readily offer internship and entry-level positions to students and recent grads, smaller firms can also offer opportunities. In addition, consumer product manufacturers and high-tech hardware and software manufacturers hire candidates to perform in promotions planning, brand management, product release, and trade show roles. Market research firms, broadcast and print media, and retailers also offer opportunities for liberal arts grads to serve in advertising capacities. Media planning, media sales, and media buying positions are hidden gems that are available to those liberal arts grads with a blend of quantitative and qualitative talents.

Banking

Graduates with knowledge of large New York, Boston, and Chicago commercial, investment, and mortgage banks are well aware of the opportunities that exist, yet liberal arts graduates in other geographic areas may think that this a field for business majors only. Liberal arts graduates should explore regional differences and consider starting banking careers in smaller cities that offer opportunities. Once trained, they can transfer to regional offices or find jobs in banks closer to their particular cities of preference. They shouldn't let geographic preferences limit their options. If they must work in a location where banks are not receptive to liberal arts graduates for entry-level positions or training programs, they should consider taking accounting, economics, and finance courses during the summer after graduation. Seniors should explore taking these courses during their final semesters or as nondegree candidates at local community colleges. These few courses will make liberal arts job seekers business-supplemented candidates, and it can take as few as three months of study to springboard to success.

Liberal arts graduates favor lending functions in commercial bank settings and analyst roles in corporate, public finance, or merger and acquisition areas of investment banking. Additional options do exist, particularly within operations, consumer banking, retail banking, and mortgage banking. Issues that are related to numerous mergers within the commercial banking industry have created a demand for candidates who possess a blend of marketing, sales, and analytical talents. Professionals who were once called lending officers are now called relationship managers, account executives, or personal bankers and reflect the trend to hire, train, and then utilize liberal arts graduates in multifaceted roles. Many are often surprised by how receptive commercial banks are to hiring liberal arts grads for internal auditing and operations positions. Don't be fooled by the auditing title. Analytical and communications skills, with as few as one or two accounting courses, qualify many liberal arts grads for these opportunities.

Investment banks continue to offer analyst opportunities for graduates from highly selective undergraduate liberal arts institutions primarily on the East Coast. While the lists of schools where investment banks recruit has expanded over the years, the profiles have remained rather predictable. These much sought after employers believe that larger pools of qualified candidates can be found at Eastern schools and because of their proximity to New York City (where most investment banks are located), graduates will survive and thrive in the Big Apple. Also, it is common for alumni of certain colleges to recruit soon-to-be grads from their alma mater. No matter how subjective and unfair this may sound, realistic job seekers develop and implement assertive strategies to overcome obstacles. Liberal arts graduates should be active, assertive, and persistent in their efforts to identify and communicate with potential employers, and they should be aware of the growing fusion of commercial and investment banking functions. Also, small boutique investment banks exist in almost every major city, so those who don't want to work in New York City can uncover some hidden opportunities. The key to competing for positions like these is showing that you have a true and sincere interest in and, most importantly, firsthand knowledge of what analysts do. Information conversations with people who serve in these roles are essential research requirements. Sending resumes isn't enough. Liberal arts job seekers must find advocates who will champion their candidacy and, via such relationships, ensure initial screening interviews.

Marketing-oriented liberal arts graduates can find challenging and rewarding opportunities within investment banks, commercial banks, retail banks, and mortgage banks. Those who are analytical and quantitative and have a drive to understand "the deal" can focus efforts on investment banking options. Federal Reserve Banks as well as state and federal regulatory agencies also offer challenging opportunities for liberal arts grads who have taken some basic economics or business courses.

Biotechnology and Pharmaceuticals

These fields offer expanding opportunities to science-oriented and general liberal arts grads. Obvious options include research and quality assurance positions for biology, chemistry, and related majors and for those who have simply taken a few science courses and are fascinated by how pharmaceuticals are developed and manufactured. While laboratory skills are required, majors are not. Not-so-obvious alternatives include sales and compliance-related positions. Pharmaceutical sales offers opportunities for liberal arts grads who have amazingly broad profiles of skills and backgrounds. Those who blend educationally focused sales personalities (ones that require sharing knowledge rather than marketing-oriented sales techniques) with the desire and abilities to learn the nature of specific pharmaceuticals are prime candidates. Calling upon physicians, nurses, and other health-care practitioners in hospitals, clinics, or private practices offers salespeople the opportunity to enter the health-care world while being a business professional. Compliance positions involve continual research and documentation to support that their research, development, and manufacturing activities meet federal standards. Most often, this occurs prior to receiving FDA approval and during clinical trials, yet it also takes place throughout the manufacturing process. Liberal arts job seekers should not be overly concerned about their majors when they explore and seek options in this area.

College Administration and Support Services

Most liberal arts graduates have spent more than 70 percent of their lives within some academic setting and 20 percent within a college or university environment. Thus, it makes mathematical, emotional, and employment sense to explore opportunities that will allow them to work in a field that is familiar, one in which they have records of success. Entry-level opportunities exist in almost all areas, including but not limited to admissions, housing, athletics, student life, development, and alumni affairs. Traditionally, it is easier to get a position working for one's alma mater, but liberal arts job seekers should not limit their searches. They should conduct research to gain focus and volunteer while in school and, if appropriate, after graduation. They should identify people and publications that will help them learn about opportunities at institutions of interest. The *Chronicle of Higher Education* and the *Chronicle of Philanthropy* are believed to be the best publications that post announcements. Also, *The NCAA News* is another useful publication that is available in print as well as on line and is a good source for opportunities. Liberal arts job seekers should begin with their alma maters and then expand to other schools within the same "leagues." Often, schools that compete with one another on playing fields and courts find candidates from their league's member schools to be more knowledgeable of and sensitive to similar issues and environments.

Yes, a master's degree (in counseling psychology, college student personnel, counseling, or higher education administration) increases one's chances for consideration, but entry-level opportunities do exist for those without advanced degrees. A relevant course or two and attendance at seminars that address fund-raising or topical issues (professional organizations offer them regularly) before or immediately after graduation can enhance one's candidacy. A day or two spent at a conference could prove very valuable, as participants meet professionals, participate in discussions of relevant issues, and enhance knowledge of opportunities (interviewing often takes place at professional events). While salaries may not be as high as other fields, particularly business, they are not as low as some believe. Other compensations and benefits often include housing and access to special recreational and technical facilities as well as the intangibles of working within a very challenging and rewarding environment. Never ignore fields nor eliminate them from job search consideration simply because salaries are perceived as low. First, individual salaries do vary from person to person and from school to school. Second, relative costs of living are usually lower in academic communities in small towns. Third, and most important, it is easy to quickly progress up salary scales in a performance-driven academic environment. Go for it!

Related opportunities include serving as a regional or national representative for Greek organizations or for topical movements, such as responsible use of alcohol. Many professional associations and study-abroad programs are housed on college campuses, so there are lobbying, editing, program management, outreach, fund-raising, and special event planning options within these organizations.

Computers and Technology

Computers and data processing are fields that some liberal arts majors think are limited to those with computer science, engineering, or related technical degrees. While some entry-level jobs do require specialized knowledge, others simply require a level of comfort with computers and their related peripherals and that candidates are familiar with and ready to expand their knowledge of related issues in order to sell, use, test, or write programming for computer hardware and software or to provide supporting services. This continues to be a high-growth field, but the perceived supply-and-demand factor should not be the only criteria for focusing an internship or job search effort on this field. Still relatively young yet sparked by unpredictable technical advances, the field is now characterized by peaks and valleys. Firms that are involved in manufacturing equipment, developing software, selling products, and providing specialized services, as well as the companies in which computers are used (almost every field cited in this publication), have revealed increasing needs for qualified professionals.

By the time they complete their undergraduate studies, most liberal arts majors have been exposed to state-of-the-art software applications and many have also developed programming skills. Even those who have not majored in technical curricula have or can quickly develop qualifications that are required to seek and obtain programming, Web site development, systems analyst, technical support, beta testing, or any number of related posts. Others who have the required communications skills, curiosity, and enthusiasm can obtain sales, marketing, promotions, and training positions. The retail activities that are associated with this field and involve sales of equipment and support services, including training and technical troubleshooting, have grown dramatically in recent years. Target markets that once only included businesses and highly skilled professionals now include almost all individuals and groups—adults and children—in work settings and at home. Opportunities now exist within fields such as publishing and multimedia services, where specialized newsletters, online information, Web sites, magazines, and graphics have been established to address the ever-expanding and unpredictable demand for the relevant and updated information that is now instantaneously available through desktops, laptops, televisions, and phones. That is why this is one of the top fields for liberal arts grads.

Like other fields that have been perceived as unreceptive to liberal arts graduates, particularly those who majored in arts and humanities, barriers can be eliminated by taking a few courses during the final semesters at school or immediately after graduation. Such courses will enhance one's computer confidence as well as competence and, as a result, increase everyone's confidence that a liberal arts grad can succeed on the job.

Consulting

For many liberal arts majors, especially those who graduate from selective institutions, management consulting is a frequently stated goal, but too few understand the realities that are associated with supply and demand (the number of positions that are available for the number of students who seek them) nor the realities of day-to-day employment as a consultant. Subjective reasoning, geographic proximity, and tradition have created some narrow parameters and perspectives. In spite of some boom times in the late 80s and early 90s and some challenging times in the mid-90s, these firms have not expanded their recruiting activities to large numbers of schools. While consulting and investment banking firms now visit more schools, the number of opportunities do not expand. Viable candidates must know what is involved in serving as an analyst, consultant, research analyst, research associate, and associate consultant. Awareness of the lifestyle issues that are associated with this time-demanding, fast-paced, and challenging yet very rewarding field is also required to be successful. Liberal arts job seekers should be prepared to document their candidacies with transcripts, standardized test scores, resumes, and cover letters. They should project analytical, quantitative, and communications skills through behavior-focused interview techniques and be able to attack problems that are posed via case-study interviews.

Large general management and strategy consulting firms are easier to find (Harvard Business School publishes a resource that documents numerous firms each year, and field-specific directories are also published annually). These organizations, cited below, know exactly how to screen candidates and have very structured recruiting programs. They have easy-to-identify entry-level positions, and while they visit only a specific number of schools, they will review all resumes they receive. They are very familiar with the potential and power of liberal arts candidates. Smaller general management, specialty, and boutique firms, including litigation support, benefits and compensation, and field-specific organizations, as well as consulting practices of the "Big 6" (accounting firms such as Ernst & Young and Arthur Andersen) and regional and local public accounting firms do offer opportunities. To be considered by this latter group, a liberal arts job seeker may have to demonstrate and document that undergraduates are used by the larger firms and, more importantly, project the research, analysis, writing, and presentation talents that are associated with a liberal arts background.

Liberal arts job seekers shouldn't be afraid to set their sights on a very selective goal like consulting, but they should be well prepared to communicate with firms in this field and always have alternative plans. The process consists of stages, which may require additional employment and academic experience. No matter the circumstance, liberal arts graduates should be aggressive and confident yet realistic. Talk to the career services professionals and those who have worked in consulting firms. It is important to conduct as many information conversations with people who are currently in this field as possible. Through these interactions and subsequent networking, liberal arts job seekers will enhance their chances of getting interviews and perhaps jobs.

Education

While it regularly receives much attention in the popular press, education receives too little consideration in the minds of qualified liberal arts graduates. Jobs, especially within private secondary schools, are available for those who seek diverse and rewarding opportunities. Liberal arts graduates should explore the possibility of working in a private or public school setting immediately upon graduation. These roles allow liberal arts job seekers to continue their active research and easily complete any additional courses that may be required of next career steps.

It is said too often that "those who can, do, and those who cannot, teach." Well, those who can **do** teach and may also wish to serve in other education-related posts. With little fear of focus, many enter these fields and establish foundations upon which diverse careers are built. Although education may not be as rewarding as some other fields in a financial sense, it can be equally rewarding and challenging in many other significant ways.

Administrative jobs and special teaching opportunities exist within public and private elementary, middle, and secondary schools. Options also exist in child-care, educational support, tutorial, youth services, special education, and other settings. Explore positions in preschool and afterschool programs; in health-care and adult-care facilities that provide more than custodial services for both the young and not-so-young; in youth services and treatment settings that deal with drug, child, or spousal abuse as well as mental health and related concerns; and in associations and special interest organizations that conduct research, disseminate information, and provide programs that are related to educational issues.

Insurance

The insurance business has long suffered from negative perceptions, but it offers many professional sales and nonsales positions for liberal arts graduates. Many sales-support positions in large companies don't involve commission sales, which is one of the most often cited reasons why many liberal arts grads do not explore this field. Underwriting, actuarial, claims, group sales, customer service, and training positions all offer challenging and professional opportunities and with time, lead to managerial responsibilities.

Large insurance companies are well known for offering diverse opportunities beyond the entry level. Those who remain in these organizations are rewarded with new and different assignments that increase year after year. Liberal arts job seekers decide which functional areas best match their interests and abilities or explore and consider hidden specialties, such as reinsurance. This field specifically requires strong analytical skills and creative thinking.

Print, Electronic, and Broadcast Media

Because creative thought, research, writing, and editing skills are the hallmarks of the liberal arts graduate, the fields of print, electronic, and broadcast media offer amazing opportunities for many. Editing and writing posts exist in all three settings. Increasingly, liberal arts graduates have supplemented a traditional curriculum with computer science and technical courses. Those who have good writing skills, knowledge of specialized areas, and the desire to write and create graphics should explore technical writing, Web page development, and related options. It is still difficult to find individuals who combine communications abilities, specifically writing and presentation talents, with more technical ones, so liberal arts majors with HTML and Java abilities have a definite advantage. Newspapers, magazines, radio, network and cable television, and soon, Web-TV stations are potential employers. Organizations such as computer and high-technology manufacturers, software developers, scientific equipment and health-care products manufacturers, consulting firms, and public relations firms do hire writers, editors, production assistants, and graphic artists. Reactive efforts are obvious, but proactive efforts that often involve networking through professional associations are critical. A liberal arts job seeker should identify these groups and then attend seminars or training classes. He or she should learn the processes involved in Web site development and maintenance, technical writing, and related production efforts and then create a portfolio (or a personal Web page) to demonstrate the desired skills. The portfolio can contain exercises that have been completed informally, through courses, or as assigned by someone in the field.

Liberal arts graduates who are interested in more traditional writing or editing roles in magazine, book, or newspaper companies should become familiar with entry-level options. Publishing institutes are offered at a variety of institutions (e.g., Stanford, University of Denver, and Radcliffe), and they can offer recent or not-so-recent graduates opportunities to develop new and very applicable skills and portfolio entries. Also, these programs offer opportunities to meet and network with others who are interested in the same field and interaction with professionals in the industry.

Volunteer experiences or internships that are obtained through personal efforts or as part of course requirements are also ways to break into the field. Within magazine settings, research and fact-checking positions are traditional first jobs. In book publishing, sales, manuscript reviewer, and editorial assistant positions offer similar opportunities. Explore all the options that are cited in the glossary under communications that involve the use of editing, writing, and production talents, but do not ignore those opportunities that are located in marketing, advertising, and public relations areas.

The ability to communicate in written forms will be tested during the job search through resumes and letters as well as through portfolios. More so than in other fields, written communiqués will be judged as illustrations of one's capability to perform on the job.

Public Relations

Those who seek to enter public relations must understand the nature of reality-based roles and responsibilities. They must be prepared to state the skills they possess to support an interest in event planning, promotions, press relations, writing, and other related activities that are associated with the field. Recalling the phrase "**publicity** relations" and thinking about how public relations resulted from losing the "i-t-y," it is easy to emphasize the clear distinction between this field and advertising and reinforce the skills that are critical to success in this field. While advertising creates strategic marketing plans, an agency's clients pay for print and broadcast media time and space to reach their target markets and implement their plans. Public relations involves creating an event, placing a story, sponsoring activities, developing promotional materials, or in some way affecting predetermined public opinion. Thus, public relations can also be thought of as free advertising.

Like advertising, liberal arts grads who seek to enter this field should undertake thorough research to understand the day-to-day functions within an agency and within corporate or other settings that offer entry-level options. Internships also abound in this field. Those who complete at least one internship do have an advantage.

Retailing

This field continues to offer numerous opportunities to liberal arts job seekers. The formal training programs of large retail firms, including department, specialty, drug, and food store chains, have traditionally provided structured and fast tracks to dynamic and rewarding careers. Liberal arts graduates can become responsible for multimillion-dollar departments or stores, with a dozen or more people to supervise, in as few as six weeks after starting a program. No retail firm hires college graduates into formalized programs or management-focused entry-level options just so that they can only be salespeople. Sales may be one of the responsibilities of an early rotation or assignment, and it is the way to enter a management track as an in-house candidate. Retailers want those who complete these programs to be senior managers and top executives as soon as possible. Very young people can hold very high rankings and well-paying positions if they use their liberal arts power to progress within this field.

Retailing is a field that has traditionally been known for low pay and long hours for entry-level positions. The hours have not changed over time, except to increase; most firms are open seven days a week (some 24 hours a day), and some have online and mail-order operations. The pay, however, has definitely improved. Retailers realized in the late 80s and early 90s that if they were to compete with other fields for the most talented college graduates, they must pay their employees accordingly. Retailing is also a field that rewards performance. If an employee produces, then he or she will be paid appropriately and be given increased responsibilities. Lifestyle issues, particularly during early years in the business, are challenging. Like college life, retailing doesn't have traditional hours but does have demanding preholiday stress. In academe, the stress was caused by midterms and finals. In retailing, it's caused by Christmas and seasonal sales. In addition to store management careers, retailing offers employment growth opportunities within operations areas, including finance, recruiting, training, facilities management, mail order, security, and advertising (through copywriting, media buying, and sales promotions roles). All are available to those who can cite these as entry-level goals.

Sales/Sales Management

Too many shy away from sales because of their stereotyped perceptions. Sales should be thought of as an arena from which many top executives have risen, not as one for men who wear plaid polyester suits and carry bulging sample cases. Sales jobs, especially those offered by consumer products and hard goods manufactures and marketers, can serve as springboards to sales management and many other areas.

Some of the larger organizations that hire liberal arts graduates into sales positions and management development paths include Procter and Gamble, Automatic Data Processing, Coca-Cola, and American Greetings. The sales opportunities that are offered by consumer products and soft goods manufacturers should also be examined carefully.

Sales opportunities also exist within banking, financial services, computers and technology, and, in fact, almost all of the functional areas that were noted in the glossary of options. Remember "S-A-L-E-S is not a four-letter word." The fifth letter is S, and that can signify starting a career. It does not limit or narrow future options. Regularly, sales positions can lead to promotions, marketing, advertising, human resources, and related options.

Again, this diversified dozen is presented to educate and motivate, not to psychically predict what field you might find appealing. Review your completed Research and Job

Search Goals Worksheet after you have examined this top twelve listing. Have your views changed? Have they been further reinforced by these specialized discussions? Have your research or job search targets remained constant? If any of these twelve areas are of particular interest to you, examine the resumes in Chapter 7. Then go for it!

The Resume and the Interview—Keys to Success

Even the most inexperienced job seeker knows that the resume and the interview are the two most common routes to securing a job. In Parts I and II, you've been able to consider your career options and, through self-evaluation and your research efforts, have no doubt come up with a list of career interests and job search goals. In Part III, you will enter the heart of your job search campaign—writing your resume and cover letters and preparing for your interview.

6

The Liberal Arts Resume: A Powerful Presentation

THE RESUME AS A TOOL AND JOB SEEKER AS CRAFTSPERSON

Because liberal arts students and graduates are truly free to enter the numerous fields discussed in Part II, to be successful they must be able to articulate goals verbally as well as in written forms—resumes and cover letters. Like clothes worn to an employment interview, a resume must project a positive image and fit both the job seeker and the circumstances. A job seeker must be comfortable with its content or format to be effective. Likewise, a job seeker should have enough confidence in his or her resume writing skills to change a resume when necessary.

THE EMPLOYER'S PERSPECTIVE

Before compiling a resume, it is helpful to understand just how it will be viewed by the prospective employer. To fill particular jobs, employers first establish qualifications that they determine as required or desirable. Once these skills—areas of expertise, personal characteristics, employment history, and other variables—are established, candidates who fit the profile are sourced, screened, and, ultimately, selected. In some cases, qualification criteria are clearly specified in job descriptions posted via printed or electronic systems, on sign-up schedules for on-campus interviews, and through third-party search firms. In all cases, interviewers maintain awareness of the desired profile. Successful internship and job seekers must do the same.

Resumes and cover letters are reviewed and interviews are conducted with a very clear set of criteria in mind. Through "behavioral interviewing" and "key-word scanning," employers develop written profiles and lists of desired skills and past behaviors that qualified candidates have exhibited. While reviewing job search documents and listening to interview responses, employers judge those candidates who match the predetermined profile as "qualified," worthy of additional consideration. Employers do **not** thoroughly read resumes, analyze content, nor critique format to determine where a candidate might fit. It remains the liberal arts job seeker's response-ability to set and articulate goals (remember step one). Once employers review documents that state goals and cite clear presentations of relevant skills and abilities, they can be inspired to consider additional options.

While this seems quite simple, it does not mean that a liberal arts job search is easy. Looking for a job or internship requires a great deal of work and is psychologically demanding. Although writing a good resume is one of the most important steps in the process, it is not the only step. A liberal arts job seeker will be successful by focusing on what a potential employer is looking for and by presenting a goal-directed image in writing and in person.

A RECOMMENDED FORMAT

While many think that there is no perfect resume, there is a format that best meets the needs of liberal arts students and grads—**a resume with structure but also with the flexibility to address the strategic objectives of the candidate.** The information that follows is an overview of this special approach.

As you read, you will learn why I believe that one format is most powerful. In order to create multipurpose and targeted versions, you must first assess the qualifications you possess, identify those that are required to perform a specific job function, and then articulate your capabilities in active, personal, and precise terms. Thus, this format forces resume writers to take responsibility for projecting their goals and qualifications onto their resumes.

Many sample resumes may appear dense, offering a great deal of information on one page. This was done to offer you, the reader, as many reference points as possible, not to encourage you to match an example word-for-word or in total length.

Components of the Resume
Now, let's review the basic components of this powerful resume, section-by-section and step-by-step, to provide a more structured approach.

Identifying Information
Your name, address, telephone number, e-mail address, and fax number appear at the top of the document. Include your present school and home addresses if both will be used during the search, particularly if home is your geographic target. If addresses or phone numbers change while your job search progresses, this information must be immediately updated, and follow-up correspondence should be sent to the employers you previously contacted. Use one line for each of the citations. All of the samples in this book illustrate space-efficient approaches that utilize bullet points or spacing to separate content.

Objective
The objective tells potential employers that you are headed in a certain direction through clearly articulated goals. It informs readers of your reasons for making contact, and it serves as a focal point from which they can review and analyze the document. This statement does not limit you nor prevent potential employers from considering you for positions other than those stated, but it does indicate your preference.

A very brief and well-written objective statement, accompanied by well-developed qualifications, can effectively communicate goals and capabilities. This "one-two" combination can focus and, thus, increase the power projected by your document. An effective combination tells potential employers clearly what you want to do, uses job titles and functions that are identifiable, and reflects knowledge of areas in which you are seeking employment. A vaguely worded and lengthy objective can confuse a reader.

Qualifications and Capabilities

Although this section is not a given for all resumes, it is particularly powerful for the liberal arts graduate. Whether titled Summary of Skills, Skills and Capabilities, Qualifications, Qualifications and Capabilities, or some variation, a section that lists a powerful profile of assets enhances a resume's effectiveness. Preferably, this section should appear immediately after the objective or as a creative blending of your objective and qualifications. When possible, the heading is preceded by a phrase that projects a clear focus. I call this a "headline" rather then a "header." A resume with well-crafted headlines can, like newspapers, tell scanning readers a great deal before they review the full content. Headline examples include Advertising Qualifications and Capabilities, Finance and Analytical Skills and Achievements, and Teaching and Tutorial Background. The more one can project knowledge of self and knowledge of a specific job, the better. Steps to creating this important component of your resume will be discussed later in this chapter.

Education

Include undergraduate and graduate study as well as overseas study, special academic programs, and, when appropriate, training seminars. Majors and minors, degrees, institutions and their locations, dates attended, and dates graduated can be included. Courses, projects, and areas of academic emphasis (if they are related to your objective) may also be included. Scholarships, honor society memberships, special awards, and grade point averages can be cited. You may wish to note your GPA in your major and minor areas of study in addition to or instead of your cumulative GPA. Some candidates note GPAs for specific periods of time, such as junior and senior years, if the information reveals positive trends and achievements. Examples of effective headlines for this section include Technical and Scientific Education; Economics and Business-Related Studies; Computer Science Education; Business, Promotions, and Marketing Degree; and Related Courses and Projects. Courses and projects can be noted under these headlines as separate categories, but you are very strongly encouraged to list both. Abbreviated course listings and dynamic project descriptions are usually well received by reviewers.

Experience

List full-time and part-time experiences, including employment, volunteer and academic projects, cocurricular projects and special events, internships, externships, and all skills that project desired qualifications. State titles you held and names of the organizations you worked for and describe your experiences in active, skills-oriented terms. Whenever possible, cite specific achievements, noting facts and figures. The most common way to present information is in reverse chronological order, with the most recent experience listed first, but headlines can present your experiences in a goal-specific order. Examples of headlines include Counseling and Tutorial Experience; Research, Analysis, and Presentation Achievements; Finance and Banking Accomplishments; and Event Planning and Promotions Experience.

Cocurricular and Community Activities

Note names of organizations, offices held, accomplishments, and special projects. Your descriptions of these activities and your roles and responsibilities should project the skills you acquired. If your activities are associated with a club, school group, or community organization that is related to your stated goal, describe them. Whether or not you received payment for your contributions should not determine where your entries appear. The nature of your achievements and their relationship to your goals should dictate how early in the document they appear. Headlines could include Leadership, Program Management, and Outreach Achievements; Community Outreach and Event Planning Experience; and Fund-raising, Leadership, and Project Management Experience.

Special Categories

While almost anything can be noted as a special category on a resume, the above-cited options address the needs of almost all job seekers. Presenting information under goal-targeted headlines is a critical characteristic of this powerful liberal arts format. Headlines include Supervisory Experience, Finance Background, Travel and Cross-Cultural Experiences, Multilingual Capabilities, and Computer Applications and Systems.

While personal interests are recommended by some, they rarely affect a job search. If you have acquired skills as a result of special interests, cite them in your Qualifications Summary or under a special headline.

References

Many resumes end with a "References Available Upon Request" statement. Although some samples do illustrate this approach, the space can also be used for more important information. An additional line that cites your goal-focused qualifications is much more significant. Also, never list references on the resume itself. Do so on a separate sheet and, when appropriate, create individualized lists for different job search targets.

References are people who can tell potential employers about your background and how you might perform on the job. These individuals may be past employers, teachers, or others who have known you in academic, employment, or cocurricular settings. Recommendations, written by those who might appear on a list of references, tell potential employers about your background and capabilities. They appear as a list of names, titles, addresses, and phone numbers.

References should be used assertively and effectively. They should be active participants in your job search. Ask these individuals if they can refer you to others as well as to resources that can help you. Keep them informed of your progress, solicit reactions to and advice about situations, and don't be afraid to ask them to contact employers directly, even if their opinions have not been solicited. A surprise testimonial from one of your references to a potential employer can be very helpful.

STEPS TO TAKE AND OBSTACLES TO AVOID

These steps have been developed to help you determine your skills and capabilities and write your resume using a systematic approach. You should review the samples in Chapter

7 to recognize resumes that will be best perceived by potential employers. Then you should review your job search targets, document your accomplishments, and cite your qualifications and capabilities that match your goals. Finally, draft your documents, revise your drafts, and then complete duplication- and distribution-ready versions.

Numerous liberal arts job seekers have used this method with very positive results, creating effective job search tools that landed challenging and rewarding internships, externships, and postgraduation jobs. Note that the total time suggested for completing your resume is between 12 and 24 hours. This does not mean that you should accomplish everything in one day; the activities should be completed over at least a few days. There are times in the resume writing process when you must stop and think or simply relax before continuing to the next steps.

Proceed through the steps one at a time. Use the following summary and target time frames to gain an idea of what is involved and to organize your efforts. Before you actually begin each step, be sure of what you want to accomplish at each stage.

Review Samples to Determine Those You Wish to Model

First, examine the sample resumes and accompanying analyses in Chapter 7. Identify which ones use the content and format that serve your needs. All are powerful examples for liberal arts graduates, but one or two might seem to match your circumstance. Photocopy samples and highlight special sections or presentations you find most appealing.

Use the Chronological Flowchart to Prepare Your First Draft

On the worksheet that follows, document your educational history, notable achievements, projects and activities, and employment experience. From this inventory, you will select the entries that will appear on your initial and final drafts. (Note education and employment experiences and achievements in order of their occurrence.) Utilize the formatted page to prepare your flowchart. Components include:

Dates. Place in the left margin. Start with the present, noting month and year, academic year, or season, and proceed in reverse chronological order, going as far back as you desire.

Educational History. Describe graduate, undergraduate, high school, and other academic or training experiences. Include special programs, such as overseas study and field-specific institutes. Cite institutions, dates attended and/or dates graduated, courses, majors, research undertaken, papers written, projects completed, credits received, and as much detailed information as you deem appropriate.

Notable Projects, Achievements, and Activities. Document cocurricular and community service activities, travel, and other achievements (including those that could appear in any of the other sections) that have given you a sense of accomplishment and are of particular note. List the experiences and describe the circumstances and accomplishments involved. Also include special academic projects and research efforts.

Employment History. List full-time and part-time jobs, internships, and other project-by-project efforts. Cite where these activities took place and the titles you held and describe the nature of your activities. At first, simply use your own phrasing. Later, you will edit this section to include more active and behaviorally oriented phrasing. You can record volunteer experiences here or under Notable Projects, Achievements, and Activities. This step often takes the most time, between 2 and 4 hours.

Review Research and Job Search Goals Worksheet and Skills Inventory

These exercises requested that you identify the skills you possess and then cite those skills that are associated with your top three job search targets. After you have reviewed your Chronological Flowchart, you may wish to rethink your analyses and note revisions in your Skills Inventory Summary that follows. Additional skills may appear, and your goals may arise. Once you have a list of your capabilities and those that are required to succeed within your targeted roles, you can easily create an objective statement and a summary of your qualifications. This activity takes approximately 1–3 hours.

Determine Objectives and Draft a Summary of Qualifications

On separate pages, note your objectives and begin to formulate a list of your assets. At first, one version may not be too dramatically different from another, but during the final stage, you will revise and clearly develop distinct documents. This undertaking may take as long as 1 to 3 hours, with most of the time dedicated to drafting your summary section. For each goal on your Skills Inventory Summary, review your existing abilities and the abilities you need to enhance, add new ones, and then transform your list into a "statement" like those appearing in the sample resumes. Put the most goal-focused statement first, followed by a prioritized order of the most significant to least significant statements.

Draft, Critique, and Then Finalize Your Resume

This is a process that takes your rough draft through several revisions in order to create a final version of your resume. Guidelines for critiquing your resume and for fine-tuning your Summary of Qualifications are presented. The total process can take 2 to 6 hours.

Drafting Your Resume

You should be ready to begin drafting your resume. On the first pass, write as freely and quickly as you can. Refrain from being overly critical at this point. Include everything you think is applicable to your job search. Don't be too surprised to find your first draft is several pages. The more comprehensive this rough draft is, the more effective your final version will be. Use a format you like, but don't worry too much about the order of entries yet.

When describing academic, cocurricular, and employment experiences, be as thorough and descriptive as possible. Use active, skills-oriented, behavior-focused phrasing. Refer to the list that follows for examples of effective words and phrases, but try to resist the temptation of using them verbatim. State your accomplishments clearly and with conviction. Be proud of what you have done. Note facts and figures, including dollar amounts when appropriate. Always refer to the sample resumes in Chapter 7 to see a "finished product."

Don't feel as if you have to write in complete sentences in all sections. It's perfectly acceptable to use "resume style," omitting articles and pronouns, especially first-person references, which do not add to the clarity of descriptions. Phrasing should make sense, but it should be as succinct as possible. Often, rules of formal grammar are stretched a bit, but they are never broken.

The Chronological Flowchart

DATES	EDUCATIONAL HISTORY	NOTABLE ACHIEVEMENTS, PROJECTS, AND ACTIVITIES	EMPLOYMENT HISTORY

Skills Inventory Summary

JOB SEARCH GOALS	EXISTING ABILITIES	ABILITIES TO ENHANCE
1		
2		
3		

Drafting Your Resume Using Action Words and Phrases

accommodated	appraised
achieved	approved
acquainted	assembled
activated	assisted
adapted	assumed
administered	attached
advertised	attained
advised	audited
advocated	augmented
altered	authorized
analyzed	

Examples:

analyzed procedures to assess efficiency and monitor outcomes

analyzed ideas and situations from varied perspectives to establish measurement criteria

applied research data to develop proposals or reach conclusions

applied theory and abstract concepts to performance-oriented work projects

balanced	conferred
built	consolidated
classified	consulted
collected	controlled
combined	converted
commanded	coordinated
communicated	counseled
conceived	created
condensed	curtailed

Examples:

created and implemented promotional campaign utilizing posters, flyers, and media coverage

conveyed positive message to the public via personal presentations and written documents

debugged	disclosed
demonstrated	discontinued
designated	discovered
designed	dispatched
determined	displayed
developed	distributed
directed	drafted

Examples:

described events or objects accurately in written documents and to customers via the phone

designed experiments and research procedures

demonstrated appropriate assertiveness and dynamic sales behavior in varied settings

documented success rate via attendance, sales, and profit figures

drafted, finalized, reproduced, and distributed promotional materials and media releases

economized

educated

eliminated

employed

encouraged

established

estimated

evaluated

examined

exchanged

executed

expanded

expedited

extended

familiarized

formulated

governed

grouped

guaranteed

guided

Examples:

evaluated information and presented analyses via PowerPoint presentations and written reports

expressed opinions and preferences in objective and diplomatic yet persuasive ways

formulated questions to clarify problems and assess attitudes

generated trust and confidence of clients and coworkers

illustrated

improved

increased

informed

initiated

instructed

interpreted

introduced

inventoried

investigated

lectured

Examples:

identified alternative courses of actions and detailed strategies to yield goals

listened objectively and utilized information gained for problem solving

maintained

managed

measured

merged

minimized

modernized

modified

motivated

observed

obtained

operated

organized

originated

planned

prescribed

procured

produced

programmed

publicized

published

Examples:

managed time and resources effectively

motivated and managed coworkers to complete daily activities

marketed self, products, and services to target constituencies

organized others to develop plans and achieve goals

recommended	strengthened
rectified	studied
reduced	supervised
regulated	supplemented
removed	surpassed
reorganized	taught
repaired	terminated
replaced	trained
reported	transferred
researched	tutored
restored	unified
simplified	updated
solved	utilized
sponsored	vetoed
stabilized	wrote

Examples:

suggested possible long-range and short-range outcomes of actions
wrote dynamic promotion materials and designed advertising brochures and posters

Critiquing Guidelines

Once your initial draft has been completed, use the Critiquing Guidelines that follow. At this stage, you should be concerned with writing style, presentation, and order of appearance. Review the samples again to identify effective phrasing, highlighting, and layout techniques. Use spell-checking options and a dictionary to eliminate all spelling errors. Your second draft should be almost ready for duplication.

After you have completed the second draft, ask a few people to critique it. Friends, family members, and faculty members are often good choices. They might be able to spark memories of achievements you may have omitted. Of course, career counselors at college and university career services facilities can offer constructive advice. Be aware that when you ask three people to look at one resume, you will hear at least nine different views. Often, you will receive contradicting suggestions. This particular liberal arts format may appear unique to some, particularly those who regularly review resumes of more experienced candidates and who don't believe in the value of focusing actions and sharpening job search tools via objectives. Unless a job search professional or a specific prospective employer has told you, "This is the format we require you to use," feel confident that your resume is appropriate and powerful. For those few circumstances that require you to create a resume that follows specific guidelines, fine. Create this special document, then use yours for other activities. Otherwise, after considering comments and incorporating appropriate suggestions, create a final version. Always proofread them. The resumes you distribute must be error free.

Review the following questions to judge the quality of your resumes. If you cannot answer "yes" to each query, examine your draft carefully and make appropriate changes. If you are critiquing an early draft, ignore those questions that refer to your final version.

Appearance

- Is it neat and easy to read?

- Do headlines stand out?

- Have you used space and font size to highlight headlines?

- Have you used CAPITALIZATION, **bold type,** *italics,* bullets (•), or varied type fonts?

- Were you consistent with the placement of headlines and content?

- Have you used the best font(s) to facilitate quick reading and present the image you want?

- Does you resume look professional and businesslike?

- Is your final draft clear and printed using a duplication-ready laser or ink-jet printer?

- Is it free of typographical errors and misspelled words?

Identifying Information

- Does your name, address(es), phone number(s), and other personal information stand out?

- If more than one address or phone number appears, did you use only one line for each entry?

- If you noted an e-mail address or fax number, do you have easy access to both?

Objective

- Does it project knowledge of your desired field and use appropriate phrasing?

- Is it brief, using job titles, functions, or skills to project focus?

- Have you considered blending the objective with a summary of qualifications?

- Do you have one multipurpose and at least two targeted versions?

Qualifications Summary

- Have you cited the qualifications you possess, linking them to your job search target and revealing that you know which attributes are attractive to an employer?

- Does this section use appropriate terminology to demonstrate your understanding of the field of interest?

- Did you use special headlines to reinforce your goals?

- Did you present your most significant and field-related qualifications first?

- Have you projected confidence in your abilities to develop new skills as well as note those you now possess?

Education

- Have you presented school(s), degree(s), area(s) of concentration, courses, projects, honors, and special certificates?

- Did you use a headline statement to reinforce special components of your educational experiences?

- Are grades or GPA (if above 3.0) presented?

- Have you highlighted objective-specific academic information, including courses and projects, using special headlines or other techniques?

- Did you cite research papers, projects, and lists of goal-related courses?

Experience

- Did you include all experiences that project your skills and accomplishments?

- Did you bullet your most significant achievements?

- Did you describe your experiences in active, skills-oriented, and functionally descriptive phrasing?

- Did you include volunteer as well as paid experiences and formal as well as informal internships?

- Did you use special headlines to identify your most goal-related experiences and to lessen the significance of other experiences?

- Under each headline, did you present information in reverse chronological order and list titles, organizations, and dates in easy-to-see formats?

- If you just listed experiences, omitting descriptions, was it for a logical and goal-directed reason?

Cocurricular and Community Activities

- Have you listed all appropriate activities, noting leadership positions, describing responsibilities, and citing special achievements?

- If you included organizations that might be controversial, have you considered how employers might react?

- Have you presented information in clear and concise phrasing, avoiding acronyms and describing little-known awards?

References

- If you closed with "References Available Upon Request," did you create a separate list that contains names, titles, addresses, and phone numbers for your references?

Overall Presentation

- Are the most important topics presented first in each section?

- If your resume is more than one page, is the most important information on the first page, and does the second page have your name and page number as a header?

- If you have developed more than one resume, did you change the order of appearance for each?

- Is your resume well organized, presenting a professional image and highlighting the most important information and a clear sense of direction?

- Can you elaborate on all elements of your resume if called upon to do so in an interview?

- Can an employer perceive you as qualified, even if he or she did not read an accompanying letter?

- Would you be proud to show a potential employer your resume?

Finalizing—Special Tips and Key Issues
Before you actually create your multipurpose and targeted resumes, here are some brief tips for special groups of resume writers and job seekers.

Freshmen and Sophomores Just Getting Started
Most likely, you are developing a resume for a part-time or summer job or for externship or internship experiences. Don't be concerned with what you have **not** done, but focus on how to best highlight what you have accomplished. While you may not have a lengthy list of sophisticated work experience, you should have a great many academic strengths and high school cocurricular achievements. Don't be intimidated by accomplishment-filled samples. Create a good resume, but spend a great deal of time supporting it with actions. Liberal arts power is always best channeled if you have focus. Identify employers within fields of interest, and communicate with potential employers within these fields. Express how much you wish to learn and what you are willing to give in return. Networking through family members, friends, and others (including recruiters and alumni who are identified through career services facilities of your school) will be effective. Also, use internship directories, especially those noted in the annotated bibliography at the end of this publication, to identify formalized internship options.

Juniors Beginning to Think About Postgraduation Options
You could be thinking that this is the last chance to obtain a great "resume-building" experience. You're probably not thinking that this is a good time to begin some of the research efforts required to establish goals, but you should. As expressed earlier, the summer is an ideal time to implement a Weeks Of Work strategy that includes information conversations, shadowing, and externships. For those concerned about the concept of resume building, the better perspective focuses on skills building, which includes completing a few courses and projects in addition to whatever summer experience you locate. Working in a retail or customer service–oriented setting could be supplemented by a course in marketing research, a brief HTML seminar, and information conversations with people in the media planning field.

Where you work (the name of the firm and type of organization) can be important, but what you will be doing (the nature of the tasks performed) and the skills and perspectives you gain are more important. If you have not completed the self-assessment and research required to identify potential postgraduation options, the summer is a great time to do so.

Do not rule out the possibility of obtaining a nonpaid career-related internship or externship for 20 hours per week in addition to a part-time paid experience. To seek these opportunities, do not be too concerned with what you cannot put on your resume. Create the best tool possible; highlight your academic, cocurricular, and employment strengths while clearly projecting your fields of interest. Take advantage of the services offered through your school's career planning and placement office for your part-time and summer job searches. Preview the services they offer. During the summer, identify local schools that might offer you some assistance. Utilize temporary agencies if needed. Network with recent grads and not-so-recent alumni. They might provide good leads for your immediate summer efforts, and they can offer insights into what you will experience in the months ahead.

Seniors Getting Ready for the Real-World Job Search

This book was written primarily with you in mind. Learn what services your school's career center offers and take advantage of them. Self-assessment, research, and goal projection are your most powerful tools. Make sure your resumes (yes, more than one version) clearly present your goals and qualifications. Create powerful documents and maintain a positive attitude while taking effective actions!

Recent Graduates Still Looking

You should explore what alumni services your school offers. Use this book as well as the other publications noted in the bibliography to create your own personal "career resource collection." Also, find people (counselors, librarians, family members, and friends) and places (career services offices, libraries, and resource centers) that can provide information as well as motivation. While you certainly should look ahead with confidence, don't be afraid to look back and analyze or reevaluate your resume, correspondence style, and efforts to date.

Follow up with people you haven't communicated with in a while, even if they have rejected your candidacy at one time. Review the Ten Steps to job search success, and determine if you need to fine-tune your game plan. Although you may be tempted to become more "open," you should stay as focused as possible. You can always add a goal or two, but don't state your goals as "anything anywhere." Take courses, seek volunteer experiences, or obtain an internship within your field of interest. Seek a shadowing or externship experience. Any or all of these options will continue your skills-building efforts, project a commitment to a field, keep you energized, and, in many instances, give you access to a career services facility. A key liberal arts skill is your ability to quickly absorb and apply newly acquired knowledge to a specific project. Show potential employers that this is the case by updating your resume to project your increased knowledge of your fields of interest and of the qualities you possess that are related to these fields.

Experienced Graduates Making a Change

Your resume is a symbol that you have begun the process of a job search. Whether you have set a job search strategy in motion by choice or because of circumstances beyond your control, don't underestimate the liberal arts power you possess and can project via a well-written resume. Your resume must project professionalism and maturity. It must be dynamic and bold. Networking and an ongoing flow of communications, both verbal and written, will be critical to your efforts. This book contains samples that are associated with relatively young job seekers, but the formats are easily transformed into ones that can be used by experienced candidates. Whether you are making a transition, seeking something completely different, or building upon earlier or current employment experiences, review and apply the information contained in this publication, even if it appears to be directed toward recent graduates. You have a proven track record of success, but you can also be the most likely to become frustrated and overcome by self-doubt. While you may have to fine-tune your research skills a bit, and it might be wise to take a skills-focused course to make more significant transitions, you do possess the liberal arts response-ability to be successful. Use it!

Your resume should be concise as possible, but it must communicate essential information. Do not limit yourself to an arbitrary length of one page before you have drafted and finalized your powerful job search tools. If you have honed it down and edited out unnecessary information and it is still longer than one page—fine! Employers do read information that is organized and well presented. If your resume is longer than one page, the first page should contain the most important information.

As documented, targeted resumes contain an objective statement and multipurpose formats do not. I encourage all liberal arts job seekers to create one multipurpose and at least two targeted resumes. Resumes with objective statements that are supported by functional descriptions of key skills and capabilities have proven the most powerful and effective.

PRODUCING RESUMES IN THE ELECTRONIC AGE

Most resumes are created using word processing software and duplicated through quality photocopying. They are "traditional," appearing vertically on an 8½- by 11-inch page. If you have a choice of word processing software, utilize one that allows you to change fonts and type size, bold, italicize, spell check, and make desired changes. The system should also be compatible with a letter-quality ink-jet or laser printer. Dot-matrix printers and daisy wheel printers are not acceptable for creating duplication-ready resumes and job search correspondence.

General Rules to Follow

Because most students and graduates have access to personal computers, computer-generated resumes and written supporting materials are preferred. Computer software offers the most flexibility and, if ink-jet or laser printers are used, the highest-quality documents at the lowest cost. Offset printing is an option, particularly for graphic-filled documents, but most resumes can be reproduced by high-quality photocopying. Professional copying services generally provide high-quality duplication and can immediately show you how your resume will look on any paper you select. In addition, these businesses usually sell envelopes that match whatever paper you select. Do not use coin-operated photocopiers, such as the ones found in libraries. The paper in these machines is not of a high quality, and your resume will not create a very positive impression. Never use a "wet paper copier" with slick thermal paper to duplicate your job search tools.

It is better to have too many copies than too few. While you can quickly put quality paper in your printer and create several copies, if you have a supply of resumes on hand, you will be able to immediately distribute copies.

When choosing a high-quality bond paper for your resume, select a conservative businesslike color. White, ivory, natural, and off-white are perhaps the best options. Beige or gray may be appropriate for more creative resumes or for contacting nontraditional employers, but bright colors, parchment paper, and creative borders should be avoided. The content of your resume and cover letters and your job search actions, not the color of the paper, will make your resume stand out. It is a good idea to purchase blank pages and envelopes (usually 9- by 12-inches so that you don't have to fold the document) to match the paper your resume is printed on. Using the identity information from your resume, you can create your own personalized letterhead for cover letters and additional correspondence. The matching presentation projects a strong and positive image.

Alternate Formats

Resumes can be traditional, a vertical "portrait" form on an 8½- by 11-inch page, or more creative, with graphically dynamic headers or borders or folded like a pamphlet. Some fields allow for more graphic and creative presentation. Options that have been effectively used by liberal arts job seekers include a resume in "landscape," a horizontal form on an 8½- by 11-inch page; a 17- by 11-inch portfolio, with the resume on the front cover and samples of works within the folder; and 5- by 8-inch or 5½- by 8¼-inch miniresumes. "Pocket resumes" and business cards can facilitate one's success when serendipitous circumstances arise during chance meetings, social functions, seminars, and other events. Other options include boldly bordered headlines, graphics, or, for those seeking journalism and communication positions, press releases and "articles" that outline past efforts. Even when developing and using creative options, always utilize a standard format. By using both creative and traditional versions, liberal arts graduates show their capacities to offer varied alternatives to clients and work within various writing and presentation styles.

While resume development software does seem easy, simple word processing programs are equally effective. Often, special software programs make amending your resume difficult and literally box you into particular formats. If you find and use resume development software that allows you to "mail merge" and develop and track comprehensive efforts, go for it, but don't become too ingrained in the process rather than the outcomes. You must always remember that the response-ability of job search remains on your shoulders.

On the Web: A Scannable Resume

When entering a resume on Web-housed databases, you may not be given the opportunity to be too independent or creative. Prompts specify required information and sometimes limit the space provided. Some do allow you to copy and paste the powerful resumes you have now created. That's ideal, but don't be concerned if you can only enter information sought via the site-specific prompts. Whatever the approach, make sure you are sensitive to key-word-search phrasing. While you should never present false information on your resume, you can be sensitive to what is presented and how it is done. Always keep in mind the nature of the positions you are seeking, the nature of their day-to-day responsibilities, and the activities they involve. When documenting your abilities, use phrases that would also be used to describe the jobs in question. If you are entering your resume into online databases, follow the instructions and carefully use basic fonts, such as 12-point Helvetica or Times. Keep horizontal content to ninety characters across. Note your e-mail address on a separate line so that the characters do not become confused with other entries. Most employers who request that you download documents will provide clear directions.

Create and use an e-mail version, which can be copied and pasted into a brief e-message. Do not use attachments; readers may not have compatible software to completely open the document and present the contents as you designed them. Close your e-message with an "originals to follow by fax" or "original copies to be forwarded by mail" statement.

Today, the most important things to remember are as follows. Rather than action verbs, you are encouraged to identify and use field-focused nouns. Key nouns may be technical, including programming languages, operating systems, and software applications or field specific, including references to techniques, equipment, functional areas, reporting structures, policies, and procedures. Don't become passive. Follow up with more time-tested approaches, like phone calls, faxes, and mailed communiqués to progress to the most critical of all job search interactions, the interview. It is easy to remain anonymous while searching for Web sites, sending e-mail, and entering resumes into databases, but it is not necessarily effective. While some predict that more and more interviews will be conducted via desktop videoconferencing, right now face-to-face communications yield the offers.

7

Sample Resumes and Correspondence

JOB SEARCH SUCCESS STORIES

This chapter presents a number of sample resumes and cover letters that you should refer to as you finalize the format of your resume. Each sample is accompanied by a discussion of the resume writer's particular situation. These analyses give you an insider's perspective, reveal challenges that the individual had to overcome, and show some creative ways for resolving such difficulties. Ideally, you should review these samples and review Chapter 6, including the exercises, to incorporate some of the ideas you will read about in this chapter.

It can be frustrating to review sample resumes of "super candidates," ones that note accomplishments that seem beyond the capabilities of most. The resumes presented in this chapter document real academic, cocurricular, and work experiences, although the names of students, schools, and employers have been changed to ensure confidentiality. These samples are from actual job seekers who obtained good jobs after graduation and have been reviewed by employers who found the formats and content appealing. Most are dense, in an effort to illustrate as many options as possible, so do not be concerned if yours does not contain the same number of entries. Your resume should be easy to scan (visually and electronically) and not appear intimidating to readers.

Review samples and analyses with an open mind. Avoid making statements like, "Look at all he has done!" "I haven't done anything," "She is interested in public relations and has worked in the field. I don't have any related work experience," and "How can I compete with people whose resumes look like this?" Samples are meant to help you write your resume and facilitate your job search, not to frustrate you. They do not set standards. Each job seeker is an individual, and you will be successful with your own background and qualifications.

Cover Letters

Sample resumes are accompanied by detailed cover letters or brief cover notes. Cover letters and supplemental job search correspondence are crucial. Resumes can tell potential employers what you have done and when you completed specific efforts. Cover correspondence presents why you are now seeking specific opportunities, the skills you have nurtured through your experiences, and how they relate to your job search goals. Letters and notes allow you to further express your interest and to cite specific accomplishments that might grab the attention of a given employer. To be powerful, cover letters must stand alone and highlight key points that are independent of the resume; they must also ignite a reader's interest in your resume. Should your resume and accompanying correspondence be reviewed separately by different people, each must present your qualifications and project your liberal arts experience in ways that make each reader want to interview you. When combined, your cover letter and resume should be more than twice as powerful.

These sample cover letters are not offered for you to copy. Documents you use must project your style and personality. Letters in this chapter are presented to inspire and offer frameworks upon which you can build individualized communiqués. They illustrate powerful approaches for letters of inquiry (when you contact potential employers to determine their hiring needs and to motivate your consideration) and for letters of application (when you respond to posted opportunities).

There are various accepted formats for business correspondence. In the electronic age, a left-justified block format is best transmitted by e-mail. Cover letters should always be addressed to a specific person, someone responsible for initiating the review process, someone who can serve as an advocate of your candidacy, or someone who can make hiring decisions. Never address correspondence to *To Whom It May Concern, Dear Sir or Madam,* or *Personnel Director.* Call to find out the name and title of the individual you should contact and to confirm address, fax, or e-mail information. College career services facilities should have names and pertinent information for many organizations of interest. National or regional professional association membership directories can also prove valuable resources. If you cannot obtain a name or are told to "send it to Human Resources," begin the body of your letter without a salutation.

Protocol

Whenever possible, fax your initial correspondence after calling to determine who should receive it and then forward a hard copy by mail. Also, if time is a crucial factor, send mailings via overnight or second-day service. Because a job search is an ongoing communication process that is not limited to initial contacts, follow up is very important. The most powerful liberal arts job seekers are assertive communicators, not passive applicants. Therefore, it is appropriate to maintain ongoing communication via follow-up actions. A powerful job search pattern alternates faxes, mailings, phone calls and e-communiqués, all of which lead to or follow an interview. After the interview, follow with a faxed thank-you note and, a bit later, with a phone call to determine the status of the decision-making process. Regularly, after receiving a rejection, follow up with a letter expressing your disappointment but appreciation for consideration. Seek additional consideration or information that will help inspire you to begin the next steps.

As with any relationship, be sensitive to those you interact with. Be assertive but not aggressive, persistent yet polite. Generally, if you are businesslike via phone, letter, fax, e-mail, and in-person communiqués, you will do fine. There may be situations when you should wait a few weeks until you contact someone again and others when you should do so immediately. Always ask when and how a next communication should be made and who should initiate it. If you have been told to wait or call back by someone, feel comfortable doing so. As your search progresses, take an occasional retrospective look at your efforts. Follow up with people you have already contacted (including references), inform them of your efforts, and seek advice and counsel. By rekindling old contacts, you may be taking actions that will recharge your overall campaign.

Joseph E. Byrne—A Case Study

From the day he entered college, Joseph thought that he would someday pursue a career in retail management. High school experiences in a multiplex cinema that were marked by quick promotions, progressively responsible positions, and wage increases, motivated his early goal formation. Bookstore sales and customer service roles reinforced his interest in retailing as a career. Joe did not know that he would major in English and minor in history, nor that he would grow more and more interested in law as a career field as he got closer to graduation. In fact, during his senior year, Joe decided to explore law-related jobs.

After speaking with career counselors, alumni who were attorneys, and faculty members, Joe determined that working for a law firm for a year or two would help him determine whether or not law would be the right choice for him. Joe created a multipurpose resume to use for on-campus interviews (the temptation of interviewing with retail firms was strong) as well as a law-focused document. His targeted resume did not show that he had law-related experience, so he depended a great deal on the Summary of Qualifications section, titled Legal Research, Writing, and Related Qualifications, to project his commitment and to highlight his skills. He also thought a great deal about the order in which entries appeared on each document and listed his experiences that were most significant to the law field earlier in his targeted resume than other less relevant educational or employment entries.

Joe also used several writing samples as evidence of his skills. He summarized some of his best research papers and created a collection of very brief abstracts to distribute to potential employers. These abstracts noted varied research topics and clearly illustrated his ability to summarize large quantities of information in abbreviated forms.

Joe decided to stay in New Orleans after graduating from Tulane instead of returning home to New Jersey and seeking positions in New York City. Joe wanted to someday attend his alma mater's law school. With functional and geographic goals in mind, Joe felt very confident that something would arise before graduation. He developed a relationship with the director of his school's career services office, contacted alumni, sought referrals from various contacts (including the local bar association and law school alumni association), and identified various sources of postings. A job search can typically take three to six months, and in many cases, it can take six to nine months. Although Joe had clearly defined functional and geographic goals, he experienced typical ups and downs of a job search. As discussed in earlier sections of this publication, one of the first things a soon-to-be-graduate should do is prepare for realistic options.

Each candidate must become comfortable with the communication process that is the job search. Joe, at first, was a bit uncomfortable with these meetings because he felt awkward explaining his seemingly newfound interest in law. While the best advice he could follow was, "Read your own resume and believe in it," words often spoken by the director of his school's career services facility, Joe still needed to learn by doing. Each new meeting, whether an information conversation or an employment interview, made Joe feel more confident. In time, he also felt more and more frustrated.

As he became better at interviewing and interacting with network members and potential employers and as graduation grew closer, he grew more concerned by the fact that he had not been offered a job.

With time and after many insightful meetings with his career services support person, Joe realized that he was being compared to many other soon-to-be graduates, with law students seeking summer positions, and with experienced legal researchers and paraprofessionals. Joe eventually realized that even after taking the liberal arts responsibility for determining and projecting his goals, he would have to take the liberal arts response-ability to act persistently and maintain a positive outlook. As graduation drew near, Joe began to make contingency plans so that he could earn an income while continuing his New Orleans job search. Realizing that it would be inefficient to move home and conduct a long-distance search in Louisiana, Joe used his retail and customer service background and his easy-to-access contacts to locate a part-time position in a local department store. Although graduation came and went, Joe felt psychologically and financially secure with his circumstances and confident that his law-related search strategy would soon yield results.

His part-time postgraduation position proved ideal in many ways. By structuring his schedule appropriately, Joe allowed himself two full working days for his job search efforts. He was able to write letters, make calls, conduct interviews, and use career services resources during these intense 48-hour periods. As a result of well-crafted notes and some alumni support, Joe was offered informal and limited access to the resources of Tulane's law school library and placement office. He also enrolled in courses in business law and legal research at a local community college and in a school that specialized in paralegal training. This increased his marketable skills, made him feel that he was taking clear goal-directed steps, and granted him access to additional resources. Of course, Joe updated his resume to cite these new experiences as they arose. The community college and paraprofessional training institution's career services office had listings of employers who sought graduates of paralegal programs and also provided information about search firms and temporary employment agencies that specialized in the legal field. As time went on, Joe became a better job seeker, and, as his access to specialized resources expanded, he got closer to his ultimate goal. Through these law-specific resources, Joe soon received an offer to work part-time with a law firm. While he declined the offer because he felt that his challenging yet predictable schedule addressed his needs and that he would receive a full-time offer, he did complete some special projects for this firm. He regularly updated his resume and changed his correspondence to note these achievements.

As summer passed and fall arrived, Joe proved to himself and others that he had the ability to juggle multiple tasks in varied settings and that he was truly committed to a full-time paralegal or legal research position. As a result, he received three offers from prestigious New Orleans firms. These offers originated through some traditional and not-so-traditional sources. One came as a result of an ongoing letter-focused relationship that followed an early rejection. Another came from a letter-writing campaign that Joe implemented in late August when he contacted all the employers who hired law school students for the summer. The last came from referrals made by members of his ever-growing network of contacts. Before accepting any of the offers, he discussed pros and cons of each position with members of his network. Joe took the job that offered him the broadest exposure to different types of litigation and clients.

Joseph E. Byrne

P.O. Box 1222 • Tulane University • New Orleans, LA 70188
504-876-2356 • jbyrne@tulaneu.edu

LEGAL RESEARCH, WRITING, AND RELATED QUALIFICATIONS
- Able to quickly understand legal concepts, correctly utilize legal terminology, and apply knowledge of computerized search programs.
- Able to develop easy-to-access documentation and complete comprehensive research and summation tasks.
- Interviewing, active listening, and analytical writing skills nurtured through course assignments, cocurricular leadership, university committees, and academic support roles.
- Proofreading, editing, and related abilities associated with various styles.
- Experience with IBM PCs and using Microsoft Word and WordPerfect software.
- Knowledge of Quattro Pro 5.0 spreadsheet and Internet-access applications.
- Experience prioritizing and completing administrative tasks accurately and on time.
- Able to work cooperatively in large and diverse staffs and with supervisors.

EDUCATION, ACADEMIC HONORS, AND COCURRICULAR LEADERSHIP
Tulane University, New Orleans, Louisiana.
Bachelor of Arts, May 1999.
Major in English. Minor in history.
Cumulative GPA: 3.32 (4.0 scale)

Dean's Honor Roll three semesters
National Dean's List 1995–96
Student Representative on Enrollment Management Task Force and Academic Regulations Committee
Served on University Tenure Committee and various other committees
Member, Pi Kappa Alpha fraternity

University College of Ripon and York St. John, York, England
Completed overseas studies in history, English, and philosophy, Spring 1996.

RESEARCH, WRITING, AND PRESENTATION EXPERIENCE
Tulane University, New Orleans, Louisiana.
Supplemental Instructor for Freshman Seminar, Fall 1998 and Spring 1999
- Assisted with lectures and discussions, held office hours, and attended meetings with other instructors.
- Supported academic and logistical efforts of required University-wide freshman general education course.

Writing and ESL Tutor, Spring 1996 and Fall 1997–Spring 1999
- Assisted students of all academic levels and with varied abilities, specifically those for whom English is a second language.
- Edited initial drafts, motivated enhanced writing skills, and proofread draft and final versions.

CUSTOMER SERVICE AND MANAGEMENT EXPERIENCE
Tulane University, New Orleans, Louisiana.
Bookstore Student Worker, Academic Year 1998–99

American Multi-Cinema, Livingston, New Jersey.
Staff Lead, Part-time, Summers 1994–98
- Hired as concessionist and promoted to Staff Lead after seven months' employment.
- As Staff Lead, supervised concession staff of thirty and trained new employees.

COUNSELING AND ADVISING EXPERIENCE
Tulane University, New Orleans, Louisiana.
Resident Assistant, Summer 1996 and Academic Years 1996–99

Bayou Rehabilitation Center, New Orleans, Louisiana.
Substance Abuse Counselor, Summers, 1995 and 1996

REFERENCES AVAILABLE UPON REQUEST

Joseph E. Byrne

P.O. Box 1222 • Tulane University • New Orleans, LA 70188
504-876-2356 • jbyrne@tulaneu.edu
2 Livingston Avenue • Livingston, NJ 07039 • 973-865-7764

SUMMARY OF QUALIFICATIONS
- Customer service, supervisory, and administrative abilities.
- Retail sales experience and achievements.
- Able to work well and cooperatively in large staffs and with supervisors.
- Active listening, analytical writing, and advising skills.
- Proofreading, editing, and related abilities associated with various research papers and styles.
- Confidence in tutorial and counseling roles with diverse students and clients.
- Experience with IBM PCs and using Microsoft Word and WordPerfect software.
- Knowledge of Quattro Pro 5.0 spreadsheet and Internet-access applications.

EDUCATION, ACADEMIC HONORS, AND COCURRICULAR LEADERSHIP
Tulane University, New Orleans, Louisiana.
Bachelor of Arts, May 1999.
Major in English. Minor in history.
Cumulative GPA: 3.32 (4.0 scale)

Dean's Honor Roll three semesters
National Dean's List 1995–96
Student Representative on Enrollment Management Task Force and Academic Regulations Committee
Served on University Tenure Committee and various other committees
Member, Pi Kappa Alpha fraternity

University College of Ripon and York St. John, York, England
Completed overseas studies in history, English, and philosophy, Spring 1996.

CUSTOMER SERVICE AND MANAGEMENT EXPERIENCE
Tulane University, New Orleans, Louisiana.
Bookstore Student Worker, Academic Year 1998–99

American Multi-Cinema, Livingston, New Jersey.
Staff Lead Part-time, Summers 1995–98
- Hired as concessionist and promoted to Staff Lead after seven months' employment.
- As Staff Lead, supervised concession staff of thirty and trained new employees.
- Also served as box office cashier and made large cash deposits.
- Worked closely with management team of six as liaison to hourly employees.

TUTORIAL AND COUNSELING EXPERIENCE
Tulane University, New Orleans, Louisiana.
Resident Assistant, Summer 1996 and Academic Years 1996–99

Supplemental Instructor for Freshman Seminar, Fall 1998 and Spring 1999
- Assisted with lectures and discussions, held office hours, and attended meetings with other instructors.
- Supported academic and logistical efforts of required University-wide freshman general education course.

Writing and ESL Tutor, Spring 1996 and Fall 1997–Spring 1999
- Assisted students of all academic levels and with varied abilities, specifically those for whom English is a second language.
- Edited initial drafts, motivated enhanced writing skills, and proofread draft and final versions.

Bayou Rehabilitation Center, New Orleans, Louisiana.
Substance Abuse Counselor, Summers, 1995 and 1996
- Under supervision of licensed therapist, counseled adolescents in substance abuse unit of treatment facility; enforced facility policies and maintained security to ensure residents' safety.

REFERENCES AVAILABLE UPON REQUEST

Joseph E. Byrne

P.O. Box 1222 • Tulane University • New Orleans, LA 70188
504-876-2356 • jbyrne@tulaneu.edu

May 13, 1999

Mr. Bernard Roberts
Director of Paralegals
Blane, Collier and Phips
One Riverview Drive, Suite 345
New Orleans, Louisiana 70189
Fax: 504-878-9313

Mr. Roberts:

I would like to interview for and ideally serve as a Blane, Collier and Phips Paralegal in your New Orleans office. Like many who express interest in a position of this kind, I desire to attend law school after several years of effective performance in this capacity. In return for the opportunity that you and your Blane, Collier and Phips colleagues offer, I offer the following qualifications:

- The abilities to quickly understand legal concepts, correctly utilize legal terminology, and apply knowledge of computerized search programs.
- The abilities to develop easy-to-access documentation and complete comprehensive research and summation tasks.
- Interviewing, active listening, and analytical writing skills nurtured through course assignments, cocurricular leadership, university committees, and academic support roles.
- Proofreading, editing, and related abilities associated with various styles.
- Experience with IBM PCs and using Microsoft Word and WordPerfect software.
- Knowledge of Quattro Pro 5.0 spreadsheet and Internet-access applications.
- Experience prioritizing and completing administrative tasks accurately and on time.
- The ability to work cooperatively in large and diverse staffs and with supervisors.

Through initial telephone and subsequent interviews, I can detail how these traits will enable me to be an effective paralegal member of a Blane, Collier and Phips research and litigation team. During the interview, I will expand upon my resume citations and, I sincerely hope, convince you that I can meet all of your technical, personal, and professional requirements. Specifically, I will share how English studies and past experiences in research, writing, and tutorial roles nurtured my analytical, research, writing, and project management talents that your firm seeks.

I will call to confirm your receipt of this fax and my writing sample and transcripts (originals to follow via mail) and to discuss appropriate next steps. With graduation on the horizon, I am eager to begin working in my career field of choice. I will be available to begin work as soon as you require.

Thank you for your consideration.

Sincerely,

Joseph E. Byrne

✔Boldly and effectively uses qualifications to highlight assets.

✔Projects writing skills through a comprehensive yet clear document.

✔Reinforces job search focus throughout.

A fax from
Joseph E. Byrne

P.O. Box 1222 • Tulane University • New Orleans, LA 70188
504-876-2356 • jbyrne@tulaneu.edu

DATE

May 23, 1999

TO

Bernard Roberts
Director of Paralegals
Blane, Collier and Phips

FAX: 504-878-9313

MESSAGE

First, thank you for a most informative and enjoyable meeting. The more I learn about Blane, Collier and Phips; about the nature of paralegal positions; and, most importantly, about realities associated with the day-to-day tasks of a paralegal in your firm, the more eager I become to receive an offer.

I hope I conveyed my qualifications in appropriately positive ways because I sincerely believe I can be a productive member of the Blane, Collier and Phips paralegal team. As discussed, I am available to start as soon as appropriate. Please, let's keep in touch regarding the next steps.

Enjoy your vacation. I look forward to hearing from you when you return. Thank you again for your continued consideration.

Attached is another copy of my resume to remind you of my background.

✔ Brief yet effective thank-you note.

✔ While written and immediately delivered letters are wonderful, faxing is an appropriate approach.

✔ Another resume is included for reinforcement.

Joseph E. Byrne

P.O. Box 1222 • Tulane University • New Orleans, LA 70188
504-876-2356 • jbyrne@tulaneu.edu

August 5, 1999

Mr. James Jerome
Jerome, Stevens and Reldan
Suite 109
1349 Crescent Place
New Orleans, Louisiana 70189
Fax: 504-878-3042

Mr. Jerome:

John Williams, Director of Career Services at Tulane University, encouraged me to contact you. Mr. Williams and I recently met to discuss my interest in the field of law, and he suggested that since you are an alumnus of both Tulane University and the Tulane School of Law, you might be willing to offer advice and guidance. I have enclosed a copy of my resume to familiarize you with my background, not necessarily to solicit consideration with your firm. While that would be ideal, I would also welcome the opportunity to conduct an information conversation. By learning more about your career, I will be better able to clarify my goals and mount a successful job search.

At present, I am looking for a paralegal or legal research position. It is my intention to gain exposure to the field and gain fundamental skills prior to applying to law school in a year or two. I would be very interested in your thoughts regarding this strategy, and I would also welcome any assistance or advice you could offer.

I do understand how busy you are, so I will come prepared with specific questions about your background and the legal profession. I will call to confirm your receipt of this fax, and I do sincerely hope to arrange a meeting at your convenience.

Thank you for your consideration of this request.

Sincerely,

Joseph E. Byrne

✔ Request for consideration, information conversation, and networking assistance that notes a referral immediately.

✔ Clarifies nature of information conversation to recipient of request.

Joseph E. Byrne

P.O. Box 1222 • Tulane University • New Orleans, LA 70188
504-876-2356 • jbyrne@tulaneu.edu

August 25, 1999

Ms. Jane Brenden
Orin and Hatch
Suite 777
Two Shell Square
New Orleans, Louisiana 70189
Fax: 504-876-3450

Ms. Brenden:

Mr. James Jerome of Jerome, Stevens and Reldan suggested that I contact you. Mr. Jerome and I recently met to discuss my current efforts to locate a law-related position.

As noted on the enclosed resume, I would like to use my research and writing skills in a law office. Academic assignments have required that I complete many research projects and a number of papers. Enclosed you will find a few abstracts of my efforts. They are intended to illustrate my abilities to conduct research and report findings in appropriate abbreviated or detailed formats. I understand through conversations with Mr. Jerome and others within your field that these are skills that are required to complete paralegal tasks.

I work well under the pressure of deadlines, and regardless of the nature of the written assignment or work-related task, I pay close attention to detail. Prior to and after graduation from Tulane University, I have learned that one must work extremely hard in order to achieve success. Work experiences have taught me that one must be prepared to work beyond the typical 40-hour work week. I am willing, ready, and able to do so for Orin and Hatch. In summary, I offer:

- The abilities to quickly understand legal concepts, correctly utilize legal terminology, and apply knowledge of computerized search programs.
- The abilities to develop easy-to-access documentation and complete comprehensive research and summation tasks.
- Interviewing, active listening, and analytical writing skills nurtured through course assignments, cocurricular leadership, university committees, and academic support roles.
- Proofreading, editing, and related abilities associated with various styles.
- Experience with IBM PCs and using Microsoft Word and WordPerfect software.
- Knowledge of Quattro Pro 5.0 spreadsheet and Internet-access applications.
- Experience prioritizing and completing administrative tasks accurately and on time.
- The ability to work cooperatively in large and diverse staffs and with supervisors.

Are there openings for paralegals or legal assistants at your firm? I will call to confirm your receipt of this fax, to discuss current and potential openings, and, I hope, to arrange an employment interview at your convenience. Thank you for your consideration.

Sincerely,

Joseph E. Byrne

✔ An excellent letter of inquiry that immediately notes the referral source.

✔ Very skills-focused presentation that projects reality-based understanding of the desired job.

Justin Blake—A Case Study

With a major in psychology and a minor in communication, Justin had a varied academic background. He also had a wide range of extracurricular, employment, and athletic experiences to his credit. By the time he graduated from college, he had worked for a cruise line, in food services, and in a recreational setting. He also held almost every position possible in his fraternity.

When it came time for Justin to decide on his postgraduation employment goals, at first he had some difficulty. After doing a great deal of research by reading articles and books and interviewing alumni about their careers, Justin decided that retail management offered the diversity he sought and the day-to-day challenges associated with his goals.

Because Justin had done so many different things, he decided it was important to present himself in an organized fashion. He created a fairly conservative resume but used a Summary of Qualifications and dynamic headlines to highlight his varied accomplishments. He had customer service experience, clear cocurricular leadership achievements, and the qualities associated with student athletes. The general qualifications and computer skills he presented would also be of interest to employers.

Justin's resume is intentionally flexible, so it can easily be adapted for various opportunities. Headlines very clearly and creatively present his qualification categories in an easy-to-screen format. His goals made early stages of his job search relatively easy because it was simple to identify retail firms, interview with them through on-campus recruiting, and contact them directly. While Justin seemed to do quite well in interviews, a problem did arise. His interest in retailing, while based on thorough research and many information conversations, seemed to wane as he went through the interview process. He wasn't getting more excited about the prospects of an offer; instead, he was less intrigued by the idea of working in the field. Justin discussed this with some of the alumni with whom he had interviewed during his research efforts. They suggested that he complete all of the retail interviews and obtain as many offers in this area as possible but that he also broaden his search to other fields.

Justin decided to develop a sales-oriented resume. Justin revived his research activities, read about other fields, talked to more people about their jobs, and attended company information sessions. During this time, a career services professional spoke to him about an alumnus who had conducted a successful job search with a nationally recognized consumer products firm and one who worked in pharmaceutical sales. After speaking with this alum, Justin became quite enthusiastic and driven toward these particular goals. Utilizing general directories that listed major consumer product and food manufacturers, Justin created a rather lengthy list of potential employers. Using the phone and fax extensively, he conducted an intense and persistent campaign. In addition, he visited several grocery stores and networked with managers to identify people who worked for many of the firms on his list. By contacting recruiters in corporate headquarters as well as professionals working in the field, Justin arranged for a few first-round interviews. His persistence and preparation paid off with invitations to continue interviewing and for ride alongs with each of the firms.

In contrast to what happened when he interviewed with retailers, the more the consumer product sales interviews progressed, the more excited he became and the more eager he was to get an offer. As deadlines to make decisions about several of his retail offers approached, he received his first offer to become as sales representative from a major candy manufacturer. Just in time, this liberal arts graduate took a sweet job.

While he credits his alumni contact and the suggestion he received from his career counselor to visit stores to conduct informal surveys, Justin's powerful and focused efforts demonstrated all of the personality traits that sales employers sought. He personified their profile and was successful.

Justin Blake

3666 Pacific Avenue • University of the Pacific • Stockton, CA 95204
209-333-8532 • jb0003@uop.edu
13 South Avenue • Millbrae, CA 93030 • 415-677-2037

Objective—Sales position utilizing . . .
- Abilities to conduct professional cold calls, nurture relationships with prospective and existing accounts, and present product qualities and profit analyses in effective ways.
- Strong public speaking and customer service skills.
- Knowledge of public relations, promotions, and event planning techniques.
- Reality-based understanding of sales gained through active research.
- Macintosh experience using Word and Internet-access applications.

Psychology, Communication, and Business Related Degree, Courses and Projects
UNIVERSITY OF THE PACIFIC, Stockton, CA
Bachelor of Arts in psychology with a communication minor, anticipated May 1999

Public Speaking	Decision Making
Principles of Public Relations	Motivation
Writing for Public Relations	Human Behavior
Communication Research Methods	Intercultural Psychology

- Planned and documented all logistical details for hypothetical Levi Strauss fiftieth anniversary celebration in San Francisco. Identified all accommodation, entertainment, and related needs. Established a timeline of required activities. Created invitations and other promotional materials, including press release and media kit. Cited efforts in detailed presentation and portfolio.
- Identified logistics for and established existing not-for profit organization, Pacific Youth Foundation. Raised funds, screened requests, and then delivered sports equipment to qualified schools and youth groups.

Athletic and Cocurricular Achievements and Leadership Roles
UNIVERSITY OF THE PACIFIC NCAA DIVISION I WATERPOLO, Fall 1995
UNIVERSITY OF THE PACIFIC NCAA DIVISION I SWIMMING, Spring 1996
SIGMA ALPHA EPSILON FRATERNITY, Spring 1996–present
Interfraternal Council Representative, Spring 1997
Eminent Treasurer, Fall 1998–Spring 1999
DELTA GAMMA ANCHOR MAN, Fall 1998–Spring 1999

Customer Service and Marketing Support Experience
TMDA CRUISE LOGISTICS, Millbrae, CA
Cruise Logistics Service Representative, Summers 1997 and 1998
- Greeted clients, addressed issues and concerns, and transported travelers from airport to pier for departures on Princess and Royal Caribbean cruises.
- Regularly responded to special needs and solved related problems.
- Transported returning travelers from pier to airport.
- Baggage Handler, Summers 1993–96

Food Services and Recreation Experience
DELTA GAMMA SORORITY, Stockton, CA
Food Server, Fall 1998–Spring 1999

ALPHA CHI OMEGA SORORITY, Stockton, CA
Food Server, Fall 1997–Spring 1998

MILLBRAE PARK AND RECREATION DEPARTMENT, Millbrae, CA
Pool Manager, Summer 1998
Lifeguard/Swim Instructor, Summers 1994–98

UNIVERSITY OF THE PACIFIC AQUATICS, Stockton, CA
Lifeguard, Fall 1997–Spring 1998

REFERENCES UPON REQUEST

A fax from
Justin Blake

3666 Pacific Avenue • University of the Pacific • Stockton, CA 95204
209-333-8532 • jb0003@uop.edu
13 South Avenue • Millbrae, CA 93030 • 415-677-2037

Date   February 24, 1999
To   Steve Stellar
          District Manager, Hershey Chocolate USA
Fax: 510-885-4888

I am writing at the suggestion of Bob Johnson. When recently speaking with Bob, I shared my desire to begin a sales career, and he encouraged me to contact you immediately regarding the San Jose option or others. I would very much like to interview for a Sales Representative position with Hershey Chocolate. Through conversations with Bob and others in consumer product sales and merchandising, I have become quite enthusiastic about and focused on my job search goals. As reflected by my undergraduate academic, athletic, and cocurricular achievements, I have been very successful in my goal-directed efforts. It is with this motivation that I request consideration for a sales position and seek to arrange a meeting with you as soon as appropriate.

My attached resume details the traits and qualities I believe are required for a successful Hershey Chocolate sales and, ultimately, sales management career. These include:

• Abilities to conduct professional cold calls, nurture relationships with prospective and existing accounts, and present product qualities and profit analyses in effective ways.
• Strong public speaking and customer service skills.
• Knowledge of public relations, promotions, and event planning techniques.
• Reality-based understanding of sales gained through active research.
• Macintosh experience using Word and Internet-access applications.

Through an interview, I can expand upon these points and describe how much I have learned in the classroom, as an NCAA Division I student athlete, as a campus leader, and as an employee of various organizations. While I have learned much to date, I know I have more to learn if I am to reach my goal of becoming a successful Hershey sales professional. I am confident that the initial training and support provided by you and your colleagues will start me off on my quest to turn my dreams into realities.

I will call to confirm your receipt of this fax (originals to follow by mail) and, hopefully, to arrange a meeting with you or one of your colleagues. Thank you for your consideration.

Sincerely,

Justin Blake

✔ An excellent letter of inquiry that immediately notes referral source.

✔ Very enthusiastically projects reality-based understanding of the job desired and a sales attitude.

Justin Blake

3666 Pacific Avenue • University of the Pacific • Stockton, CA 95204
209-333-8532 • jb0003@uop.edu
13 South Avenue • Millbrae, CA 93030 • 415-677-2037

March 11, 1999

Jane Carden
General Mills
77564 East Center Parkway #555
Pleasanton, CA 94565
Fax: 510-654-0283

Ms. Carden:

Thank you for meeting with me at University of the Pacific. Now that I have had a chance to reflect on our interview and, most importantly, on the opportunities that are integral to the Sales Management Associate career path, I am even more eager to take the next steps.

I have attached another copy of my resume to remind you of my background. I am an achievement-driven person who seeks to meet the challenges of and reap the rewards associated with a General Mills career. I want my performance to allow me to move up the career path, and I am excited about my potential to affect sales efforts in various geographic regions. It is with this enhanced motivation that I request continued consideration for a Sales Management Association position and seek to arrange additional interviews as soon as appropriate. I hope to hear from you regarding the status of my candidacy.

Thank you again for your continued consideration.

Sincerely,

Justin Blake

✔ Thank-you note that continues to project enthusiasm and a sales-oriented tone, a must for sales positions.

Justin Blake

3666 Pacific Avenue • University of the Pacific • Stockton, CA 95204
209-333-8532 • jb0003@uop.edu
13 South Avenue • Millbrae, CA 93030 • 415-677-2037

February 24, 1999

Human Resources
Johnson & Johnson Medical
2500 Southwest Boulevard
Arlington, TX 76010
Fax: 817-784-5400

I would very much like to interview for a sales position with Johnson & Johnson Medical. Through conversations with people in pharmaceutical/medical product sales and other related fields, I have become quite enthusiastic about and focused on my job search goals. As reflected by my undergraduate academic, athletic, and cocurricular achievements, I have been very successful in my goal-directed efforts. It is with this motivation that I request consideration for a sales position and seek to arrange a meeting as soon as appropriate.

My attached resume details the traits and qualities I believe are required for a successful Johnson & Johnson sales career. These include:
• Abilities to conduct professional cold calls, nurture relationships with healthcare professionals, and present product qualities in effective ways.
• Strong public speaking and customer service skills.
• Knowledge of public relations, promotions, and event planning techniques.
• Reality-based understanding of the field gained through active research.
• Macintosh experience using Word and Internet access applications.

In an interview, I can expand upon these points and describe how much I have learned in the classroom, as an NCAA Division I student athlete, as a campus leader, and as an employee of various organizations. While I have learned much to date, I know I have more to learn if I am to reach my goal of becoming a successful pharmaceutical sales professional. I am confident that the initial training and support provided by Johnson & Johnson will start me off on my quest to turn my dreams into realities.

I will call to confirm your receipt of this fax (originals to follow by mail) and, hopefully, to arrange a meeting with you or one of your colleagues. I am very willing to relocate for the opportunity to become a member of the J&J team. Thank you for your consideration.

Sincerely,

Justin Blake

✔ An excellent letter of inquiry that uses goal-specific qualifications.

✔ Strong opening paragraph that focuses on target and projects sales profile.

✔ Very skills-focused presentation that projects reality-based understanding of the desired job.

Teri Annette—A Case Study

Teri realized two things as early as her high school senior year. First, she wanted to actively explore and pursue a career in public relations. Second, she didn't want to major in the field as an undergraduate. These two realizations came as a result of discussions with and observations of a live-in role model. Teri's older sister began a career in public relations when Teri was in high school. Through observation and active solicitation of information, Teri gained valuable insights and advice about completing broad liberal arts undergraduate studies, enhancing writing skills, and completing as many internships as was possible. Following recommendations of people within the field and personal interests and motivations, Teri enrolled at a school that would allow her to major in English and, if she desired, take some business courses.

While she sought the most liberal arts–oriented education possible, Teri strategically completed technical courses via summer classes at a local community college. Through these courses as well as an overseas studies experience, Teri was able to learn specialized vocabulary and continued to build a portfolio of her work, including news releases, event plans, promotional correspondence, flyers, posters, and feature articles. Through the contacts her sister had and a structured internship program offered via the community college, Teri obtained three very challenging internships. Through the community college, Teri also became actively involved in and a leader of the student affiliate chapter of the national Public Relations Student Society of America. This enhanced her continued career development and nurtured her relationships with local Public Relations Society of America members. Through luncheons, special skills-building seminars, and regularly distributed publications, she became aware of opportunities and networked with professionals. Teri's resume revealed a goal-driven individual who also excelled in cocurricular roles and never shied away from the four-letter word, "w-o-r-k." Because she amassed such an impressive and lengthy list of achievements, Teri had to create a two-page document. At first, she was concerned that her resume was too long. After consulting her sister, some of her sister's colleagues, and friends she had met through the Public Relations Student Society of America, Teri determined that it was acceptable to use a two-page document as long as the first page contained all of her most important information.

The resume was a hybrid of the conservative and the creative and used a pleasant font and two different bullet points for citing her experiences and noting her key achievements. Headlines reinforced the breadth and depth of Teri's background as well as the focused nature of her undertakings. Teri led with her strengths. She also determined that she would include a miniportfolio with every initial letter she sent to prospective employers. Teri reviewed the materials she had developed for course, on-the-job, and cocurricular projects and then refined a few in order to create the very best possible collection of her work. Each sample of work was preceded by a brief explanation of the goals and rationale behind it. Using this approach, Teri didn't have to be present to support her professional potential.

Within each collection were a resume, a cover letter, a reference list, sample works, and a well-crafted and finely edited news release that creatively and humorously summarized Teri's efforts to find a job. The news release was particularly well received by those who reviewed her job search packet.

Because Teri was very focused in her geographic and functional goals, her strategy was easy to develop and implement. Business journals of targeted cities listed top 25 public relations firms as well as hi-tech and consumer product manufacturers and travel and tourism groups, which were Teri's top three job search targets. She then reviewed these lists with her sister and other industry contacts in order to determine potential referral links. While doing so, she asked permission to use individuals as references and asked if she could use network members' names in correspondence. She also reviewed local printed and online want ad sources and responded to appropriate postings.

Very quickly, Teri gained numerous formal and informal interviews. At first, Teri was surprised by how easy initial screening discussions were and how nicely things progressed. Soon thereafter, she grew a bit frustrated and anxious about how rigorous second- and third-round discussions were and how long the process seemed to take. While Teri was often granted continued consideration and frequently became a "finalist," many positions went to someone with "a bit more experience." Continued coaching from her professional contacts resulted in an expanded portfolio and a better "show-and-tell" technique. Teri maintained her confidence and persistence because she remained busy at her internship activities and employment settings.

Ultimately, she was offered an intern position with a major firm. This title was a bit misleading, and, emotionally, Teri was a bit concerned as she interviewed for the job. In this case "intern" was used to identify a pool of talented beginners who rotated through various departments and projects for a specified period of time. After she completed the apprentice period, internal interviewing and networking yielded Teri a more permanent assignment on a client team.

Teri did follow in her sister's footsteps, but she was striking out on a clearly defined path with a sense of confidence and willingness to creatively address any obstacles or intersections that might lie ahead.

Teri Annette

7566 Greenback Lane • Santa Clara, CA 95610
415-729-2164 • tan@aol.com

Public Relations, Event Planning, and Editing Qualifications

- Special event planning and implementation talents gained through internships, academic projects, competitions, and cocurricular leadership roles.
- Ability to transform plans into strategies and then into detail-oriented realities, often using volunteers.
- Professional training in and experience with media relations, including press kit development and distribution as well as newsletter and tabloid production.
- Editing, writing, and design skills to draft and finalize documents, brochures, and promotional pieces.
- Skills gained from courses that include Journalism and Persuasive Writing, Communication Case Studies and Problems Principles of Public Relations, Communication Research Methods, and Public Speaking.
- IBM PC experience using Windows, Word, PageMaker, PrintShop, and Internet-access applications.

Public Relations Internships and Field-Study Achievements

THE OAKLAND ZOO, Oakland, CA
Public Relations Intern/Special Event Coordinator, Fall 1998–Spring 1999
- Served as Coordinator for fortieth anniversary celebration. Planned series of special events and fund-raisers, and developed related press kits, news releases, invitations, and promotional materials.
- Chaired planning meetings attended by zoo staff members, board members, and volunteers.
- Drafted, edited, and finalized all solicitation correspondence, flyers, and other published documents.
- Created, produced, and distributed tabloid that featured yearlong goals, activities, and historical highlights.

BIG BROTHER AND BIG SISTER, San Jose, CA
Public Relations Strategy Case Team Member, Spring 1998
- Identified mission and strategic plans for local chapter through interviews with Senior Manager and staff members as well as a thorough review of written materials.
- Analyzed data to developed Plans Book that contained potential press releases, fund-raising events, community outreach activities, and other marketing efforts.

INTERNATIONAL PUBLIC RELATIONS FIELD STUDY, Germany and England
Field Study Participant, Summer 1998
- Through site visits and seminars, met professionals of various publications, corporations, and firms.

GENERAL MOTORS INTERNSHIP, Santa Clara, CA
Public Relations Department Intern, Spring 1998
- Planned promotional event for Santa Clara Chevrolet-Geo and Truck World.
- Created and presented options, then implemented plan approved by client.
- Assisted with logistics associated with campus carnival and designed brochures to enhance knowledge and sale of products to college target populations.
- Created minipromotion at local shopping mall to target larger market.

Public Relations, Event Planning, and Promotions Projects

- Planned hypothetical fiftieth anniversary for Disneyland. Identified key tasks, created timeline, and documented logistics for gala New Year's celebrity-filled event. Created press releases, invitations, and related materials for anniversary celebration and simultaneous grand opening of a new theme attraction.
- Created press kit and brochure used by local certified massage therapist. Kit contained news releases, biographical profile of owner, historical feature on message therapy, and promotional materials.
- Researched and presented 2-hour team-building workshop. Identified issues, created handbook and exercise materials, conducted minilectures, and facilitated group activities.

English, Journalism, and Public Relations Training

SANTA CLARA UNIVERSITY, Santa Clara, CA
Bachelor of Arts in English with communication minor, May 1999

EL CAMINO COLLEGE, Mountain View, CA
Completed summer courses in public relations and journalism, Summers 1997 and 1998

Teri Annette

Page Two

Retail Sales, Marketing, and Administrative Experience

MERVYN'S, Mountain View, CA
Sales Associate, Winters and Summers 1997–99

MACY'S, Santa Clara, CA
Merchandise Display and Stock Assistant, Part-time, Summers 1995–97

KIDS MART, Palo Alto, CA
Sales Associate, Spring and Fall 1995

Collegiate Cocurricular Achievements and Leadership

ALPHA PHI SORORITY, SANTA CLARA UNIVERSITY
Executive Board Member, 1997–99
Community Service Committee, 1997–99
Ultimate Volleyball Fund-Raising Committee, 1996
Panhellenic Delegate, 1996
Member, 1996–99

EL CAMINO COLLEGE PUBLIC RELATIONS STUDENT SOCIETY OF AMERICA
Fund-Raising Coordinator, 1997–99
PRSA Liaison, 1997–99
Member, 1997–99

SANTA CLARA UNIVERSITY ENTERTAINMENT AND SPECIAL EVENT PLANNING
COMMITTEE
Committee Member, 1996–98

SANTA CLARA UNIVERSITY FOUNDER'S DAY
Planning Committee Member, 1997–98

A fax from Teri Annette

7566 Greenback Lane • Santa Clara, CA 95610 • 415-729-2164 • tan@aol.com

Date	April 15, 1999
To:	Michelle Gleason Waggener Edstrom 3421 Southeast 6th Street Suite 298 Bellevue, WA 98004
Fax:	206-654-8754

Susan Wright, our mutual professional acquaintance, friend, and SCU alumna, was right. You are a very open, honest, and inspirational person. Per yesterday's enjoyable conversation, I would very much like to interview for the entry-level account management, media relations, and event planning position. As noted on the attached resume, for more than four years, I have actively sought and obtained the academic and practical experiences that are required to start and build a successful career in public relations. Now, having gained diverse skills and perspectives through broad-based public relations capacities for the Oakland Zoo, **I am confident I can be a successful member of the Waggener Edstrom public relations team in Santa Clara.**

I have learned a great deal inside the classroom and through challenging and rewarding experiences. Serving as a key public relations representative of the zoo, contributing to the planning and implementation of a General Motors Internship special event, and expanding my knowledge of industry practices through an Intentional Public Relations Field Study have taught me a lot. The skills I offer include:

- Special event planning and implementation talents gained through internships, academic projects, competitions, and cocurricular leadership roles.
- The ability to transform plans into strategies and then into detail-oriented realities, often using volunteers.
- Professional training in and experience with media relations, including press kit development and distribution as well as newsletter and tabloid production.
- Editing, writing, and design skills to draft and finalize documents, brochures, and promotional pieces.
- Skills gained from courses that include Journalism and Persuasive Writing, Communication Case Studies and Problems Principles of Public Relations, Communication Research Methods, and Public Speaking.
- IBM PC experience using Windows, Word, PageMaker, PrintShop, and Internet-access applications.

While proud of the above and confident that I can quickly contribute as a Waggener Edstrom professional, I realize I have so much more to learn. I will be an ever-curious, continually improving, and client-focused professional. Through an interview, I can begin to learn about your expectations for entry-level staffers, expand upon the above, and, I hope, convince you that I have the qualifications and motivations to succeed.

I will call to confirm your receipt of this fax (originals and miniportfolio to follow by express mail) and to discuss the next steps. I hope to share my comprehensive portfolio with you and other appropriate Waggener Edstrom professionals; news releases and other documents contained in this collection illustrate the potential I possess.

Thank you for your consideration and assistance. It's so great to identify alumnae who can be role models, mentors, and job search advisers. Thank you so very much.

✔ An excellent letter of inquiry that immediately notes a referral contact.
✔ Uses goal-specific qualifications.
✔ Strong opening paragraph that focuses on a target and projects commitment to public relations.
✔ Very skills-focused presentation that closes with a request for an interview and to show her portfolio.

Teri Annette

7566 Greenback Lane • Santa Clara, CA 95610 • 415-729-2164 • tan@aol.com

June 15, 1999

Lynn McCormick
Frost & Sullivan
653 Charles Road
Mountain View, CA 94043
Fax: 415-681-4542

I would like to interview for the entry-level account management, media relations, and event planning position that was recently posted in the Public Relations Society of America newsletter. Bill Winter, current Vice President of Membership for PRSA of the Bay, encouraged me to apply for this opportunity. As noted on the attached resume, for more than four years, I have actively sought and obtained the academic and practical experiences required to start and build a successful career in public relations. Now, having gained diverse skills and perspectives through broad-based public relations capacities for the Oakland Zoo, **I am confident I can be a successful member of the Frost & Sullivan public relations team.**

I have learned a great deal inside the classroom and through challenging and rewarding experiences. Serving as a key public relations representative of the zoo, contributing to the planning and implementation of a General Motors Internship special event, and expanding my knowledge of industry practices through an Intentional Public Relations Field Study have taught me a lot. The skills I offer include:

- Special event planning and implementation talents gained through internships, academic projects, competitions, and cocurricular leadership roles.
- The ability to transform plans into strategies and then into detail-oriented realities, often using volunteers.
- Professional training in and experience with media relations, including press kit development and distribution as well as newsletter and tabloid production.
- Editing, writing, and design skills to draft and finalize documents, brochures, and promotional pieces.
- Skills gained from courses that include Journalism and Persuasive Writing, Communication Case Studies and Problems Principles of Public Relations, Communication Research Methods, and Public Speaking.
- IBM PC experience using Windows, Word, PageMaker, PrintShop, and Internet-access applications.

While proud of the above and confident that I can quickly contribute as a member of the Frost & Sullivan team, I realize I have so much more to learn. I will be an ever-curious, continually improving, and client-focused professional. Through an interview, I can begin to learn about your expectations for entry-level staffers, expand upon the above, and, I hope, convince you that I have the qualifications and motivations to succeed.

I will call to confirm your receipt of this fax (originals and miniportfolio to follow by express mail) and to discuss the next steps. Thank you for your consideration and assistance. I hope to share my comprehensive portfolio with you and other appropriate Frost & Sullivan professionals; news releases and other documents in this collection illustrate the potential I possess.

Sincerely,

Teri Annette

✔ An excellent letter of application, with immediate citation to the posting source and a referral contact.

✔ Uses goal-specific qualifications.

✔ Strong opening paragraph that focuses on a target and projects her commitment to public relations.

✔ Skills-focused presentation.

Teri Annette

7566 Greenback Lane • Santa Clara, CA 95610
415-729-2164 • tan@aol.com

April 16, 1999

Susan Wright
PRx
Suite 298
1876 Ninth Street
San Jose, CA 98004
Fax: 408-476-9876

Susan:

As the attached cover letter documents, I recently communicated with Michelle Gleason of Waggener Edstrom. I will call her tomorrow to discuss the appropriate next steps. Thank you so very much for referring me to Ms. Gleason. She was most enthusiastic and helpful. I am optimistic that our communications will yield an interview with the Santa Clara office.

Also attached are copies of additional letters I recently sent as well as a copy of my miniportfolio. You have been so supportive to date. Any additional leads or advice would be much appreciated. I will keep you informed of how all progresses. Don't be surprised when I get to the interview stage and I ask you to conduct a role-play interview.

As I stated in the letter to Michelle, it is so wonderful to have a fellow SCU alumna as a mentor, role model, and, yes, friend. If you feel comfortable, would a call to Michelle supporting my candidacy facilitate my efforts to be interviewed?

Thanks again and again.

Sincerely,

Teri

✔ A blending of a thank-you note and follow-up letter.

✔ Contains a request for a supporting phone call by a network member to a potential employer.

8

The Interview: Making Your Best Impression

SOME GENERAL GUIDELINES

Throughout this book, I've made the point that a liberal arts graduate is more likely to have a more comprehensive blend of abilities and perhaps a wider range of experience than his or her counterparts in engineering and business programs. In addition to expressing these assets in written correspondence, the interview is a perfect opportunity to let this advantage shine through. Resumes and cover letters help to secure an interview. Having accomplished that, here are some general preparatory steps to take for the interview. They involve the "four Ps"—preparation, presence, participation, and poise.

PREPARATION

Link your skills to the requirements of the job.
The exercise that follows provides a framework for linking characteristics you gained from course work, employment, internships, volunteer, and cocurricular activities to your job search and interview targets. Read your resume before each and every interview! Be prepared to discuss its key points. By completing the Preinterview Exercise, you will develop employer- and job-specific Qualification Connections and be able to cite specific examples of where and when you used your personal capabilities to achieve desired results. As a result, you will more clearly and concisely match your qualifications to the requirements of specific positions.

Be familiar with all of your paid and volunteer experiences so that you can discuss your accomplishments in active terms.
When possible, cite facts and figures to document your successes and project pride in your personal performance. Your resume, combined with the Preinterview Exercise, will prove extremely effective when documenting, recalling, and sharing important data.

Be prepared to articulate goals.

This does not mean predicting the future or knowing exactly where you will be in five years (a typical interview question). You should be ready to discuss the functions you wish to perform on the job and possible directions you might take over time. Thus, you must be able to share with others the results of your research efforts. Never state, "I don't know," when queried about professional objectives. Think about the job you are interviewing for and project possible career paths associated with that job as your prospective goals.

Know your strengths and weaknesses.

We all have them, and this is one of the most often asked interview questions. Share two or three strengths and cite examples of how they relate to the position you are interviewing for. Describe how they can be foundations upon which you can build a successful career. Identify and honestly state a weakness as a "skill or experiential deficit" that relates to your field of interest, but quickly mention ways in which you can improve upon your deficiencies. Don't leave a weakness "hanging," even after you have revealed that you know what must be done to enhance a particular skill. Close with an example of what was once a weakness but is now a strength, specifically one that is associated with your functional goals.

Research the field, function, and firm (in that order) as thoroughly as possible.

Remember, you are interviewing for a specific job within an organization, not just with an organization. Do not spend inordinate amounts of time learning trivial details from annual reports or shareholder information that appears on Web pages. Do understand the big picture. Be knowledgeable about the company's history, geographic locations, general methods of doing business, products, services, mission, reputation, proposed growth or redirection, organizational structure (specifically of the area within which you wish to work), and recent events of particular note. Most importantly, you must know about the specific job you are interviewing for and state your interest in terms of the skills you have to serve within specific roles and responsibilities. Explain what you can do for the company within the context of the job. Always ask for preinterview information directly from the company. While college and university career services facilities and reference librarians can be very helpful when you need to locate written materials and online resources, those who work for the organization, specifically the person who has identified you as a good candidate, are best able to provide accurate and timely information. Don't feel awkward about asking for written materials or the names of people to communicate with informally before an interview. They will be impressed that you asked and, in most cases, very willing to provide the data. Research should never be done in secret!

Call friends, family members, and alumni who might know something about the organization or about the people who will interview you.

The more people you talk to and the more you share with interviewers about your conversations, the better. It's not name-dropping when you mention that you discussed the job in question with others, that you learned a great deal through your discussions, and that your enthusiasm increased after your conversations. Do not limit preinterview research to paper-and-pencil activities. People-to-people efforts are often more easy to talk about, and they give you a better point of reference for interesting exchanges.

Prepare appropriate and thoughtful questions.

Focus queries on the day-to-day tasks associated with the job, the atmosphere within which you will be working, the goals of immediate supervisors, and how performance is judged and rewarded. Through your questions, show and tell how interested you are and that you can see yourself in the job. The answers you receive will prove valuable as you conduct post-offer analysis.

PRESENCE

Personal appearance and behavior are very important.

The way you dress, speak, and carry yourself are parts of the image you project to a prospective employer. Your image is subjectively judged while your skills are objectively analyzed. You should dress as though you had already been hired for the job you are seeking, erring on the side of being too businesslike or conservative. With the increasing popularity of business casual, what to wear to an interview has become less clear for some candidates. Although you may someday interview for a job that does not require business attire, suits for both men and women still remain the best choices for success. A positive personality can be projected through conservative and traditional clothing; if your ensemble speaks too loudly, what you say about yourself might not be heard. You can take off a suit jacket and roll up your sleeves to be more casual, but you cannot quickly excuse yourself and put on your suit in the nearest restroom.

Be aware of body language and posture, but don't worry about every gesture or movement.

Find a comfortable and balanced position in your chair. Face the interviewer, and express yourself in natural and effective ways. Eye contact does enhance communication, but don't stare or appear too stiff. Avoid mannerisms that indicate tension or nervousness (easier said than done), and be natural when using hand, body, and facial gestures. Be expressive when appropriate. Let your personality shine through. Enjoy talking about yourself and meeting new people. Be enthusiastic and positive. Imagine how great it would be to actually get the job.

Avoid slang and trite phrases.

Use proper grammar and a varied vocabulary. Whenever you can, use vocabulary that is specific to the job for which you are interviewing. Show that you know the common language that is related to the industry or job function. Speak clearly and audibly. Maintain a positive and optimistic attitude without being arrogant. Express confidence in your ability to perform tasks that are associated with the position. Don't dwell on negatives or overly criticize situations or people, particularly past supervisors. If you do speak about people and situations that could have been more positive, do so in an intelligent and analytical manner. Be analytical, not critical. Don't ever speak crudely, even if your interviewer uses a few common vulgarities.

Be honest and sincere.

By being yourself, you are giving the interviewer the best opportunity to judge whether or not a match exists. Don't give easy reasons to reject you. Don't express interest in other fields while interviewing for a specific job. Don't state, "I don't know," when asked about goals. Don't tell prospective employers that you might go to graduate school someday soon if you know that it is not a requirement for advancement within that firm. Stay focused. You are interviewing for a particular job, not simply sharing everything and letting employers judge what's important.

PARTICIPATION

Be an active listener and a response-able participant, not a passive respondent.

Elaborate on answers when appropriate. Refer to earlier questions and answers and, regularly, to your resume. Use the resume as a common point of reference that you and your interviewer share. In some ways, it serves as a menu of potential interview topics that you both can choose from. Paraphrase and summarize to remind an interviewer of important points. Be sure to ask questions if you need elaboration. Ask one question related to the job in the first 5 minutes of every interview. Then, use information gained during the remainder of the conversation.

Think about what you would look for in a qualified candidate, then connect yourself to the job via these qualifications.

Don't leave it up to the interviewer to make connections between statements on your resume and your potential to perform on the job. Sharing insights into what motivates you to perform will powerfully project your abilities and attitudes during this important job search exchange. Ask for clarification of vague or open-ended questions. Use this opportunity to bring up favorable information that has not yet been discussed. Don't panic when asked questions that seem to have no specific answer, such as, "Tell me about yourself."

Answer questions by highlighting your abilities, attitudes, and actions. Project liberal arts power.

You share response-ability with the interviewer. If you leave an interview without providing the information that you think qualifies you for the job, it is not because you were not asked the "right" questions. You did not take advantage of the opportunity to powerfully link your past to your desired future. Go into each interview with a strategy and predetermined key points. Utilize the Preinterview Exercise to enhance your participation, but remain flexible so that you can flow as the interview takes a variety of directions. Prior to expressing answers, think about the job and then share your responses through a focal phrase. Don't offer free-floating qualifications. Anchor your responses to what you know are the responsibilities of your target position.

POISE

Participation and practice yield poise.

Practice makes you increasingly comfortable with interview situations. Practice with a counselor, friend, or even alone. Utilize lists of typical interview questions to inspire your potential answers, but when doing so verbalize, don't memorize them. This is a conversation, not an examination. You must maintain your composure in an anxiety-provoking situation.

If you try to memorize specific answers, you will be creating more concern for yourself, not less. You know yourself and you know what you want to do, so don't stress, just share your personal qualifications with an attentive listener. Don't fret if you have to wait to be interviewed or if your discussion is interrupted by phone calls or other circumstances. The interviewer may use a dramatic and stressful style to test you. Stay cool and in control!

End every interview with an understanding of what might happen next and who should contact whom and when. Follow with a faxed or e-mailed thank-you message. Mailed notes take too long to affect decision making, but you should follow quick communiqués with ones that are a bit lengthier and mailed. Make follow-up phone calls if you haven't heard something by the agreed-upon date. Ask one or two references to call on your behalf if you really want the offer. Be persistent, patient, and polite in all follow-up activities. You want ongoing actions to reinforce your positive traits.

THE PREINTERVIEW EXERCISE

Before each interview, reproduce and complete the following exercise on the back of your resume. This will organize your thoughts and clearly identify what to highlight during the exchange. Using these notes, focus your liberal arts power specifically on your job search target. Review your notes prior to the interview, and use them during the interview. Don't be distracted by this worksheet, but do refer to it during your discussions. The interviewer might refer to your resume as a point of reference to inspire questions. You should do the same to inspire answers. Never attempt an interview without a copy of your resume to use as a reminder of your qualifications. You should also bring some extra copies with you in case you unexpectedly meet additional interviewers.

EMPLOYER AND JOB

Concisely note the organization and describe the position you will be interviewing for.

1. _____

2. _____

3. _____

THREE QUALIFICATIONS CONNECTIONS (QCs)
Cite three key points that make you qualified for the position.

Review your resume's Qualification Summary section and then identify three of your cited qualifications or define broader connections that clearly match the position's required qualifications. In general, you are completing the statement, "For this job, my three key assets are . . ."

1. _____

2. _____

3. _____

147

THREE LIBERAL ARTS EXAMPLES
Note three anecdotes that illustrate your ability to succeed on the job.

Your stories should support the three Qualifications Connections you cited earlier and link skills you used to take goal-directed actions to achieve desired results. First, very briefly note each story. Then, identify the *actions, results,* and *tasks* that were associated with your accomplishments. Last, cite the key *skills* you used and enhanced as a result of each particular experience.

1. **A**ctions: _____

    Results: _____

    Tasks: _____

    Skills: _____

2. **A**ction: _____

    Results: _____

    Tasks: _____

    Skills: _____

3. **A**ction: _____

    Results: _____

    Tasks: _____

    Skills: _____

THREE EMPLOYER QUESTIONS (EQs)
List three questions you would like to ask the interviewer.

Ask one question in the first 5 minutes of the interview in order to use the response as the discussion progresses.

1. _____

2. _____

3. _____

The following illustrates how a candidate might use this activity to prepare for an interview for a sales position in a pharmaceutical firm.

EMPLOYER AND JOB
*Concisely note the organization and describe the position
you will be interviewing for.*

Sales Representative position with Oncogenetics, a laboratory that specializes in oncology and genetic testing. I will complete training and then be a assigned territory in any geographic area.

THREE QUALIFICATIONS CONNECTIONS (QCs)
Cite three key points that make you qualified for the position.

Review your resume's Qualification Summary section and then identify three of your cited qualifications or define broader connections that clearly match the position's required qualifications. In general, you are completing the statement, "For this job, my three key assets are . . ."

1. "I know I can do the work and work well with health-care professionals because I've already worked with such people in medical and laboratory settings."

2. "I have a very strong desire to utilize my science background, curiosity about medical issues, and sales-oriented personality to achieve and grow in a sales career."

3. "I have taken many science-related courses, specifically biology classes, so I understand the technical aspects of being a pharmaceutical sales representative, and, more importantly, I know that I can enjoy the day-to-day tasks."

THREE LIBERAL *ARTS* EXAMPLES
Note three anecdotes that illustrate your ability to succeed on the job.

Your stories should support the three Qualifications Connections you cited earlier and link skills you used to take goal-directed actions to achieve desired results. First, very briefly note each story. Then, identify the *actions, results,* and *tasks* that were associated with your accomplishments. Last, cite the key *skills* you used and enhanced as a result of each particular experience.

1. Improved step-by-step customer service–oriented ordering, inventory control system, and sales at Rochester Pharmaceuticals.

    Actions: Reviewed existing steps through discussions with peers and customers; created written proposal noting potential improvements; presented to supervisor and brainstormed concerns; finalized new steps; and trained others to implement. Set sales goals via assessment of customer needs.

    Results: Created and implemented streamlined approach that utilized computerized database as well as written backup to improve the turnaround required to receive and ship materials, specifically special orders.

    Tasks: Data collection, identifying alternatives, judging potential difficulties, analyzing strengths and weaknesses, negotiating with supervisor, documenting undertakings, and training coworkers.

    Skills: Used Microsoft Access and Microsoft Excel software. Wrote and edited proposal. Interviewed colleagues and customers. Trained and diplomatically persuaded others to use the new approach.

2. Served as Research Assistant in Biology Department

Actions: Assisted with tissue analysis of amphibians with neurotransmitters and blockers. Assessed transmitter effect on skin secretion. Completed numerous histological studies, made permanent mounts, and documented efforts. Documented activities in daily and weekly reports. Conducted library research.

Results: Completed all techniques accurately and noted efforts clearly in reports. Enhanced technical vocabulary and understanding of special laboratory techniques.

Tasks: Completed dissections. Conducted testing. Utilized techniques and equipment, including embedding, microtome usage, permanent mount and staining histological sections, SDS-PAGE to characterize proteins, polarameter, micropipet usage, culturing bacteria on agar plates, UV/VIS, atomic absorption spectrophotometer, NMR, and IR spectrometer.

Skills: Completed laboratory testing. Wrote and edited reports. Conducted library research. Increased technical vocabulary and understanding of genetics as well as histology.

3. Completed Nursing Home Rounds with Consultant Pharmacist.

Actions: Shadowed pharmacist, interacted with patients, took notes, updated residents records, explained drug dosage and potential side effects, and conducted information conversations with nurses, physicians, physical therapists, and recreational therapists. Reviewed and reacted to articles related to nursing home care.

Results: Enhanced understanding of residential care and varied disorders associated with aging. Learned about roles associated with pharmacists and various health-care professionals. Created journal of activities.

Tasks: Monitored activities of pharmacists and others. Noted observations in journal. Read articles and wrote analyses pertaining to health-care issues.

Skills: Interacted with residents, patients, and health-care professionals. Gained knowledge of health-care issues and specific prescriptions for varied disorders. Enhanced health-care vocabulary.

THREE EMPLOYER QUESTIONS (EQs)
List three questions you would like to ask the interviewer.

Ask one question in the first 5 minutes of the interview in order to use the response as the discussion progresses.

1. What is the nature of your formal and informal training, and what would I learn first?

2. What particular products will I be responsible for marketing, and will there be a sales goal for each?

3. How will my performance be evaluated, and how will I be able to enhance any deficiencies?

SCREENING, CALLBACK, AND BEHAVIORAL INTERVIEWS

The actual process of interviewing can be a bit confusing. Will you be called only once to speak with a number of people on the same day? Will you have to go through this nerve-racking experience several times, working your way up the chain of command? Each organization works differently, but in general, it is most likely that you will first go through a screening interview or informational session with a representative from the human resources department.

After you have successfully introduced yourself to this interviewer and projected your potential, you will be invited to complete a callback. In most cases, this involves a lengthy stay at corporate or regional headquarters in order to complete two to four interviews. If a human resources professional conducted your first interview, the callbacks will be conducted by your potential colleagues and supervisors. To be best prepared:

1. **Be aware of the process from the hiring organization's perspective.** When seeking to hire, organizations most often **S**creen (review resumes and conduct first interviews over the phone, in person, and/or on campus), **S**elect (make offers to those few individuals they feel are qualified, usually a fraction of those they initially screen), and **S**ell (convince candidates to accept their employment offers). When you've been invited to visit a firm after an on-campus interview or after an initial conversation, you have, in most cases, entered the selection phase. Always remember to frame your answers to interview questions within the context of the specific job.

2. **Follow up with the person who conducted your first screening interview.** Thank him or her and request advice about how to prepare for the next steps. Often, these individuals will turn into effective coaches and offer a great deal of support and guidance. Ask if he or she can refer you to someone who is currently in the desired position. Information conversations are critical. Don't be concerned if your screening interviewer remains objective and offers little concrete assistance. A career services professional can counsel you at this stage.

3. **Prepare at least as well as you did for your initial screening interview.** Do background reading again. Contact alumni who work for the organization. Review your materials, your notes, and, most importantly, your resume (and cover letter if appropriate). Don't get overconfident because you've cleared the first hurdle. Prepare yourself to make a targeted and effective presentation. Review and revise your Preinterview Exercise before callback activities.

4. **Prior to any interview that requires travel, inquire about travel arrangements and reimbursement procedures.**

5. **Know your agenda.** Find out how your day will be structured, who you will be seeing and when, and whether other candidates will be interviewed at the same time. Be prepared for a long day of interviews. **Be consistent in your answers to questions.** While you may be saying the same thing for the fourth time, it is the first time each interviewer hears your answer. Don't appear

bored. Treat everyone with respect, and assume **everyone** you meet (even in informal situations) will have input into the hiring decision.

6. **Be prepared to answer, "What would you do in this situation?" and behavioral types of questions.**

7. **Be organized.** Bring extra copies of your resume with you. Carry a small portfolio that can hold a note pad, extra resumes, copies of correspondence, research notes, and recruiting materials, a list of questions you would like to ask, and accommodations and travel information. Know who is coordinating your visit, and contact that person if you have any problems or concerns or meet unexpected delays. If the interview is out of town, have enough cash and/or a credit card to deal with unexpected expenses.

8. **Don't be surprised if you are asked to take a personality or aptitude test, and be able to cite your achievements.**

9. **Salary and benefits issues may arise.** It is appropriate to address these issues toward the end of the interview but ideally after an offer has been made. Be prepared to state what a realistic range might be or, if you are experienced, exactly what you are looking for.

10. **State, "I definitely want this job!"** Enthusiasm and interest in the organization are judged very positively.

11. **Post-offer analysis occurs after an offer is received.** Get the offer first. Conduct analysis after. Don't shy away from assertively going for an offer, even if you have some questions and concerns. Remain enthusiastic.

Following these guidelines will help you project confidence, a key component of any callback interview.

The behavioral interview is an increasingly popular approach for second- and third-round assessments. This technique is an attempt on the part of the interviewer to quantify and objectify a traditionally subjective process. It is based upon the following principles: past behavior is the best predictor of future behavior, more recent behavior is a better predictor of future behavior than older behavior, and trends in behavior are better predictors than isolated incidents. Therefore, the interviewer will present what-did-you-do-when-scenarios or ask you to identify past incidents when you used certain behaviors to achieve a task or reach a goal. Interviewers have determined the nature of desired behaviors and use a preestablished checklist to determine if you have the qualities that are required to succeed in a particular job.

- Be prepared for open-ended questions and don't become rattled by them.

- Note-taking by the interviewer is not unusual; don't interpret it as negative or positive.

- Interviewers may seek clarification or contrary evidence of your statements by continually probing; don't become rattled or express frustration.

- Rapport-building questions, as well as silence, are normal aspects of a behavioral interview.

To prepare, review the questions below and then clearly identify three to five Liberal ARTS examples. Briefly note these examples on a copy of your resume and take the resume with you to the interview, but don't be too surprised or get upset if you are asked not to use your notes. Don't memorize answers to typical questions, but be prepared to expand upon your liberal ARTS anecdotes.

QUESTIONS OFTEN ASKED AND QUESTIONS TO ASK

Use the following list of questions to stimulate thoughts and inspire you to make intellectual and emotional connections to behavioral pictures you wish to verbally paint for interviewers. The exercises already presented, not just the questions, should facilitate this process.

- Describe a time when you faced problems or stresses at work that tested your coping skills. What did you do?

- Give an example of a time when you could not participate in a discussion or could not finish a task because you did not have enough information.

- Give an example of a time when you had to react quickly to come to a decision.

- Tell me about a time when you used your oral communication skills to get an important point across.

- Can you tell me about a job experience in which you had to speak up and tell other people what you thought or felt?

- Give me an example of when you felt you were able to build motivation in coworkers or subordinates.

- Tell me about a specific occasion when you conformed to a policy even though you did not agree with it.

- Describe a situation in which you felt it necessary to be very attentive of and vigilant to your environment.

- Give me an example of a time when you used your fact-finding skills to solve a problem, and then tell me how you analyzed the information you found to come to a decision.

- Give me an example of an important goal you set, and tell me about your progress in reaching this goal.

- Describe the most significant written document, report, or presentation you've completed.

- Give me an example of a time when you had to go above and beyond the call of duty in order to get a job done.

- Give me an example of a time when you were able to communicate successfully with another person, even when the individual may not have personally liked you.

- Describe a situation in which you were able to read another person effectively and guide your actions by your understanding of his or her individual needs or values.

- What did you do in your last job in order to be effective in your organization and planning? Be specific.

- Describe the most creative work-related project you have completed.

- Describe a time when you felt it necessary to modify or change your actions in order to respond to the needs of another.

- Give me an example of a time when you had to analyze a person or a situation carefully in order to be effective in guiding your action or decision.

- What did you do in your last job to contribute toward a teamwork environment? Be specific.

- Give an example of a problem you faced on the job and how you solved it.

- Describe a situation in which you were able to positively influence the actions of others in a desired direction.

- Tell me about a situation in the past year in which you had to deal with a very upset customer or coworker.

- Describe a situation in which others within your organization depended on you.

- Describe your most recent group effort.

- Describe the most challenging customer or coworker you ever interacted with, and tell me how you dealt with him or her.

- Why are you interested in this particular field?

- What academic achievements are you most proud of?

- Why did you choose your major, and how does it relate to your goals?

- What classes did you find most stimulating, and did they nurture your job-connected skills?

- What would you like to be doing in five years?

- What are your greatest strengths and weaknesses?

- How would you describe yourself, and how would others describe you?

- How would you characterize career-related success?

- What are your three most significant employment or cocurricular achievements?

- When did you use persuasive skills or sales talents to achieve a goal?

- Why should we hire you?

- What are your long-term career goals?

- How have your academic experiences to date prepared you for a career, and what are your future academic goals?

- Looking back, what would you do differently in your academic, cocurricular, and practical experiences?

- What was your most difficult decision to date, and how did you go about making it?

- Why did you attend your alma mater?

- What research projects have you found most rewarding and why?

- What do you think it takes to succeed within the job you are being interviewed for?

- What lessons have you learned from your failures or mistakes?

- Are your grades fair reflections of your academic abilities and intellectual potential?

- What are your geographic preferences, and are you willing to relocate?

- What concerns do you have about this job and our organization?

- How would you describe this opportunity to friends and family members?

- What additional information do you need to determine if this is the right opportunity for you?

- What first motivated you to interview with us?

Now that you have reviewed these general queries, develop a list of questions that would apply to a specific job that matches your job search target. Conduct a practice session and have a friend or family member ask you these questions. There are no right or wrong answers to particular questions. Your responses during an interview must always seem well conceived yet spontaneous. It's always best to think of this interaction as a conversation, not an inquisition. Thus, it is best to complete this exercise aloud, even if you are doing so alone.

1. *Why did you major in, and what does your major have to do with this career field?*

2. *What courses did you do best in and why?*

3. *What are your greatest strengths and weaknesses?*

4. _____

5. _____

6. _____

7. _____

8. _____

9. _____

10. _____

Also, meet with a career services counselor before and after your early interviews. Seek advice and guidance. Share how you feel about your performance. Identify key concerns, but don't overanalyze or dissect each and every interview. Build your confidence.

Questions you might ask potential employers during an interview or during a preinterview information conversation include:

- How would you describe the job in terms of day-to-day roles and responsibilities?

- What qualities are you seeking in a candidate?

- What type of person would most likely succeed in this job?

- What advice would you give to someone who is seeking to achieve goals quickly?

- What should I expect of myself over the first few months on the job?

- How will my performance be judged and by whom?

- What characteristics are needed to succeed within this organization and within the specific role of this position?

- What are the best things about the job and the most challenging requirements of the position?

- Who would have the highest expectations or be the most difficult to impress?

- What is the typical career path and time frame associated with career development in this field?

- How will I be trained to enhance my skills?

- Who last served in this position, and what is he or she doing now?

- What goals do you have for the person who will serve in this job?

- What project would you expect to be completed first, and what would be involved?

In summary, to be a powerful liberal arts interviewee:

- Whenever possible, call a few days before the interview to confirm your meeting and to arrange an information conversation with an alum or a recent hire.
- Don't be shy! **Cite achievements with pride.** Interviewers have half an hour to get to know "you." Don't think there is a "right" answer. Your opinion counts!
- When asked a "technical question" that you don't know the exact answer to, talk the interviewer through how you would go about finding out the correct answer.

- Ask questions when invited. Also, you should ask one or two early in the interview to acquire clarification about job roles and responsibilities. This will help you throughout the conversation.
- Practice with a friend or family member. Don't memorize. Be yourself. **Visit with a career services counselor before and after your first three interviews.**
- Take a copy of your resume with you to the interview, with the Preinterview Exercise and Liberal ARTS examples noted on the back.
- Refer to your resume and cite examples by stating, "As noted on my resume," when appropriate.
- Remember that you are **interviewing for a specific job,** not just with a firm.
- Focus on the nature of the job you are interviewing for when addressing most questions. Think about the specific job and consider what will be expected of you before responding.
- Always ask about the next steps and when they might take place.
- State, **"I want this job,"** or, "I do want to take the next step because I want to work for your firm!"
- Prepare for the callback interview as well as you did for the first.

SOME CLOSING THOUGHTS

I hope this book has given you, the powerful liberal arts job seeker, the information, tools, and motivation to conduct a successful job search. I hope I have shown you the value of analysis and research and the benefits of focusing, and sometimes narrowing, your initial career goals. I am convinced that if you take the advice in this book, you will find a job that utilizes the skills and abilities you developed as a liberal arts major. Now that you are prepared to answer the question, "What are you going to do with a major in *that?*" I wish you the best of luck in your chosen field.

IV

Additional Resources

To follow are additional resources to help you in your job search efforts. Appendix 1 includes a number of worksheets that have been referred to throughout the text. If you follow these exercises step by step, you will be better prepared to approach your job search with a clear focus. Photocopy the forms and complete them as many times as necessary. Appendix 2, The Internet as a Job Search Tool, presents ways to use the Internet to search out job opportunities as well as how to respond to them and follow up with employers. Appendix 3, Job Search Resources, suggests a number of publications to help you in your job search.

APPENDIX 1

Worksheets and Exercises

RESEARCH AND JOB SEARCH GOALS WORKSHEET

Review the glossary of options as well as any notes you have made. Identify five research goals—fields or jobs you wish to learn more about. Your list may be based on intuitive reactions or on more objective analysis, including personal experience you may already have with particular fields and jobs. As you note these initial job search goals, don't be too analytical or feel constrained. Simply document them below.

Research Goals: List Five Fields or Jobs

1. _____

2. _____

3. _____

4. _____

5. _____

Next, research the fields or jobs using the criteria discussed in Chapter 2. A quick trip to your school's library or career services center, a visit to a local public library, or a review of trade publications might provide enough information to complete effective research. You should duplicate the following page, creating separate worksheets for each of the fields or jobs you have an interest in. Take notes. In-depth exploration will enhance your analysis and allow you to prioritize.

Field/Job:

_____

_____

_____

Job Description:

_____

_____

_____

Qualifications:

_____

_____

_____

_____

Education/Training/Experience:

_____

_____

_____

Organizational Structure:

_____

_____

_____

_____

Entry-Level Options:

_____

_____

_____

Work Environment and Conditions:

_____

_____

_____

Earnings and Outlook:

_____

_____

_____

_____

Be thorough, but don't dwell on your efforts. Give yourself enough time, but don't fixate on research. Once your research is complete, rank the fields or jobs in order of preference in the spaces below.

Job Search Goals: Top Three Career Choices

1. _____

2. _____

3. _____

From your original list, identify the three research goals that you would like to identify as Job Search Goals. You can change these goals whenever you wish; listing these choices will not limit you in any way. You will be asked to use these jobs or fields in subsequent exercises.

Your job search goals will be communicated to potential employers through a targeted resume that features an objective statement and a summary of qualifications statement. Your potential employer will assess your skills and employability by what you include in your resume. It is the responsibility of the liberal arts job seeker to be career articulate. Employers will judge you not only by your ability to perform tasks that are required by a job function but also by your liberal arts background and your knowledge of the fields and functions that you stated as goals. Your career vocabulary must also include fluency in skills and qualifications. The Skills Inventory that follows will assist you with resume writing, skills analysis, and with establishing a postgraduation skill-development strategy.

Goal setting, although critical, is only the first of the Ten Steps to job search success. Do not expect that offers will magically appear once you have set your goals or begin sharing your objectives with others. Job search success hinges on your assertiveness and your proactive and reactive strategies. While stating goals is crucial, actions always speak louder than words.

Skills Inventory

The following exercise asks you to pinpoint your skills and abilities and the areas you need to enhance. Once you document your skills and analyze the skills that are required to enter the fields or jobs that are your targets, you can focus your resume to highlight these skills and, if need be, develop a postgraduation skill-building strategy.

To complete the Skills Inventory, first think about your most significant accomplishments and experiences. These can include academic, employment, and cocurricular achievements. Recall what made them so important and why you were able to accomplish what you did. Then, after making a copy of the exercise for future undertakings, check off the abilities that you used to gain these achievements. At this stage, do not be too analytical when deciding which abilities to check. Later, you will be asked to identify personal priority skills, those you believe to be your strongest, and to cite job-related skills, those that are associated with your Job Search Goals.

After you have checked your abilities, answer the following questions:

- Do some Skills Realms have more check marks than others?
- Do some Major Skills Categories have more check marks than others?
- Do there seem to be patterns of Abilities?
- Are the patterns consistent with your beliefs about the skills you would like to use on the job, or are they limited by your past experiences?
- Are there abilities that, in general, you would like to enhance?

Skills Realms

1. ANALYTICAL REALM

ANALYZING AND EVALUATING

_____ quantitative or statistical data
_____ services or programs
_____ performances of groups or individuals
_____ value of objects or services

CLASSIFYING

_____ objects or people into categories
_____ status of applicants or applications

ESTIMATING AND APPRAISING

_____ cost of services or programs
_____ time requirements of services to be performed or programs to take place
_____ physical space required for services or programs
_____ number of people or items required for services or programs

EXAMINING

_____ financial records
_____ procedures and policies
_____ physical objects or locations

RESEARCHING

_____ information from libraries or written sources
_____ information from obscure sources
_____ backgrounds of groups or individuals
_____ historical information
_____ information from people via interviews
_____ information from physical evidence
_____ information for immediate use
_____ information for continued research

2. COMMUNICATIONS REALM

BUYING

_____ for resale to the public
_____ for resale to distributors or retailers
_____ for use by organizations or for events

CORRESPONDING

_____ by answering inquiries by mail or phone
_____ by initiating contact by mail or phone

DISTRIBUTING

_____ to individuals
_____ to places for resale

EDITING

_____ book manuscripts
_____ newspaper or magazine articles
_____ papers, reports, or proposals
_____ for grammatical errors
_____ for style or format

INTERPRETING AND TRANSLATING

_____ languages
_____ technical data into lay terms
_____ complicated ideas into clear language

READING AND PROOFREADING

_____ large amounts of information quickly
_____ for errors or style
_____ to synthesize abstracts

REPRESENTING AND RECRUITING

_____ representing an organization to the public
_____ recruiting employees or volunteers
_____ promoting a point of view
_____ soliciting funds or aid

SELLING

_____ products or ideas to individuals
_____ products or ideas to large groups
_____ in a store
_____ door-to-door
_____ by phone
_____ products or services in high demand
_____ products or services where demand is created

SPEAKING

_____ publicly to audiences
_____ in small groups
_____ by developing or using presentation materials

WRITING

_____ copy for sales or advertising
_____ fiction
_____ essays
_____ reports or proposals
_____ journalistic copy for print or broadcast
_____ abstracts synthesized from volumes of data or other information
_____ quickly under deadline pressure
_____ slowly for accuracy, style, and content

3. CREATIVE REALM

ARRANGING AND DISPLAYING
_____ materials and equipment for a show
_____ furniture and fixtures
_____ products for sale
_____ wall or window displays
_____ landscapes

DESIGNING
_____ layouts for newspapers or magazines
_____ layouts for advertising or promotional artwork
_____ brochures, flyers, or posters
_____ artwork
_____ audiovisual materials

PERFORMING
_____ in a theatrical production
_____ in a musical production
_____ in a promotional demonstration

PRINTING
_____ using standard equipment and processes
_____ using desktop software and hardware
_____ freehand or in calligraphy

SKETCHING, PAINTING, AND PHOTOGRAPHING
_____ diagrams, charts, or graphs
_____ pictures of people or things
_____ illustrations for a story, idea, proposal, or report
_____ for artistic purposes
_____ for advertising or promotional purposes

4. INTERACTIVE REALM

COACHING, DIRECTING, AND TUTORING
_____ athletic teams
_____ theatrical productions
_____ academic subjects

COUNSELING AND ADVISING
_____ on personal problems
_____ on academic issues
_____ on financial issues
_____ as resource person, referring to professionals or to reference materials
_____ in groups or clubs within an academic environment

HANDLING COMPLAINTS
_____ by listening and responding verbally
_____ by listening and responding in writing
_____ by reading and corresponding
_____ by taking actions
_____ by calming tense situations

INTERVIEWING
_____ to determine attitudes
_____ to gather employment information
_____ to collect sales or marketing data

MEETING THE PUBLIC
_____ by receiving and greeting
_____ by giving tours
_____ by displaying or selling products
_____ by conducting in-person surveys
_____ by conducting telephone surveys

TEACHING AND TRAINING
_____ in a classroom or academic setting
_____ in a recreational setting
_____ in a business setting
_____ groups
_____ individuals
_____ physical activities and sports
_____ academic subjects
_____ self-improvement
_____ work-related performance skills and ideas

5. ORGANIZATIONAL REALM

MANAGING
_____ performance and productivity of others
_____ information or data collection
_____ activities of groups or individuals
_____ by delegating tasks
_____ a store
_____ an event

PLANNING
_____ an event
_____ a trip
_____ a system or program
_____ sales, advertising, or promotional activities
_____ based on cost/benefit or financial criteria

RECORDKEEPING
_____ numerical data
_____ files and records
_____ database systems

SUPERVISING AND OVERSEEING
_____ work of others
_____ physical plants, apartments, or buildings
_____ systems and procedures
_____ policies and programs

TIMING
_____ tasks to be completed in a given period
_____ events to begin and end as planned
_____ efficiency of others

UPDATING
_____ information for day-to-day use
_____ filing systems
_____ policies and procedures
_____ biographical information
_____ databases

6. PHYSICAL REALM

ATHLETICS
_____ performing or coaching a sport or event
_____ demonstrating or selling equipment
_____ planning or promoting an event
_____ managing business aspects

CONSTRUCTING
_____ houses or buildings
_____ mechanical or electronic devices
_____ objects, such as furniture, fences, or platforms

PROTECTING
_____ people
_____ objects or buildings

REPAIRING
_____ mechanical or electrical devices
_____ cars or trucks
_____ home or building components

7. QUANTITATIVE REALM

ACCOUNTING AND BOOKKEEPING
_____ maintaining financial balances
_____ maintaining accounts receivable and payable
_____ tracking sales revenues versus costs
_____ keeping records of actions or transactions versus costs

BUDGETING
_____ costs of projects or systems
_____ monitoring spending
_____ developing cost-saving techniques or plans

CALCULATING
_____ by hand or with a simple calculator

COMPUTING AND DATA PROCESSING
_____ using desktop computers
_____ using laptop computers
_____ using mainframes
_____ for simple calculations
_____ for statistical analyses
_____ for database management
_____ using packaged software
_____ writing software and programming
_____ explaining hardware or software to others

8. SCIENTIFIC REALM

LABORATORY AND MEDICAL WORK
_____ setting up equipment or instruments
_____ using equipment or instruments
_____ designing controlled experiments
_____ caring for laboratory animals
_____ handling specimens
_____ inspecting objects or specimens
_____ examining people or animals

MEASURING
_____ to obtain accurate readings from devices
_____ to assess skills or conditions

TREATING AND DIAGNOSING
_____ animals
_____ humans

Identify your top three Skills Realms as well as your top skills categories and abilities within each Realm.

	SKILLS REALMS	SKILLS CATEGORIES	ABILITIES
1			
2			
3			

Your research has identified the roles and responsibilities of the specific positions you are interested in and the skills that are required to enter a given field. Note your three Job Search Goals and enter the required abilities you now possess and the skills you may wish to enhance.

JOB SEARCH GOALS	EXISTING ABILITIES	ABILITIES TO ENHANCE
1		
2		
3		

You have now targeted the abilities that can increase your chances for attaining your job search goals. You should now be able to complete a resume and focus your interview skills.

APPENDIX 2

The Internet as a Job Search Tool

In the electronic age, job seekers can use the Internet to search for job postings, research potential employers, and transmit cover letters, resumes, and other communiqués. Whether conducting efforts in person, over the phone, or via the Internet, your ultimate goal is to secure an interview and then an offer. While the largest majority of opportunities found on the Internet are still in technological fields, resources are available for those seeking options in other fields. This appendix will teach you to develop and implement individualized and effective strategies. Most college career services offices, academic libraries, and public libraries offer Internet access as well as articles and books to aid cyber-search efforts. There are many ways to use the Internet during your research and job search efforts. You can explore online want ads and the home pages of companies you might want to work for in search of posted opportunities. You can post your resume on electronic bulletin boards, your own Web page, and specialized databases or list your resume with an electronic search firm. Search engines, including Yahoo!, Infoseek, Alta Vista, Lycos, and Excite, can provide links to a number of Web sites. Most search engines have career links (identified by headings like Classifieds, Careers, Employment, and Jobs) on their home pages.

Agent services, available through some Internet service providers and Web sites, search for employment matches for their users. Users must register with the service (provide personal information, such as name, address, phone number, occupational goals, and areas of interest or a resume) and when the service finds a potential job posting that fits the user's criteria, it sends an e-mail message to the user. Most services are free of charge to users. Be a bit wary of any firm that requires a fee. (This includes online, telephone, and walk-in services.)

As discussed throughout this book, liberal arts job seekers should implement targeted strategies. Most sites allow job seekers to target searches by geographic, skill, title, field, company, and other criteria. Review several sites before selecting one to use. Some, such as JobTrak, StudentCenter, and CareerCity, are oriented toward soon-to-be and recent grads. Others, including Tripod, focus on internship opportunities. Online yellow pages, including http://www.bigbook.com, http://www.the-yellowpages.com, http://www.yellowweb.com, http://www.bigfoot.com, and http://www.switchboard.com, can help to locate street addresses, phone numbers, and e-mail addresses of potential employers.

Increasingly, colleges and universities are creating well-linked Web sites that offer registration services, postings, alumni networks, and other resources. Often, these services are limited to students and alumni, but some offer access to everyone. If you have set geographic parameters, check the Web sites of nearby colleges and universities for job opportunities.

General and field-specific discussion groups can also offer information and motivation for long-term job search efforts. Job search coaches, counselors, and field-specific experts are regularly on line and available for interactive discussions.

Research efforts also include requesting and conducting online information conversations. Employees of your targeted fields are accessible through e-mail directories that are linked through industry and company Web pages. Professional association membership directories are increasingly accessible on line, as are alumni networks. When conducting these queries, start with a brief request for advice and assistance, list three questions you would like answered and then ask for a response via your e-mail address. I recommend the following queries: What are typical entry-level job titles and functions of jobs within this field? What abilities, personal qualities, or special talents do you believe contribute most within this field and within jobs like the ones you have held? What advice do you have for someone who is interested in this field and job function? Can you refer me to others in the field who would participate in information conversations or can be contacted for employment consideration?

The Internet can be counterproductive for some. Students who seek information on the Web and spend hours to find it when the same information could be accessed in minutes via published resources are not conducting effective research. Always ask a reference librarian or a career resource specialist for assistance. Blend traditional efforts with electronic ones to be powerful and productive. Don't send e-messages and then wait for a reply. Don't forward your resume via the Internet and then wait. Take one action, then another.

There are many Web pages that offer some form of job search assistance. To follow are the Web addresses for some widely used sites.

Academic Position Network
    http://www.apnjobs.com/
AdOne Classified Network
    http://www.adone.com
America's Job Bank
    http://www.ajb.dni.us/
American Management Association
    http://www.amanet.org
Career Exposure
    http://www.careerexposure.com
Career Mosaic
    http://www.careermosaic.com
CareerPath
    http://www.careerpath.com
Career Site
    http://www.careersite.com
Career and Resume Management
    http://www.crm21.com
The Catapult
    http://www.jobweb.org/CATAPULT/catapult.htm
Chronicle of Higher Education
    http://www.chronicle.merit.edu

Cool Works
> http://www.coolworks.com/showme

College Grad Hunter
> http://www.collegegrad.com/internships/

E-span
> http://www.espan.com

Employease
> http://www.employease.com/bweb/careers.html

Environmental Careers
> http://www.eco.org
> http://www.environmental-jobs.com

Good Works
> http://www.essential.org/goodworks

Institute of Electrical and Electronic Engineers
> http://www.ieee.org/jobs.html

Interim Services
> http://www.interim.com

Internet Career Connection
> http://iccweb.com

International Internships
> http://www.studyabroad.com

JobBank USA
> http://www.jobbankusa.com

Job Center
> http://www.jobcenter.com/

Job Hunt
> http://www.job-hunt.org

JobSmart
> http://www.jobsmart.org/

JOBTRAK
> http://www.jobtrak.com

Med Search America
> http://www.medsearch.com

Monster Board
> http://www.monsterboard.com

Online Career Center
> http://www.occ.com

PursuitNet
> http://www.tiac.net/users/jobs/

Recruiters Online Network
> http://www.ipa.com

Smithsonian Internships
> http://www.si.edu/youandsi/studies/infell.htm

Society for Human Resource Management
> http://www.shrm.org

Student Center
> http://www.studentcenter.com

TOPjobs USA
http://www.topjobsusa.com
Tripod
http://www.tripod.com
TV Internships
http://www.tvjobs.com/intern.htm
Walt Disney World Internships
http://www.careermosaic.com/cm/wdw/wdw1.html
Washington D.C. Internships
http://www.interns.org
http://www.dcinternships.org

HOME PAGES AND WEB RESUMES

Liberal arts job seekers can create personal Web pages that showcase their resumes, projects, employment experiences, cocurricular achievements, and portfolios. There are many books, seminars, courses, and consultants who can teach liberal arts job seekers how to build a home page. User-friendly software, including PageMill, simplifies the process for those who do not know Java or HTML programming. Job seekers should build focused and resume-centered pages and attached them to a college or university site. Creating and launching a personal Web page clearly demonstrates high-tech abilities, but job seekers should not assume that employers will find them. Job seekers should refer to their Web addresses on resumes and in correspondence. They should also register their sites with search engines and through other methods.

If you use an e-resume, there are basic suggestions to follow.

- Do not underline or use italics as highlighting techniques.

- Use traditional, easy-to-scan fonts, including Helvetica and Times, and left-justify all copy.

- Do not use graphics such as shadowing, boxes, or columns.

- Use career-specific phrases, including nouns and active verbs as well as headlines with function-oriented labels, to facilitate the identification of your document through a key-word search.

- Do not attach a resume to an e-mail message; copy and paste it into the message.

- List your e-mail and Web addresses on separate lines.

E-MAIL, SNAIL MAIL, AND TELEPHONE TECHNIQUES

You should recall step six of the Ten Steps: **Call first, then fax or e-mail, and, finally, mail resumes and cover letters to people on the hit list and in the job search network.** While I do encourage initial use of faxes and e-mail, once you have done so, mail copies of job search communiqués to your potential employers. Be thorough but thoughtful. Don't transmit or mail too many resumes too often to the same people, but feel confident to communicate when appropriate.

When calling, do leave messages via voice mail. Even if it is your first contact with a prospective employer or job search network member, leave a polite and professional message that contains your phone number and/or e-mail address and request that he or she respond to your call.

The more often that candidates use the phone, the more likely they are to be successful. Those who are comfortable using the phone will accelerate their job search efforts. Always **CALL . . .**

- **C**onfirm who you are speaking with and clarify your job search circumstance to ensure that you are speaking with an appropriate person about your situation and can follow up later.
- **A**ssess the status of your candidacy, determine whether or not your resume and cover letter were received, and, whenever possible, arrange an interview or an information conversation.
- **L**eave messages that briefly outline your circumstances and clearly cite what you would like to happen next.
- **L**eave your phone number, fax number, and e-mail addresses to facilitate follow-up communiqués.

Using this acronym, outline your thoughts and create phone scripts prior to your contacts. Don't memorize or read the scripts, but do organize what you would like to say. Also, remember that you can always call back if you forget to address a particular point. The following is an example of an exchange and a worksheet.

C	**C**onfirm who you are speaking with and clarify your job search circumstance to ensure that you are speaking with an appropriate person about your situation and can follow up later.	"Hello. My name is Joseph Byrne. With whom am I speaking? I've recently faxed Bernard Roberts regarding a paralegal position with Blane, Collier and Phips. I would like to confirm that my resume and cover letter were received and, if possible, arrange an interview. Can you connect me with Mr. Roberts?"
A	**A**ssess the status of your candidacy, determine if your resume and cover letter were received, and arrange an interview or information conversation.	"Mr. Roberts's office? Yes, I'm Joseph Byrne. I faxed my resume and cover letter yesterday. Could you confirm that it was received, and would it be possible to arrange an interview? May I speak with Mr. Roberts or someone else who might be able to clarify the status of my candidacy and schedule a meeting?"
L	**L**eave messages that briefly outline your circumstances and clearly cite what you would like to happen next.	"Yes, I would like to leave a voice mail message. Thank you. Mr. Roberts, this is Joseph Byrne. I would like to follow up on the fax I recently sent. Did you receive my resume and cover letter? Could I meet with you to discuss my candidacy?"
L	**L**eave your phone number, fax number, and e-mail address to facilitate follow-up communiqués.	"Please call me at 504-876-2356 or e-mail jbyrne@tulaneu.edu. Thank you."

Duplicate and then complete this template to create an informal script. Document your thoughts, but don't become stiff, read your script, or get overly nervous if situations require that you deviate from it and be spontaneous.

C	**C**onfirm who you are speaking with and clarify your job search circumstance to ensure that you are speaking with an appropriate person about your situation and can follow up later.	
A	**A**ssess the status of your candidacy, determine if your resume and cover letter were received, and arrange an interview or an information conversation.	
L	**L**eave messages that briefly outline your circumstances and clearly cite what you would like to happen next.	
L	**L**eave your phone number, fax number, and e-mail address to facilitate follow up communiqués.	

APPENDIX 3

Job Search Resources

Because liberal arts students and graduates must conduct research to set goals and develop a list of prospective employers, printed resources remain critical to their success. The following is an up-to-date list of resources that provide all of the information required to complete the Ten Steps. Most of the resources are available through online and traditional bookstores. College career centers as well as public and college libraries should also have many of them.

American Jobs Abroad by Victoria Harlow and Edward W. Knappman. Detroit: Visible Ink Press, 1994. Identifies various firms with overseas opportunities. Indexed by geographic, functional, and other criteria, this is an easy-to-use publication.

The Back Door Guide to Short-Term Job Adventures by Michael Landes. Berkeley: Ten Speed Press, 1997. Addresses the needs of those seeking internship and externship experiences. It contains many creative community service and skills-building opportunities.

Breaking into Advertising by Jeanette Smith; *Breaking into Film* by Kenna McHugh; *Breaking into Television* by Dan Weaver and Jason Siegel. Princeton, N.J.: Peterson's, 1998. Step-by-step plans, advice, and anecdotes illustrate how to get your foot in the door and how to build a career in these exciting fields.

Career Advisory Series: Healthcare, Newspaper, Magazines, Mental Health and Social Work, Marketing and Sales, Medical Technologies and Technicians, Radio and Television, Public Administration, Education, Public Relations, Film and Video, Performing Arts, Therapy and Allied Health Professionals, Environmental, Physical Sciences. Detroit: Visible Ink Press, 1993. Contains concise descriptions of field and functional options and addresses job search strategies. Like many books of this kind, appendices list potential employers, professional associations, and educational options.

Career Choices for the 90's (series): *Art, Business, Communication and Journalism, Computer Science, Economics, English, History, Mathematics, Political Science and Government, Psychology.* New York: Walker Publishing Company, 1990. Each book contains job search and graduate school information and presents recommended career paths.

Careers for (series): Animal Lovers, Bookworms, Caring People, Computer Buffs, Crafty People, Culture Lovers, Environmental Types, Fashion Plates, Film Buffs, Foreign Language Aficionados, Good Samaritans, Gourmets, Health Nuts, History Buffs, Kids at Heart, Music Lovers, Mystery Buffs, Nature Lovers, Night Owls, Numbers Crunchers, Plant Lovers, Shutterbugs, Sports Nuts, Travel Buffs, Writers. Lincolnwood, Ill.: VGM Career Horizons, 1996. *A creative and expanding collection of publications that focus on skills and interests.*

Careers in (series): Accounting, Advertising, Business, Child Care, Communications, Computers, Education, Engineering, Environment, Finance, Government, Health Care, High Tech, Journalism, Law, Marketing, Medicine, Science, Social and Rehabilitation Services. Lincolnwood, Ill.: VGM Career Horizons, 1995. *One of the most often used and easiest to read set of career publications. Instills the vocabulary required to state goals and complete internship, externship, and job search efforts.*

Career Planning Today, Third Edition, by C. Randall Powell. Bloomington, Ind.: Indiana University Bloomington, 1995. *Without focusing on needs of liberal arts students, it overviews goal setting, resume writing, employer identification, and interviewing.*

CareerXRoads by Gerry Crispin and Mark Mehler. Kendall Park, N.J.: MMC Group, 1998. *Discussion of Internet search activities and listings of Web sites that offer field-specific and general information and career services.*

Great Jobs for . . . Majors (series): Psychology, History, English, Communication, Business, Sociology, Foreign Language, Engineering. Lincolnwood, Ill.: VGM Career Horizons, 1997. *Even if your particular major does not appear in a title, reading a few of the books in the collection should inspire you to prioritize fields of interest.*

Guide to Mass Media Internships: Print and Broadcast by Ronald Claxton. Boulder, Colo.: University of Colorado. *A collection of various options within print and broadcast areas. Effective way to find internships, externships, and entry-level options.*

Guide to Your Career by Alan B. Bernstein and Nicholas R. Schaffzin. New York: The Princeton Review, Random House Inc., 1996. *Alphabetical listing of job descriptions and fields.*

Harvard Business School Career Guide: Management Consulting, Finance, Boston: Harvard Business School Publishing, 1997. *Specialized books written by and for M.B.A.'s.*

Hidden Job Market. Princeton, N.J.: Peterson's Inc., 1998. *Extremely valuable for those seeking high-tech options, this book lists employer names, addresses, phone numbers, and Web addresses and is indexed by field and geographic criteria.*

Internships 1999. Princeton, N.J.: Peterson's Inc., 1998. *Annually published book that identifies internships and creatively offers insight into potential externship and postgraduation opportunities. Basic information on resume writing and job search in the* preface is informative and motivational. Offers good indexing by geographic, field, and other special criteria, which makes it easy to use.

Internships by Sara Dulaney Gilbert. New York: Arco, 1997. Another annually published work that identifies internships. Offers good indexing by geographic, field, and other special criteria, which makes it easy to use.

The Internship Bible, by Mark Oldman and Samer Hamadeh. New York: The Princeton Review, Random House Inc., 1997. Annually published internship directory that also offers insights into broad and challenging potential externship and postgraduation opportunities. Like others, it offers good indexing by geographic, field, and other special criteria, which makes it easy to use.

The Job Bank Series. Holbrook, Mass.: Adams Publishing, 1997. Annually published series of geographically focused employer directories. Currently available for Atlanta, Boston, Carolina, Dallas–Fort Worth, Denver, Detroit, Florida, Houston, Los Angeles, Minneapolis–St. Paul, New York, Ohio, Philadelphia, Phoenix, St. Louis, San Francisco, Seattle, Tennessee, and Washington, D.C.

Job Opportunities: Business Majors, Engineering and Computer Science Majors, Health and Science Majors. Princeton, N.J.: Peterson's Inc., 1998. One of the best series of employer directories. Facilitates internship, externship, and postgraduation job search efforts. Indexes refer readers to brief profiles, with names, addresses, and basic identifying information for potential employers.

Jobs '98 by Kathryn Petras, Ross Petras, and George Petras. New York: Simon and Schuster Inc., 1997. Offers insight into numerous internship, externship, and postgraduation opportunities. It offers information by geographic, field, and other special criteria, which makes it easy to use.

The Job Vault by Samer Hamadeh, Mark Oldman, and H. S. Hamadeh. Boston: Vault Reports, Inc., 1997. Another encyclopedic listing of employers, indexed by fields and geography. In addition to names, addresses, phone numbers, and Web addresses, this publication offers good getting started and preinterview information. It is an excellent first resource to use to start developing a hit list of potential employers.

Making a Mil-Yen Teaching English in Japan by Don Best. Berkeley,: Stone Bridge Press, 1994. A specialty publication that highlights popular postgraduation options. For those who want to test teaching as a career, begin an international career, or bridge from commencement to first jobs, this is a must-read resource.

Naked at the Interview by Burton J. Nadler. New York: John Wiley & Sons, Inc., 1994. Used in tandem with the other must reads, job seekers will be well prepared to ace the interview.

National Directory of Arts Internships, edited by Dian Robinson. Los Angeles: The National Network for Artists Placement, 1996. Composed of a collection of various options in music, photography, performing arts, arts management, and other areas.

150 Best Companies for Liberal Arts Graduates by Cheryl Woodruff and Greg Ptacek. New York: John Wiley & Sons, 1992. This corporate and government listing offers basic organization and job function information. It is a good hit list publication.

100 Best Companies to Work for in America by Robert Levering and Milton Moskowitz. New York: Plume, 1994. A broad compilation of employer profiles that can assist with internship, externship, and postgraduation activities. This is a simple alphabetically presented collection of information on various employers.

The Ultimate Job Search Survival Guide by Paul Dyer. Princeton, N.J.: Petersons, Inc., 1998. A comprehensive career guide that leads the reader through the important phases of self-discovery, skills assessment, and goal setting as well as resume writing and interviewing.

US Directory of Entertainment Employers. Van Nuys, Calif: EEJ Publishing, 1998. An exceptional annual publication that can be used as a comprehensive employer listing for those seeking internships, externships, or entry-level opportunities in the entertainment field. Lists advertising agencies, television and film production houses, lawyers, public relations firms, agents, recording studios, film studios, and many other prospective employers.

Vacation Work's Teaching English Abroad: Talk Your Way Around the World! by Susan Griffith. Princeton, N.J.: Vacation Work, 1997. A more comprehensive guide that offers information for those interested in this popular postgraduation option.

Work, Study, Travel Abroad: The Whole World Handbook, edited by Lazaro Hernandez and Max Terry. New York: St. Martin's Press, 1995. A valuable publication for those seeking international options.

INDEX

FIND A LIFETIME OF LEARNING AT PETERSON'S ON LINE!

Knowledge gives you the power to perform and to succeed— and petersons.com puts the power at your fingertips!

At **petersons.com** you can

- Explore graduate programs
- Discover distance learning programs
- Find out how to finance your education
- Search for career opportunities

Looking for advice on finding the right graduate program?
Look no further than the **Enrollment Message Center at petersons.com!**

- Explore program options by discipline
- E-mail program contacts for more information
- Best of all? **It's FREE**

Peterson's gives you everything you need to start a lifetime of learning.

And it's all just a mouse click away!

Peterson's Enrollment Message Center ADMISSIONS ADVISORY SERVICE

The Enrollment Message Center is an advisory service providing admission news from colleges and graduate schools wanting to contact students like you who are looking for the right institution.

Maybe you are looking to transfer, reassessing your choice of colleges, or just looking to learn more about graduate programs. Whatever your situation, if you're not yet committed to a college or graduate program, use Peterson's Enrollment Message Center, now, to contact institutions that are able to provide you with an enrollment opportunity.

PETERSON'S
Princeton, New Jersey
www.petersons.com
Keyword on AOL: Petersons
1-800-338-3282

Wait! There's more!➜